10.00

SAROYAN

SAROYAN
A BIOGRAPHY

LAWRENCE LEE
AND
BARRY GIFFORD

UNIVERSITY OF CALIFORNIA PRESS
Berkeley · Los Angeles · London

To my mother, and to the memory of my father.

L.L.

To Mary Lou, who knows what it's all about.

B.G.

University of California Press
Berkeley and Los Angeles, California

University of California Press, Ltd.
London, England

Grateful acknowledgment is made for permission to reprint:
"Zip" by Richard Rodgers and Lorenz Hart. Copyright ©
1951, 1962 by Chappell & Company, Inc. Copyright renewed,
international copyright secured. All rights reserved. Used by
permission.

First California Paperback Printing 1998

Designer: Gloria Adelson

Library of Congress Cataloging-in-Publication Data

Lee, Lawrence, 1941–
    Saroyan : a biography / Lawrence Lee and Barry Gifford.
      p.   cm.
    Originally published: New York : Harper & Row, c1984. With new
pref.
    Includes bibliographical references and index.
    ISBN 0-520-21399-8 (alk. paper)
    1. Saroyan, William, 1908–   —Biography. 2. Authors,
American—20th century—Biography. I. Gifford, Barry, 1946–
II. Title.
PS3537.A826Z77   1998
818'.5209—dc21
[B]   97-31389
                                                              CIP

Printed in the United States of America

1 2 3 4 5 6 7 8 9

The paper used in this publication meets the minimum
requirements of American National Standard for Information
Sciences—Permanence of Paper for Printed Library Materials,
ANSI Z39.48-1984. ∞

Every person in the world is a character who deserves the kind of definitive biography that heirs authorize on behalf of famous men. . . . But of course everybody doesn't get what he deserves in the way of a written life. He himself can't write his life, he can't imagine it, he can't think it, and nobody else will do these things for him.
—William Saroyan, *Letters from 74 rue Taitbout*

A man and his friends are liars to one another. They are friends only of one another's best. . . . A man is not a guilty thing, he is an innocent thing, as he himself knows.
—William Saroyan, *Rock Wagram*

Our Willie is in one place, the world is in another.
—Lucy Garoghlanian, William Saroyan's maternal grandmother, *circa* 1922

This edition is dedicated to
the memory of Lawrence Lee, 1942–1990

CONTENTS

ILLUSTRATIONS

Preface to the Paperback Edition

SAROYAN'S SENSE OF THE PAST

I met William Saroyan in 1979, when he was 70 years old and I was 32. I had recently completed the editing of his last book to be published during his lifetime, *Obituaries*, an unusual, idiosyncratic memoir that would be nominated the following year for an American Book Award in autobiography. (Saroyan lost the competition to Lauren Bacall's more traditional effort.) We had never met before, communicating exclusively by letter and telephone, though Saroyan's partial deafness made the latter difficult, often causing him to become extremely frustrated and to lose his temper and hang up in a fury. I learned not to take these explosions personally. Saroyan would usually dash off a letter or card to me immediately after prematurely ending one of these conversations, beginning the missive at the point we had broken off.

The occasion for our meeting was to celebrate the impending publication of *Obituaries*. Saroyan insisted that we have lunch at the Sheraton-Palace Hotel in San Francisco. Also present at the luncheon were Donald S. Ellis, the publisher; Herbert Gold, the novelist; and Pennfield Jensen, the magazine editor, who acted as official photographer for the occasion.

I greeted Saroyan at the entryway to the Garden Court restaurant. I was a bit surprised that he was two or three inches shorter than I—I'm slightly under six feet tall—perhaps because the booming voice I'd heard over the telephone had caused me to envision him as an extra-large, Burl Ives-sized man. Saroyan's old-country mustache was huge, however, and turning white; and he wore his thinning hair long in back and on the sides. He instantly charmed me by saying, "Do you know why I suggested we meet here?" Saroyan then gestured toward the spacious Garden Court, waving a hand at the magnificent high roof. "The food here isn't much these days," he said, "but I wanted you to have an idea of how grand things used to be, to have a sense of the past."

While we ate and drank and talked, I became convinced that Saroyan intended to evoke this sense of the past for himself as much as or more than he wanted it for the rest of us. "In the old days," Saroyan prefaced every other remark that afternoon. "Back in the 30s," he'd say, or "Once, before the war."

At one point he whispered to me loudly, "See that waiter over there? He's a Slav, maybe a Czech." I told Saroyan that I thought the man was a Latin. "No," he barked, "a Slav. Look at the slant to his jaw, the eyes." "*Señor*," I called to the waiter. "*Quantos años trabaja usted aqui?*" "*Veinte dos años*," he replied. "Where are you from originally?" I asked. "*España*," he said. "Barcelona." I turned and looked at Saroyan. "I was in Barcelona once," he said to the waiter. "A beautiful city." The waiter nodded and smiled and moved away.

When the five of us walked out of the hotel after lunch, Saroyan took one look at Pennfield Jensen's old gray Cadillac parked in front and said, "That's a classic! A '54. I had one." "It's a '55," said Penn. "I've got to ride in it," said Saroyan, clearly enthused. "In the passenger seat, in front." Penn opened the door and Bill, as he had asked us to call him, got in, slammed it shut, rolled down the window and propped his elbow on the side.

Saroyan looked marvelous in the old Cadillac; he was thrilled at the prospect of riding in such grand fashion through the streets of San Francisco, as he had a quarter of a century before. It was great to see him sitting there, too; it enabled us to visualize Saroyan as he had been in the prime of his life, as he wished us to see him. Smiling, slapping his hand against the weathered roof of the magnificent, garish hunk of tin, Bill Saroyan appeared the embodiment of a finer, grander and simpler time, one he knew was worth remembering.

Barry Gifford

PREFACE

He was one of those people who seem to have been more plentiful a generation or two ago, men and women whose last name alone said it all, who were terribly and totally famous without being prizefighters or dictators: Garbo, Einstein, Chaplin, Lindbergh, Gershwin, each name a little biography unto itself.

In his neighboring bailiwicks of authorship and the theatre Hemingway and O'Neill already had achieved this kind of last-name notoriety when our man came on the scene. In the late thirties and early forties they were his only rivals for this degree of total public recognition. Steinbeck and Faulkner were achieving this sort of familiarity, and the theatre had Odets, Hellman, Thurber, and Wilder among its bright, freestanding surnames. His name was entirely the equal of theirs.

His life itself is another matter, to be discussed shortly by many voices. Here at the start let us concentrate on his ambition to turn his beautiful and unusual surname into a household word. The task was planned as carefully as an alpine expedition. Along the way he sought out others who had achieved fame before him: Sibelius, Shaw, Mencken. Still others were friends whom he came to regard as enemies: Cerf, Shubert, Mayer. On his long way down he was helped or hurt by other men who had sought and won fame: Gulbenkian, Zanuck.

As generations of new names crowded his own off the bookshelves and the marquees—Mailer, Kerouac, Styron, Cheever, Vonnegut, Capote, Beckett, Albee—he retreated into himself, laboring daily to set his record straight. In his writing and his interviews he often would address his biographers directly. We were to have a total documentary record of his life to rely upon. This meant not simply the manuscripts, letters, and journals, but the grocery receipts, restaurant checks, laundry chits, and jam labels. Bulging file folders of travel brochures and the resulting train and airplane tickets. Parimutuel tickets, too—the losing ones. Jars of coins and bent bits of jewelry picked up off the streets of four continents. Bowls and boxes of rocks, which spoke to him of a special beach, a particular companion, a certain afternoon's walk and conversation. It was a trove to rival the storehouse of Charles Foster Kane or the tomb of Tutankhamen in its complexity and potential for meaning, if not in bulk or treasure. The idea was for all of this to become available to scholars chosen by the foundation created and named by and for himself, an organization to be financed by the royalties that have flowed uninterrupted since 1934, when everyone first heard his name.

We are not the chosen scholars. A hundred or so conversations provide the fine detail of his story as told here. Some of our sources are not quoted by name. Material from all the witnesses has been used in the narrative that binds the excerpts from the conversations together. For the rest of the story we have relied on conventional sources and method: journalism and Saroyan's own voluminous autobiographical writings.

But it is our living sources who star here. We wanted the book to be their story as well as his, to be a group portrait and a social history, to tell a dozen other tales of war and ambition and gambling and prejudice and the theatre. As a journalist and a novelist, each of us has absorbed a bit of the other's discipline, and we wanted a story that, while as accurate as we could possibly make it, was first of all a story. If we have done our job right, it also will provide the basis for an understanding reading of his works themselves.

We have chosen to let some of the voices contradict each other on factual matters, ruling only when available documentary evidence makes one view or the other plainly correct. We have held back only recollections with inventions or embroidery that would prove embarrassing to a speaker, and have withheld the identity only of those whose presence or actions would bring pain to them or to their immediate survivors.

Whether the venue is Hollywood, Paris, Park Avenue, or the orchards and dusty alleyways of Fresno, California, *circa* 1920, the people whom we tracked down are a marvelous gang of talkers, and finding and hearing them was a splendid adventure for us.

We thank them for authorizing this book by the gift of their own voices.

PART ONE
1940-1950

CHAPTER ONE

SAROYAN

1. THE GREATEST WRITER IN THE WORLD

A few minutes after midnight on the last morning of 1940, William Saroyan went to the basement workroom of the new house his words had bought for him and began typing a play he had decided to entitle, in the spirit of the season, *A Cup of Kindness*.

The action would be set, he decided, in an old frame house on Red Rock Hill near Quintara Woods in the Sunset District of San Francisco. This was the neighborhood where Saroyan sat, chain-smoking Chesterfields and typing in swift, percussive outbursts. Unlike the mouse-ridden old house he imagined for his protagonists, the Webster family, Saroyan's own house was sturdy and up-to-date, one of half a city of "Sunstream Homes," which promoter Henry Doelger had built, despite the Depression, on San Francisco's last low hills before the sea. At one time the district had been thought to be uninhabitable because of its dense and persistent fog, but now it was a middle-class redoubt and Saroyan's house there was intended to become the lifelong home for his mother and for the maiden sister who answered the telephone, kept the scrapbooks, and was a quiet and steadying influence in a family of outspoken grudges and passions.

In the family of the play Saroyan began writing that night the mother is missing, driven away by the eccentricities of her husband, a genial crackpot of Old Testament stripe. The daughter is a saintlike creature who believes herself to be worshiped by the household mice, who bring her offerings of flowers. There are two Webster sons. The younger, Owen, is a dreamer who composes one-word novels:

> "Tree."
> "Trees?"
> "No. *Tree*. One."
> "Well, what do you say about it?"
> "I don't say anything about it. I just *say* it. *Tree* . . ."

The older brother, Harold, has left San Francisco for fame and fortune in New York, and for most of the play he is to be represented by an offstage cornet solo of one of Saroyan's favorite songs, the sweet and mournful "Wonderful One," written by Paul Whiteman and Ferde Grofé.

In creating the Webster family Saroyan was not committing autobiography. His own father had been dead for thirty years. His mother, asleep upstairs out of earshot of his typing, remained a towering presence in her son's life. Saroyan's sister was nothing like the ethereal Agnes Webster of the play.

But inside Bill Saroyan were both of the Webster brothers—Owen, the poetic homebody, and Harold, conqueror of the distant city.

The homebody half of Saroyan was never more at home than here in his basement workroom with its pine-paneled walls. There was a big fireplace he could use to ward off the chill of the fogs or to stare at for inspiration. There were ceiling-to-floor shelves for the books that accumulated daily—the latest volumes from the New York publishers mixed with items from the nickel tables at San Francisco's second-hand stores. To the right of the fireplace sat an expensive player piano. There was a radio-phonograph console, too, but the cornet in the workroom was wishful thinking. For all his love of music, the only "instruments" Saroyan could play were the pianola and his mechanical harmonica. There were a bicycle and dominoes and his tennis racket. His polished work table was an old solid-oak affair he had bought used, stripping away six layers of paint to reveal the grain. The cane-bottomed chairs, recently recaned, dated back to the farmhouse near San Jose where Saroyan's father had died, and Saroyan always thought of them as part of his legacy from that mysterious figure, although they were far from being valuable antiques. He told his friends that if he had his way the workroom would contain more: a stage, puppets, a movie projection system, gym equipment. But the workroom as it was and its small adjoining bedroom were all that he needed for now. The view from the work-table window was the Pacific Ocean, a featureless gray stripe two miles away. But whenever that scene from the workroom became too narrow, the walls too close, the pleasures of two cities were his to command. This house of his mother's on San Francisco's Fifteenth Avenue was the west pole of a two-coast existence shared by very few people in those last months before America was drawn into World War II.

Coast-to-coast air travel was a two-day suspense story with multiple layovers, but Saroyan already was a veteran of that new adventure. The club cars and private drawing rooms of the comfortable cross-country trains were an equally natural habitat for him. On this December midnight he would have been entirely welcome in the Cub Room of the Stork Club, where Manhattan's most glittering debutantes were exhibited, or in the rich gloom of Jack and Charlie's "21," or across the street from that outpost of wealth in the barely-controlled madness of the joint run by comedian Jack White, where sirens and bells announced the comings and goings of the famous. By the same token, Saroyan could have spent the evening at any of several social altitudes on the hills of San Francisco: in mideastern splendor at Omar Khayyam's, at the ritzy Garden Court of the Palace Hotel, or in the dim, *avant-garde* milieu of the Black Cat. Sally Stanford, the city's reigning madam, would have been pleased to scramble some eggs for him before he returned by Cadillac to his house in the avenues.

At the Stork or "21" he was accustomed to a really good table, at Jack White's to a four-alarm entrance. At Sally's, if not the loveliest girl, at least the lion's share of the hostess's attentions. In both of his cities he demanded and received the pleasures and recognition reserved for the very biggest of big winners. His movement toward this fame had been a tropism: the way a seedling seeks the light, Saroyan had turned to face the fat flashbulbs popping from the Speed Graphics at Grand Central, in the Cub Room, at the foot of the airliner stairway.

Although still a young man, thirty-two years old on this particular morning, Saroyan had devoted twenty-three years of his life to this climb, and while the fame and honors already achieved might appear to the naked eye to be the summit of reasonable ambition, to Bill Saroyan, in this last winter before America joined the war, they were simply a plateau like the others already achieved and surpassed.

Everyone knew who he was.

His name itself was a fabulous stroke of luck for this expert at self-invention. A wit had remarked that it made him sound like his own disciple.

Saroyan. It was exotic and familiar at the same time. Familiar, of course, because of Saroyan's own exertions on its behalf, which made the name the only word most people had ever heard in that strange tongue. The Armenian syllables spoke of Asian stretches east of Trebizond, the bright emptiness of a country that had taken leave of the map itself, Armenia. Everyone understood in a vague way that the circumstances behind Armenia's relatively recent disappearance had been horrible. Armenians starved en masse and emphatically declared their suffering and their anger at history and the Turks. In the mind of the public all this heavy historical freight had become connected with the young writer who at every turn reminded his readers that he was part and parcel, blood and bone, of this tortured race older than Rome, older than Egypt, than Babylon, older than the Jews.

Saroyan's writing, however, was such a canny mixture of Old World suffering and New World optimism that it spoke of the simplicity, durability, and resilience of his lost homeland rather than of Armenia's pain and suffering. Just as Saroyan was the only Saroyan anyone had ever heard of, any and all other Saroyans necessarily his satellites, he was also the only Armenian whom most people could name in a pinch. Because his fame was so wide and his work so lovingly accepted, the Armenians themselves celebrated him as avatar and ambassador. Before he was thirty he had been heroized by the Armenia-in-exile that survived in such places as Jerusalem, Paris, Boston, and in the shadow Armenia reconstructed within the Soviet Union near the borders of the old lost land. Had old Armenia survived as a nation, Saroyan would have been a postage stamp by 1940, if not a coin.

As it was, just as his name was known to anyone in America who read a magazine, listened to the radio, cared about the theatre, or visited a bookshop, the face was familiar, too—and without the benefit of television. The nose was an Ararat of a nose, as noble a landmark as Armenia's sovereign mountain where Noah disembarked. The jaw was strong, the lips were full. His eyes were large and black and bright, with dark crescent brows, which overshadowed their attentiveness, and long lashes, which softened their intensity.

Saroyan was short and solid, stocky without being heavy, and his choice of clothing sometimes conveyed a prosperous-peasant look, which may have been studied, practical, or a bit of both. There was the dark overcoat of good quality, but a size too large, which he often wore tossed over his shoulders, its bulk emphasizing its utility as the impresario's cape. Shopping for sturdy shoes, he had chosen ski boots for their workmanship without knowing what they were, tried them on, fell in love with them, bought them over the clerk's explanations and protests, wore them everywhere. As a busy New York bachelor he found doing laundry troublesome, and so it was easier sometimes to buy new white shirts by the dozen. His suits themselves were invariably dark, his ties silk and subdued. Bill Saroyan was loud, but his clothing was not.

The crowning fixture was the hat. Everybody wore a hat in those days, but Saroyan seemed to wear his hat all the time, indoors and out, and he did not wear it to camouflage baldness. The hat sat at a sharp angle, Saroyan's black wavy hair spilling out. The crown was high, the brim was narrow, and the tilt was theatrical. This particular hat worn this particular way was his emblem. Saroyan's name and face spoke of the country that his parents had fled in terror, and he bore his Armenian heritage proudly, but the hat and the tilt of the hat told everybody that the man who wore it was Armenian as apple pie.

Whatever its source, Bitlis or Fresno, Saroyan's braggadocio was tempered with enough sweetness and self-mockery to make it an engaging trait. His monumental self-esteem was, in fact, the very heart of his public image, like Jack Benny's stinginess or W. C. Fields's fondness for the bottle. Saroyan's journey from obscurity to fame and playful arrogance had been endlessly retold. It was an all-Armenian boy's version of Cinderella, utterly devoid of supernatural intervention, a plot anyone could understand:

A runty kid from an immigrant family decides at a very early age to devote his life to art. He cannot draw, sculpt, paint, sing, play, or compose. Once he can read, at the age of eight, he determines to write, and he begins to write almost immediately, suffering almost twenty years of rejection. In time, a great Depression settles upon the land, making many millions of Americans just as poor as the boy's own family. While his relatives work at drudge jobs, mocking his dreams, he completes a small and nearly perfect work of art. This tale, "The Daring Young Man on the Flying Trapeze," not only contains the facts of his life and times, transforming them into art; it is so good that it comes to redefine and to speak for the very genre of the short story itself—in a sense, for all storytelling. The boy, by now a young man, mails his story away to a pair of distinguished editors of short stories, who publish it with full attentiveness to its remarkable qualities. The critics agree that it is a masterpiece and, most miraculous of all, the adoration of the public is equally great and proves to be even longer-lived.

"The Daring Young Man on the Flying Trapeze" relates the last hours of a young writer with a single penny in his pocket. He is out of work, out of hope, out of time. Although he is starving to death, art comes first. He stops by the public library to read Proust. He goes to the writing table at the YMCA for the ink and paper he needs to work on his "Application for Permission to Live," a work otherwise un-described in Saroyan's brief story.

Proust completes his masterpiece by having his hero resolve to begin the gigantic tale the reader is just finishing. Art and life connect in an unusually satisfying way. On a miniature scale, something very similar happens in "The Daring Young Man on the Flying Trapeze." As Saroyan's nameless young hero pitches forward into oblivion, a poetic vision of the unity of the universe flashing through his starving synapses, Saroyan himself zooms from oblivion to blazing fame. The un-qualified success of his short story amounted to signed and sealed approval of Saroyan's own application for permission to live. The writer in Saroyan's story dies unknown, but in so marvelous a fashion that a happy ending is created for the author himself.

How close were the facts of the story to Saroyan's own life? The readers could not know, and a typographical error in *Story* magazine, which first bought and published it, made Saroyan seem ten years younger, the tale the work of a sixteen-year-old boy, not a twenty-six-year-old man. With a forenote to his very next story Saroyan began a monologue to his readers that would continue to his death, and from beginning to end this running commentary on his work gave full credit to himself as the secret of his own success. Saroyan would come to acknowledge influences as various as Maupassant and Zane Grey, but there was no living mentor who had touched him directly—no teacher, no editor, no particular colleague to recognize or to thank.

So, from the beginning of his public career, Saroyan stood alone as a self-made writer, and in his interviews and essays and forewords he was at great pains to emphasize the speed and effortlessness with which he wrote. Revision was for someone else. In feature journalism, as in a Norse epic, he was Saroyan-who-wrote-a-story-a-day-for-a-month or Saroyan-who-wrote-the-Pulitzer-Prize-play-in-six-days.

To friends and strangers alike Saroyan would announce himself as "the world's greatest writer," a self-embroidered mantle worn in all weathers. Only a Hemingway could be, and was, offended by Saroyan's cheerful assertiveness about it. Saroyan's first publisher, Bennett Cerf, delighted in repeating the story of the hotel operator who "called up, chuckling, and said, 'Mr. Cerf, the greatest author in the world is here to see you,' and I said, 'Send Mr. Saroyan up.'" Almost as often as he told the story, which was often indeed, Cerf confessed to having invented it as a publicity stunt. ("Bill came to believe these things really happened.") But many another friend recalls Saroyan using the title on the street or with a bartender: "The greatest writer in the world wants to buy some drinks for his friends!" To a stranger squinting at him on a street corner, trying to match up the man with the remembered photograph in the Sunday roto, Saroyan was only too pleased to confirm the suspicion. The pleasure was theirs. It was, indeed, the greatest writer in the world.

Already he had given birth to his own adjective. "Saroyanesque" had vivid meaning. A Saroyanesque character was a sweet eccentric—a whore with a gold-plated heart, a doddering old Scot with a battered bugle, a wide-eyed kid whose energetic innocence made a reader or theatregoer see the world the way it looks after a morning rain.

The most Saroyanesque character of them all, of course, was the man himself, who, at a relatively tender age, found himself hardening into an archetype of popular culture. Just as the intellectual entertainer Alexander Woollcott had been enshrined in Kaufman and Hart's *The Man Who Came to Dinner*, Saroyan recently had been impersonated by Keenan Wynn in a comedy called *The White-Haired Boy*, a farce by Mrs. George S. Kaufman and a young collaborator she secured for the occasion. Director George Abbott's exertions were unable to keep the play going past its Boston tryout, but the audiences who did see it saw the Saroyan figure riding a child's tricycle, hugging his plump ethnic momma, reveling in himself as he loved the world with a great and good heart.

Saroyan had been notified that the creators of *Pins and Needles*, the garment workers' revue that represented Seventh Avenue on Broadway, had decided to lampoon him in their new edition. Would he care to write the sketch himself? And the very title of "The Daring Young Man on the Flying Trapeze" had been merged into the Saroyan mythos, irresistible to those who spoke or wrote or joked or, on occasion, sang about him. Yip Harburg, that most adroit of Broadway lyricists, had been inspired to pen a song about Saroyan with no particular show or composer in mind. (It ran in *Variety*.)

THE BLARING YOUNG MAN

There's a charm you can't destroy in
Saroyan—
It's Saroyan's all-out joy in
Saroyan.
He's the subject that he talks on.
Loves the very ground he walks on—
It's the dear eternal boy in
Saroyan.

There's a *soupçon* of Tolstoy in
Saroyan,
Eddie Guest and Eddie Foy in
Saroyan,
He's the left man and the right man,
He's Walt Whitman and Paul Whiteman,
Yes, you'll find the real McCoy in
Saroyan.

There's *haute monde* and *hoi polloi* in
Saroyan,
Flatfoot floogy and floy floy in
Saroyan;
He's the cream in his own coffee,
He demands a Bernard Shaw fee—
For there's gold . . . and no alloy in
Saroyan.

There's hey hey and some 'oi 'oi in
Saroyan;
Mills Hotel and the Savoy in
Saroyan;
He is Carthage, Rome, Des Moines!
He's Gigantic and Sequoian!
But at best—he's most annoyin!
Saroyan!

2. BILL VS. BROADWAY, 1940

Working alone in his mother's basement on that last midnight of 1940, mapping out his new assault on Broadway, Bill Saroyan faced several obstacles and enemies, real and imagined.

Perhaps the biggest shadow across his path was something called the well-made play, which was the commercial theatre's stock-in-trade. Its characters and components had moved beyond simple custom and convention and now functioned according to a secular liturgy. Plots marched from first-act exposition through second-act development to third-act climax. The characters themselves had to reflect the standard personnel of a stock acting company, if for no other reason than visions of royalties from repeated stock productions. These rules were to be avoided or experimented with only at great peril.

Saroyan had been at pains to stretch and break the rules from the outset. His playwriting career reached back five years, to 1935 and his first visit to New York after Random House published his short-story collection, *The Daring Young Man on the Flying Trapeze*. He had told Bennett Cerf that he wanted to write plays, and Cerf had assumed that the young man from the West Coast was ignorant of the theatre. This was untrue. Even Saroyan's boyhood hometown, Fresno, was a one-night stand for touring companies, and Bill had seen duplicates of Broadway productions that settled in for longer runs in San Francisco and Los Angeles. Indeed, Saroyan had sampled Broadway itself during a daring reconnaissance east that he had made as a teenager, scouting territory for future conquest.

In his 1935 visit, Saroyan was taken by Cerf to one of the biggest hits, the aviation melodrama *Ceiling Zero*, starring Osgood Perkins, an actor now best remembered as Tony Perkins's father. As Cerf told the story, "After the first act—it was quite a hit and the lobby was crowded—we walked out for a breather, and I said to Bill, 'Well, what do you think of a Broadway show?,' expecting him to be bowled over. Bill said, 'So that's a Broadway show. For God's sake, I could write a better one than that in twenty-four hours.'" On his first visit to New York Willie Saroyan had stayed at the Twenty-third Street YMCA, but on uptown walks he gazed longingly at the Great Northern Hotel on West Fifty-seventh Street as the pinnacle of sophistication. The gilt of the Great Northern was tarnished even then, and its day was definitely over by 1935 when Saroyan fulfilled his fantasy by staying there. And it was there one morning that Saroyan read in "News of the Rialto" in the *New York Times* that he was at work on a play. It was untrue, but not unreasonable, and Saroyan spent a few days before sailing to Europe locked in his room, transforming his impressions of New York into the short play *Subway Circus*.

It was four seasons later, 1939, that the play reached the stage mounted by the Group Theatre, whose institutionalized spirit of rebellion provided a comfortable shelter for Saroyan's maverick impulses. The Group was not so idealistic and theoretical that it would thumb its nose at success, and it had struck up an arrangement with the powerful firm of producers who called themselves the Theatre Guild and commanded not only theatre leases and subscription audiences, but serious attention. When the Group's workshop production of *My Heart's in the Highlands* continued on Broadway under Guild sponsorship, Saroyan achieved praise for what might be called the homemade play. Its lovable characters were understandable to anyone familiar with Saroyan's short stories. Saroyan translated to the stage with perfect ease and a sense of belonging there.

Saroyan's second play, *The Time of Your Life*, was stillborn in New Haven under Guild sponsorship, and its director, a Group Theatre veteran, was jettisoned by the producers along with his treatment of the world-in-a-barroom story as a fantasy. The experienced trouper who played the lead, Eddie Dowling, then joined forces with Saroyan himself to restage the play in a spirit of gritty realism, and the magic seemed brighter because of the new contrast between theme and style.

Even seasoned players who were in the cast of *The Time of Your Life* acknowledged that Saroyan was capable of getting good performances out of actors. Thus, for his third play—it was 1940 now—he was officially listed as co-director, again with Eddie Dowling.

But this third play, *Love's Old Sweet Song*, contained structural flaws that Saroyan refused to fix. He had written a two-act play, the form reserved for musicals, and then he had insisted on turning it into a three-act play. This could have been interpreted as a nod in the direction of convention, but in the case of *Love's Old Sweet Song* it was a tactical error. The play interrupted its tale of middle-aged romance with the arrival of a group of Okies. The Dust Bowl satire was aimed at proletarian literature and *Time* magazine, among other targets, but it led to an early climax. There was more play than plot, a whole extra act, and the leftover fantasy curdled into a not-so-funny surrealism.

This was all the ammunition that Saroyan's Broadway opponents needed, and by this point in 1940 he had plenty of them. *The Time of Your Life* had been a controversial triumph, but a triumph nonetheless.

Telegraph messengers deliver wires throughout Saroyan's dramatic works. Here, Peter Fernandez sets the plot of *Love's Old Sweet Song* in motion by reciting to Jessie Royce Landis the text of the telegram he has mislaid, that telegram itself the invention of a practical joker. (Vandamm)

"Never interrupt a pitch. At least not a high pitch." Walter Huston as Barnaby Gaul in *Love's Old Sweet Song.* A few weeks earlier, Saroyan had seen him open in *A Passenger to Bali* and was convinced the play would run. Lawrence Langner of the Theatre Guild timed the curtain calls and advised Saroyan that Huston would soon be available. He was. (Vandamm)

"*Time Magazine* is assembled every week by intelligent men all over the world," said Alan Hewitt, as the magazine salesman. He then proceeded to recite the seventy-four names on the masthead (including not-yet-famous ones like Whittaker Chambers and John Hersey) in his second-act *tour de force* in *Love's Old Sweet Song.* Arthur Hunnicutt and Doro Merande are the spellbound Okies, Cabot and Leona Yearling. (Vandamm)

The characters and acting were so good that the audiences and critics cared very little about the almost total absence of plot. But not all of the critics. Walter Winchell still preferred a loud musical with pretty chorus girls. *Time's* Louis Kronenberger professed bafflement. The most dangerous enemy was Burns Mantle of the *Daily News*, who edited the yearbook of *Best Plays*. For more than twenty years, Mantle's volumes had celebrated and enshrined the well-made, three-act play.

When award-giving season arrived in the late spring of 1940, the lines were drawn for a battle between two distinct schools of drama, the well-made play versus Saroyan's rumpled, unmade plays. Firmly on Saroyan's side was the dean of the drama critics, George Jean Nathan, whose very creed was the purity of art. He had been observing Broadway on those terms since 1904, writing his opinions for *The Smart Set, Vanity Fair* and now, in 1940, *Newsweek*.

Nathan considered himself a discoverer of new theatrical worlds, and since he had lifted both Eugene O'Neill and Sean O'Casey from obscurity, he had the credentials to prove it. Saroyan had been his particular enthusiasm since *My Heart's in the Highlands* the year before, and Nathan had worked diligently behind the scenes to advance the young playwright's cause. He helped arrange casting and production of the later plays. He staged accidental meetings that blossomed into contract negotiations. He generally pushed and promoted the young playwright's career in a manner not expected of a critic.

Nathan was the most powerful man on Broadway without a direct financial interest in the theatre. In later years exertions such as Nathan made on Saroyan's behalf might have tarnished a critic's presumed detachment and neutrality. In 1940, they amounted to friendly boosterism. Perhaps the most interesting aspect of the relationship between Nathan and Saroyan was that the younger man accepted the older's efforts in gratitude and genuine friendship. Editors and agents already had fallen by the wayside, and many a professional quarrel and separation lay in Saroyan's future. George Jean Nathan, with his big, gentle eyes and his slightly antiquated manners and tastes, was an unlikely promoter of literature's pushy hotshot, but the friendship was firm. Saroyan never would enjoy another like it.

The very day after *Love's Old Sweet Song* opened, the Drama Critics Circle held their annual meeting at the Algonquin Hotel. Everyone present, wherever they stood on the Saroyan question, knew that his new play would fail in short order. (As it did, vanishing in early June,

Saroyan (cocked hat) and George Jean Nathan, who was old enough to be Bill's father—twenty-six years older. Saroyan was Nathan's third great theatrical discovery (after O'Casey and O'Neill), and no one else in Saroyan's career would play quite so warm or nurturing a role. (Courtesy Aram Saroyan)

just as Broadway's audience evaporated with the heat.) But that left the question of *The Time of Your Life*. Nathan believed, and argued to his colleagues, that, if ever art had reached the commercial stage, this play was it. And the Critics Circle, he had no need to remind them, existed to defend art against a very specific threat, overrated commercial plays.

The threat emanated from Morningside Heights, where the trustees of Columbia University administered the Pulitzer Prize in drama each spring. Five seasons earlier the university had given the $1,000 prize to *The Old Maid* by Zöe Akins. In 1936 the Pulitzer went to Robert E. Sherwood for *Idiot's Delight*. Nathan and his colleagues preferred Maxwell Anderson's verse drama *Winterset*, and they created the Critics' prize to say so. (The Critics, however, gave no $1,000 check.) In subsequent seasons the Critics and the Pulitzer committee had found plenty to disagree about. In 1937 the Critics again had honored Maxwell Anderson for *High Tor* (art), while the Pulitzer committee preferred Kaufman and Hart's *You Can't Take It With You*. Perhaps the sharpest difference between the two prizes occurred in 1938, when the Critics selected John Steinbeck's *Of Mice and Men* while the trustees of Columbia honored Thornton Wilder's synthetically folksy *Our Town*.

In the 1940 voting, Saroyan faced heavy competition. On the art side there was *Key Largo*, another of Anderson's verse tragedies. Critics who preferred entertainment to political messages had *The Man Who Came to Dinner*, perhaps the best-made of all Kaufman and Hart plays. There was even a compromise candidate the Winchell-Mantle crowd could, and did, vote for without losing face, Robert E. Sherwood's antiwar message play *There Shall Be No Night*, which was also a very commercial play, starring the Lunts and featuring a handsome young actor named Montgomery Clift.

The crowded field worked to George Jean Nathan's advantage as the balloting proceeded, and by the time the last vote was taken, the prize was Saroyan's, with critics as important as Brooks Atkinson and John Mason Brown adding their approval. The Critics' citation, undoubtedly written by Nathan himself, praised the play's "exhilarating demonstration of the fresh, original and imaginative talent he has brought into our theatre" and "the depth of its honest joy." Arrangements were made for Saroyan to receive the award the following week during a coast-to-coast radio hook-up featuring scenes from the play and speeches by the critics and the backers. The Pulitzers had nothing like that.

Nathan and the other journalists delighted in upstaging the rival prizes by announcing their Critics award the day before Columbia published the Pulitzer list. On the Thursday that the Critics met and voted, Saroyan already was back in San Francisco, at work in his mother's basement, recovering from the tryout weeks and the evident financial failure of *Love's Old Sweet Song* and writing hard on new scripts. Loyal to his friend Nathan, Saroyan had told the columnists before he fled New York that he would reject the Pulitzer if ever it was given to one of his plays, but that the Critics' prize was "a great distinction," and it was one he accepted cheerfully when he was notified.

But the following morning, the Columbia committee agreed with the Critics Circle for the first time ever. Saroyan had won the Pulitzer as well. It was Robert Giroux, then a junior editor at Saroyan's publisher, Harcourt, Brace and Company, who had the mixed pleasure of calling California with the news.

"I was speechless after phoning to tell him he'd won the Pulitzer Prize for his play *The Time of Your Life* when he replied, 'I won't accept it. They should have given it to me for *My Heart's in the Highlands*,' whereupon his refusal made front-page news."

Saroyan was not the first to refuse a Pulitzer. Sinclair Lewis had turned it down in 1926 when it was awarded for his novel *Arrowsmith*. But Saroyan's refusal crowded out of the spotlight 1940's other winners, such as Carl Sandburg in history and Mark Van Doren in poetry.

Saroyan sent Columbia University a long telegram explaining himself and pointing out that he had warned them "four or five or six or seven weeks ago that in the event my play was awarded the Pulitzer Prize, I would have to reject the award." Columbia's provost regretted, he said, that the warning had not reached the university in time. The $1,000 check would be sent anyway. If Saroyan did not cash it, it would revert to the Pulitzer fund. Saroyan was, as he had said himself, "powerless to deny the work whatever distinction the Pulitzer board has given it."

The prize had given Saroyan a marvelous soapbox, which he delighted in using for days, publishing to the wire services and the eastern newspapers his communiqués to the Pulitzer committee. "Art must be democratic, but at the same time it must be both proud and aloof," he told them. "It must not be taken in by either praise or criticism. Wealth, I am sure, cannot patronize art, and the strange impulse of wealth to seek to do so is, I believe, a curious example of noble bad taste. . . . A poverty-stricken nation with a great art is a greater nation than a wealthy nation with a poverty-stricken art."

This was far from a political war cry on Saroyan's part, however. The *Daily Worker*, newspaper of the Communist party, had attacked him that very week as "the most charming and original evader in the American theatre . . . a bright young man who spins fantasies that look like 'the real thing' and make you forget the real thing."

There were no Tony awards in 1940. Antoinette Perry, for whom that prize is named, was still an active director that season. The two prizes amounted to a sweep of Broadway's highest honors, and this robbed Saroyan of the underdog role he had enjoyed playing in his first skirmishes with the theatre. It also made him an object of interest to new producers, and new money was exactly what he needed in the summer of 1940 as he retreated to his mother's basement to work on new play scripts.

Contrary to the further accusations of the *Daily Worker*, Saroyan's plays had provided no shortcut to riches for Saroyan or for his backers. *Love's Old Sweet Song* was the very last play of his the Theatre Guild was willing to take a chance on. They would give him an option or two in the future, but never another production. They had lost money on his first play, *My Heart's in the Highlands*, and they had lost money on *The Time of Your Life* itself, which had closed a month before the two awards were announced. The prizes, however, were the Guild's cue to revive *The Time of Your Life* with its original cast and to attempt to make a profit with it. The afternoon of the Critics' prize, even before the Pulitzer announcement, Eddie Dowling announced the play's return to Broadway in the autumn, to be followed by the national tour that had been judged too risky.

But Dowling's enthusiasm for this unquestioned hit did not dim his good sense about Saroyan's work. Dowling's commitment as director and actor in *The Time of Your Life* had made it convenient for him to decline Saroyan's latest script, a fantasy called *Sweeney in the Trees*. The name of the play had been borrowed from Irish legend, but it was a fuzzy fantasy devoid of Celtic content. Even if he had been enchanted with Saroyan's new effort, Dowling was leery of the young man. The out-of-town notices had been excellent for *Love's Old Sweet Song* while it was still in its original two-act form. It was Saroyan, two days before the Broadway opening, who had come to the Booth Theater with his agent to demand it be changed into a three-act play. Brushing aside the objections of his seasoned co-director, Dowling, Saroyan had made an impassioned speech to backers and cast members. From the stage of the Booth he had told them that his reputation was more important than mere profit. He had couched the argument as Nathan would, as a matter of art versus commerce, and he had won. The morning after the bad reviews, Saroyan had telephoned the Theatre Guild to say, "You had better put the curtain back the way it was in Baltimore."

What Saroyan must have known, although he never acknowledged it in his published memoirs, was that Eddie Dowling, co-producer with the Theatre Guild, was producer in name only. The silent partner was Lee Shubert, impresario of impresarios, and by backing Dowling he had lost money twice now on Bill Saroyan. As far as Lee Shubert was concerned, there would be no third time.

Thus, in the summer of 1940, even as Saroyan was invited to lunch with the Roosevelts at Hyde Park, to pose for an eight-page spread in *Life* magazine, he was struggling with whispers that he was box-office poison. Stage whispers carry a long way, but the two prizes had made him bankable again. The proprietor of the Cape May, New Jersey, Playhouse agreed to an August tryout week for *Sweeney in the Trees*, and Saroyan announced that he would be producing and directing it for Broadway by himself.

There was a final obstacle to Saroyan's work that summer. It was the war that had begun a year earlier in Europe. In September, 1939, the day after Hitler invaded Poland, Saroyan had begun work on a play he called *The Well-Known Soldier*. It was a tract about a seventy-year-old man and his small adopted son who conducted antiwar operations out of a trench in their front yard. As Saroyan's reputation soared in mid-1940, José Ferrer optioned the play for a summer tryout at the Bucks County Playhouse in Pennsylvania.

"The present state of the world makes it seem unnecessary to publish anything but the most pertinent writing," Saroyan had written to *Hairenik,* the journal published from Boston for Armenian-Americans.

> One thing I see continuously in the newspaper crystal is death. I hereby predict that Benito Mussolini, Adolf Hitler, Josef Stalin, and an eighty-eight-year-old farmer in Czechoslovakia named Gropka are going to die. I further predict that when each of these men dies he shall stop breathing and begin to decay. . . . I predict still further also that at the very moment when each of these men dies at least one child shall be born into the world. I predict still further that when each of these men dies the

world will not know the difference, the sun will rise in the morning and
descend in the evening; rivers will go on flowing; the four seasons will
come and go as they always have; seeds will grow out of the earth and
bring forth their produce; and all living things will go on living.

Saroyan's attitude about the war was a mournful pacifism tempered
by the odd mixture of joy and guilt in the heart of any living Armenian, a survivor of a race that already had endured mass slaughter,
although much of the world seemed unwilling to remember that or to
ponder its meaning.

But, by June of 1940, events in the war were so grim that such simple pacifism seemed flimsy. Norway, the Netherlands, Belgium,
France had fallen to Hitler. The British had just fled the continent,
swimming for their lives, and the invasion of England itself seemed to
be at hand. The Republicans had chosen a presidential candidate,
Wendell Willkie, who stood on a plank of non-intervention, and President Roosevelt was campaigning for his unprecedented third term by
feigning a no-war policy.

Saroyan would not be drawn into direct political activity. His luncheon at the summer White House was a spur-of-the-moment occasion
for him. The invitation had come not from the First Lady but from the
playwright Sidney Kingsley. The affair itself was packed with writers
and theatre people, including Katharine Hepburn. Miss Hepburn, as
Saroyan recalled long afterward, "was carrying under her arm a stationery box, the contents of which rattled as she bounded about, and
so I was unable not to ask, 'Are they in that box, Miss Hepburn—all
the answers?'

"The elegant lady gave me a very icy look and said, 'It's none of
your business what's in the box, Mr. Saroyan.'"

Even so conservative a force as Henry Luce, creator of *Time* and *Life*
magazines, was propagandizing that summer for direct American en-
try into the war. In those days before television, the newsreel was a
potent medium, and Luce's "March of Time" documentaries were seen
by more moviegoers each week than read his magazines themselves.
The collapse of Europe in the face of Hitler had inspired Luce to produce a full-length "March of Time" feature, *The Ramparts We Watch*,
whose skillful propaganda infuriated Saroyan. "If you and others as
fortunate or unfortunate as yourself feel that the waging of a war is an
activity involving spiritual values, then you must not hesitate to lead
the way and give up what little you have," Saroyan wired Luce. "Your

properties, your annual profits, everything you have. Which is little enough for the good things that shall be saved." The implication was that war should be reserved for those who believe in it. Saroyan clearly did not. War on the warmakers was the theme of *Something About a Soldier*, as he now had retitled his pacifist play, *The Well-Known Soldier*. But most of his writing that summer of 1940 was not political. There were prefaces for the collection of his first three Broadway plays. There was yet another play, *Across the Board on Tomorrow Morning*, again written with Eddie Dowling in mind, a fat, center-stage role as ringmaster of a New York nightclub that was a microcosm of society, much like the San Francisco barroom in *The Time of Your Life*.

In the long view, Saroyan's most important writing project that summer was an excursion into his childhood, the finishing touches he was putting on a collection of sketches that retrieved the world of Fresno, California, in the years from 1915 to 1925.

Capitalizing deftly on his recent prizes, Saroyan had dashed off a poetic memoir, "The Saroyan Prizes, 1908–1939," which *The New Yorker* had printed. Its recitation of childhood victories was plain autobiography:

. . . Holder of the First Prize for Street Sales, The Fresno *Evening Herald*, 1917;
Twice Winner of the Around-the-Block Race, 1918 . . .
Winner of Highest Third-Grade Binet-Simon Intelligence Rating, "Far Above Average, Although Poor at Arithmetic" . . .
First to Climb Geggenheimer's Water Tank And Drop a Cat;
Most Frequent Visitor of the Public Library;
Borrower of the Most and Best Books . . .

Saroyan had dabbled in autobiography before, but never as directly as in the collection he finished that summer. *My Name Is Aram* never has gone out of print. Its opening story, "The Summer of the Beautiful White Horse," had been rejected more than a dozen times before it was bought by Edward Weeks of the *Atlantic,* who asked to see more like it. There already were more, and Edward J. O'Brien, who edited the annual of *The Best Short Stories*, also encouraged Saroyan to write more of these charming souvenirs of a sunny boyhood in California's Central Valley. The resulting volume was a selection from twenty or so "Aram" sketches, which had been published in half a dozen magazines.

The opening story manages to make horse theft appealing. The Saroyan figure, Aram Garoghlanian, and his "crazy cousin Mourad" steal a farmer's horse and keep it for a whole summer, returning it to him "stronger than ever . . . better-tempered, too." The story was a fantasy and variation on a tiny kernel of truth:

> HENRY SAROYAN: The cousin's father had a farm on the outskirts of Fresno, and I think their *neighbor* had a white horse.
> And if he stole it, it was just a kid prank. It wasn't meant with any intention of keeping the darned horse, because we had one.
> We used to go there in the summers and help pick peaches and various other fruits that were on the farm, so there was no need for another horse.

Bill's brother, Henry, his cousin Archie, and a multitude of other Saroyans, Papazians, and Bagdasarians move through the book half-disguised. But, while Saroyan's closest relations truly did struggle for decades, others thrived. The uncle of "The Pomegranate Trees," whose mistake was to plant a difficult crop no one in America yet wanted or even understood, survived that experience. Bill's dreamy Uncle Mihran was not so dreamy as the story made him out, and Saroyan's practical Uncle Aram brokered crops whenever possible, often leaving the big risk to others.

By the time *My Name Is Aram* went to press late in 1940, the cheering that had greeted *The Daring Young Man on the Flying Trapeze* had died down a bit. Edmund Wilson already had remarked on the fickleness of his fellow critics for faulting Saroyan on a variety of grounds ranging from false optimism to a lack of politics. Their main complaint was his refusal—failure, as they viewed it—to publish a novel, the quintessential American literary performance. *My Name Is Aram* was not the long-awaited Saroyan novel. But, as a suite of stories reminiscent of Sherwood Anderson's *Winesburg, Ohio,* Saroyan's new book came very close to being what the critics wanted. Saroyan follows Aram from early boyhood to his first ventures away from the Central Valley of California, and the controlled tone of voice and the sureness of its effects strongly suggest a novel. It was promptly purchased by the Book-of-the-Month Club as the first selection for 1941.

Late in August, 1940, Saroyan boarded the streamliner *City of San Francisco,* returning to New York recharged and resupplied with literary properties and ideas. Not two but three of his plays were to receive tryout performances in the closing weeks of summer stock. Two of them were opening on the same night, José Ferrer's production of *Something About a Soldier* in Bucks County and a tryout of *The Hero of the World* at Roslyn, Long Island.

At Cape May, New Jersey, the play was Saroyan's favorite among his new crop, *Sweeney in the Trees*, and one of its stars was Julie Haydon, close companion of George Jean Nathan. Miss Haydon, a striking blonde with a husky whisper of a voice, had created the role of Kitty Duval, the prostitute heroine of *The Time of Your Life*. She would recreate that role with Eddie Dowling when the production reopened in September. Meanwhile, like other leading players in those days before truly air-conditioned theatres, she had followed the audience to the country—in this case, the Jersey shore.

JULIE HAYDON: Ten plays in a row, a different starring role every week for ten weeks. Saroyan—the darling, the *great* man—wrote a play in which there was a part I might play, and it was called *Sweeney in the Trees*, and he allowed us to use it as our last play of the summer.

He arrived to see his play, bringing a Saroyanesque atmosphere with him. He sent word ahead that he was going to entertain us at supper after the play. And after the play—this theater was right on the edge of the Atlantic and it was pitch dark, there wasn't a light to be seen, a very dark night—he said, "Follow me."

"Follow me!" And we could see our own way only sort of by the luminous surf, the light from the surf. And we walked along the water's edge it seemed for endless miles, down this dark way. Suddenly, he turned to the right up this dark avenue, not a light in sight. Everyone was asleep. What do you suppose we suddenly found? A light in a doorway. It was an Armenian restaurant.

In the play, Jim Lark is a fellow who doesn't think much of money, and he tossed his money away in the play. So I said, "I'll impress Saroyan," and I took three precious dollar bills and flung them into the wind as we entered the restaurant. And he ran after them and picked them up. He said, "Don't do that! That's *money!*"

"There is an angry purity, and a fierce pride, in her . . ." Saroyan's description of Kitty Duval, the husky-voiced hooker of *The Time of Your Life*. Julie Haydon made the part her own. (Vandamm)

Anyway, we got inside, got a table, and there was a girl in the play at Cape May that I knew would be right for the part of Elsie the nurse in *The Time of Your Life*. (The girl who was playing Elsie was being married and wouldn't rejoin us when we reopened.) So I wanted Saroyan to discover this girl, Marylin Monk, who was in this company. So we cooked up a little play together, Marylin and I, that she would call me to the telephone. Then I would invite her to sit where I was, next to Saroyan, and then he would naturally see that she was right for the part. And then I would go and sit in the telephone booth and pray for a few minutes, come back, and she would be Elsie Mandelspiegel.

And it happened! That's the way he cast his own plays. He'd just go along the street. He'd go into an Automat and see two Filipinos and cast them in his play. He'd go down to Greenwich Village and get an old broken-down poet, have him play. He'd find a hatcheck girl at the Stork Club, give her a beautiful part. He loved people from real life—unschooled actors.

For two months that fall, Saroyan starred as himself up and down the length of the theatre district. The official story was that he was preparing to produce and direct *Sweeney in the Trees* himself, with backing from the Shuberts, and thus he was casting the production. But he had held his conversation with the Shubert office very early during that New York visit, and it was clear that they were not giving him the money. Mr. Lee Shubert must have been especially rankled by any approach from Saroyan. It was this Shubert brother who had wanted to close *The Time of Your Life* after its legendary opening-night disaster in New Haven, had been argued out of it, and then had suffered the agony of a play that lost money for months despite rave notices. In addition, José Ferrer had cooled toward *Something About a Soldier* after the tryout week in Bucks County. He dropped his option. Not even Saroyan was pretending that this play belonged on Broadway, or between the covers of a book, for that matter.

But these were minor setbacks. Saroyan remained convinced that nobody knew better than he how to produce and direct his own stuff. It was simply a matter of getting rid of the other people. One of his closest and most seasoned theatre friends was the caricaturist Al Hirschfeld, who realized that the playwright's great luck in saving *The*

Time of Your Life had hardened Saroyan's belief that he was a born showman, not to be argued with.

> AL HIRSCHFELD: It *worked*. So that gave him the confidence, and the lack of respect for directors or designers because he figured, "These guys are *futzers*, for Christ's sake." He can handle this whole thing himself.
>
> But he forgets that the whole pattern had been set by the time that he got into it, so that the other plays that he directed didn't have that clarity.
>
> He didn't trust anybody. He wanted to do it all himself. And the theatre is a cooperative art, it is not a one-man proposition. You can do Shakespeare a million different ways, as you can do Saroyan, and Bill— We used to have arguments about this until all hours of the morning. He said, "There's only one way to do it, and I'm going to do it that way, and anybody else who wants to do it, let 'em do it, but *I* don't want anything to do with it."
>
> And that was a terrible thing that happened to him. He never realized that all of that other stuff—the craft that went into making it for months, starting fresh with a new script—that's a different kind of thing. It can't be done with just a hail-fellow-well-met and saying, "Well, okay, do it your way." Consequently, a lot of his plays suffered after that.

Saroyan was cynical in his forecast of the new drama season in the fall of 1940:

> Act I. By God, that calls for talent, doesn't it? Thinking, too. Act I. Then a little stuff, then a little more stuff, some acting, some personality, a lady with years of experience, a little more stuff and then Intermission. By God, Intermission . . . One after another until it's Act III. The last act. A little more stuff, the voice lifted, steady, the speech clear and full of innuendo, the air tense, the eyes wild, and then he says and then she says, and the guy across the aisle says, "Yesterday I saw Evie again and she looked like hell, poor kid." And then a little more stuff, and then what is it? It's art, it's drama, it's the new season. Cheer up. Everything's going to be all right.

At first, it was. *The Time of Your Life* reopened late in September, 1940, to notices even warmer than it received at its first appearance a year earlier. Brooks Atkinson of the *Times* was especially delighted with the work of the actors. This important critic had been on Saroyan's side from the first, and without prompting from George Jean Nathan. But he also had reservations about Saroyan, which he was willing to put into print. Atkinson said that, while love and sentiment were uppermost in Saroyan's mind, the plays he wrote "offer no instance of a love that is a union and represents a surrender of self. As an egoist Mr. Saroyan may not know that such a thing exists, but as an artist he ought to take it on faith." Saroyan was quick to snap back, "It so happens that I know all about it, and believe that it is the ultimate of selfishness." Atkinson printed the letter. Saroyan was like an unpaid extra hand on the drama staff of several New York papers, and philosophical skirmishes with critics could, and did, run for months of Sundays.

While Saroyan was fencing with the critics in print, his friend Hirschfeld was trying to shore up Bill's reputation with quiet diplomacy. Hirschfeld's ink caricatures of the new productions already were a front-page fixture of the *Times* drama section, and Hirschfeld's boss-of-bosses, as well as Brooks Atkinson's, was Lester Markel, cultural czar of New York's premier newspaper by virtue of his Sunday editorship.

AL HIRSCHFELD: Lester Markel kind of had a love-hate thing about Saroyan.

He said, "What about that phony friend of yours?"

I said, "Why do you keep calling him phony? What is phony about him? I mean, for God's sake, you're so used to phonies that you can't recognize a genuine human being when you see one. I mean, here's Cliff Odets, who hangs around Sardi's and smokes an author's pipe and he's got a shepherd dog, and you think that's an author.

"Don't forget that Bill comes from Fresno. I've seen him with his family out there. They play leapfrog at night. You can't do *that* in New York without being accused of being an eccentric. So *he* comes into Sardi's and acts like he's in a bar up in San Francisco." (That's what made him an eccentric, you know. He was just being himself.)

And so Markel finally said, "Well, listen. Why don't you have him come up to my house for dinner one night? I'd like to get to know this fellow. He's an interesting character."

So I said, "Well, I'll ask him."

I asked Bill. He said, "Sure, I'd love to," so we went up there for dinner, to Markel's. And Markel's daughter was there. And Markel was *enchanted* with this daughter of his, who was a very lovely girl, a young girl then.

So we had dinner, and during the course of dinner the usual arguments went on: Markel with his snide remarks and Bill laughing them off as though he didn't hear them. It was a delightful evening.

When we had finished with dinner, Bill said, "By the way, there's a thing going on in the Village. If you want to know, Lester, about the people that I hang around with, come with me. Bring your daughter. We'll all go down to the Village. There's a reading of poetry tonight."

So we all got into Mr. Markel's limousine and rode down to the Village, and it was at Eli Siegel's apartment, who was a poet who wrote something like "Hot Afternoons in Montana," something of that nature.

People used to hire Siegel to get out of their leases. He would scream so that people would call the police.

As we came into the room it was—well, either Siegel or—who was that other fellow, who used to write just *numbers*? Had six pages of them in *transition*—Abraham Lincoln Gillespie.

It was one of those, but I think it was Siegel, who was reciting this poem of words. Just abstract words, but all four-letter words.

As we came into the room, we hear, "FUCK! SHIT! WHORE! BASTARD! LOUSE!"

This went on and on.

Markel, with his daughter, he thought Bill had planned this. Unbelievable. Walked out. Would have nothing to do with Bill again. He was furious with everybody.

Aside from Nathan, Saroyan's personal taste in journalists ran not to the critics who spent their time writing about the shows, but to the columnists who drank with the stars after the curtain came down.

Gossip columnist Leonard Lyons was his closest newspaper friend, and that friendship stretched on for decades, reaching beyond Sardi's and Lindy's and into Lyons's own home, where Saroyan met inhabitants of the upper reaches of café society, such as pianist Eddie Duchin and financier Bernard Baruch. In profile Lyons resembled a gentle ant-eater. His noble nose instantly impressed Saroyan's mother and won her to his side on a later visit to California.

Another member of their circle was Jimmy Cannon, one of the earliest of the intellectual sportswriters. Saroyan recalled Cannon's encounter with Clifford Odets, the playwright whose self-assurance matched Saroyan's, but who lacked Saroyan's spirit of self-mockery: "Last night, Clifford Odets came up to me at Toots Shor's and he said, 'Jimmy, I wrote about you in my journal this morning.' I didn't know what to say. Should I have said, 'Gee, thanks loads, I guess I'm famous now. I'm in your journal. When is it coming out? My own stuff always comes out tomorrow, will your journal come out after you've been dead fifty years, or what?'"

Drifting through the night alone or with members of his floating stag party, Saroyan would make mental notes. A man talking angrily to the air outside the entrance of Lindy's: "I'll have him in my next play." The Fifty-seventh Street Automat: "Seven girls who ought to be in one of my plays." He would venture to an upstairs joint on Allen Street to see belly dancing to kanoun and oud. A block or so east was Café Society Uptown, where Barney Josephson mixed progressive politics with equally adventurous jazz. Josephson showcased black artists like Billie Holiday, Lena Horne, and Mary Lou Williams with none of the self-consciousness that sometimes afflicted the jazz impresarios. The uptown branch of Josephson's experimental club opened in October, 1940, and Saroyan was among the first customers.

Saroyan was never more the man about town than when he was about town with George Jean Nathan, who had commanded his own corner table at "21" since the restaurant's speakeasy days. Nathan was twenty-six years Saroyan's senior, fifty-eight that autumn, but the two shared an eye for beautiful women.

JULIE HAYDON: They had a marvelous time together. For years they'd go—do the town. First, they'd see all the pretty girls they liked in all of New York. That would take quite a few hours. They would start at Lillian Gish's and have tea with her. Then they would go downtown. There was a beautiful girl who sang in the Village, called Frederika, and they'd spend a few hours talking with her. And they had a marvelous way of listening to the

beautiful young talents who really needed them for
encouragement and to lean on.

There were innumerable young actresses, dancers, singers
George discovered. Frances Langford, she would visit New York.
At that time she was a very slight, very dark little girl, very
slender, and she was almost—she would break your heart. And
she looked like a tiny little sister to George, who had these great
beautiful, dark eyes.

And he was, really, to so many young people—young *women*—
he was their mentor, or "Dutch uncle" as he called it. And at the
same time, he was Prince Charming.

He was really a romantic man, and at the same time everyone
felt more themselves with him than with anyone else. They were
both more themselves when they were together. They were just
like brothers, except that George was older.

Saroyan's principal flame in New York that season was a stunningly
beautiful young actress whom Nathan had escorted as well. Joan Castle was a child star grown up, splitting her career between Broadway
and the movies. Nathan, she recalls, "liked actresses. He went with
Lillian Gish, Julie Haydon, and he took me out a great deal. Why, I
don't know. I wasn't anything like those two women." (She met his
stringent standards of attractiveness and charm.)

"I lived at the hotel across the street from the Algonquin, the Royalton. Nathan was there, Benchley was there, Dottie Parker was around.
And Julie Haydon would come in with an enormous armful, a *huge*
bouquet of flowers and say to Red, the night manager, 'Put these in
Mr. Nathan's box.' Well. The box was *that small*. And then she would
float out again."

Everyone found Saroyan and Joan Castle an attractive couple, and
whether marriage had occurred to Saroyan or not, the idea had—if
only briefly—to Joan Castle: "Romantic young girl, man of the hour.
Perfect, certainly."

Years after, Saroyan recalled the night in Sardi's when he and Jimmy
Cannon, the brainy sportswriter, pretended to quarrel over Joan. "She
suddenly said, 'Look, I need the publicity, do me a good turn, go out
in the street and have a fight about me—Leonard Lyons is here, and
he'll report it. And Arto Demirjian is here with his camera and he'll
photograph it. And it'll be on the front pages all over the country. And

"He used to send me telegrams, and I would send him telegrams, expressing great devotion, endless love, things like that. . . . That was funny, since we both were in New York." Joan Castle, the lovely actress who married, not Saroyan, but a fellow actor and then, later and longer, a nonwriting member of England's Sitwell clan. (Billy Rose Collection)

I'll be famous. Will you? Please.' " But Saroyan remembered that Cannon balked: " 'Joan Castle's not in a play, and she hasn't just published a book, so what's the publicity going to be *for*?' "

For its own sake, actually. The clubs and the columns were a special case, a sub-genre of show business and society themselves. While Saroyan might do everything in a theatre except the essential thing, get up on a stage and act, he was willing to play out a romance in public. The affair with Joan Castle had begun with an accidental meeting at Sardi's.

JOAN CASTLE: I think it was an opening-night party, and I think Kazan was there, Elia Kazan, and Bill Saroyan and several other newspaper people. Naturally, actors always get together and Saroyan was the man of the hour at that time, and I was very interested in meeting him, which I did that evening.

He took me by the arm and said, "Let's get out of here," and we walked up Broadway, cut across Fifty-second Street, and there was a funny nightclub across from "21" that Bill loved—lots of comedians [Jack White's]—and that's where we spent the rest of the evening.

It eventually got in the columns. He used to send me telegrams, and I would send him telegrams, expressing great devotion, endless love, things like that. That made it into the columns and that was funny, since we both were in New York. You couldn't do it now if you tried. You can't *find* a Western Union office, so that fun is out of our lives.

Everything he said seemed genuine at the time. I don't know how genuine it really was. There was a boyish charm and a guilelessness. He was a pure spirit. I mean *we* all thought he was. He had his little vices, like gambling, but he wasn't much of a drinker to my memory. But he was always a writer, and that meant a lot to us.

There was a wonderful Armenian restaurant in the Fifties, the Golden Horn it was called, and we used to dine there practically every night, because he felt very at home in that restaurant. The owner adored him, and it was quite a coup to get Saroyan. He probably didn't have to pay for the food.

He used to love to draw people out to find out (actually that was the writer's mind) *everything*. Your thoughts. Your background. What you're going to do with your life.

He loved Robert Burns, and there was one lady in Bobby
Burns's poetry he used to read about all the time, and he said I
was like her. I was in total ignorance. I'd never read Bobby Burns
until Saroyan introduced me.

He used to say that I had an old soul, and I didn't understand
that. Said I was an *old soul*.

Well, that's what he saw, anyway.

I was absolutely fascinated by him, but there was a restrictor in
me that said, "This is a very dicey fellow. He's very eccentric in
his own way."

And he said I had to come to Fresno, where he lived, and see
that part of the world. Of course, I never went because I don't
like the West Coast, I'm sorry to say (except San Francisco).

But he used to fantasize. He would say, "I can see you on the
ferry . . . coming across San Francisco Bay. Stomping on grapes."

All sorts of foolishness. And he always talked about the *old
country*, where he had never been, until he made a lot of money
and I think eventually he went to some country that *used* to be
Armenia.

But even in this lightest of romances, like some comedy by Samson
Raphaelson or Philip Barry, "There was a dark side, which I didn't
like," she recalls. "He was very jealous, had a wide jealous streak in
his nature. You'd talk to somebody too long, he would sort of move in
on you and get feisty. You know how gregarious theatre people are,
and he didn't like that. He was very possessive.

"He could talk to someone, that was all right. You were with him,
and that was it."

Despite the gaiety of the circles that Bill and Joan moved in that fall,
the world situation hardly could have been more grim. Roosevelt was
winning his third term while pledging to keep America out of the war,
London was being pounded in the Blitz, and Churchill was now Prime
Minister, although Britain's ability to stave off Hitler remained an open
question. Although Roosevelt kept up his campaign rhetoric about
neutrality even after the election had passed, conscription plans already were law. Selective Service registration had begun on October
16, 1940, and at age thirty-two William Saroyan was liable to be
drafted. In his past lay a brief enlistment as a teenager in the California
National Guard, a term of peacetime service he had been free to resign.
(He had only signed up, he explained, because he was hungry.)

Saroyan had his personal reasons for considering himself exempt from World War II, but the legal grounds for his exclusion from the draft rested on his role as principal support of his mother, who was then fifty-six years old.

The very day after the draft began, Saroyan made an uncharacteristic political gesture, appearing as a speaker at a dinner to raise money for anti-Fascist writers in Europe who had been uprooted by Hitler's triumphs. He shared the platform with Pearl Buck, Edna Ferber, Fannie Hurst, and Louis Bromfield—and with Clifton Fadiman, who in review after review in *The New Yorker* delighted in missing the point of Saroyan's work. (Gertrude Stein produced similar mock bafflement in Fadiman.)

A week after the dinner, Saroyan was back in San Francisco, the city he had chosen instead of Fresno or New York as his hometown for draft-registration purposes.

And he was in a rage. Before leaving New York he had approached the Chase National Bank to borrow $15,000 to produce *Sweeney in the Trees*. Small as the sum may sound against the eventual seven-figure costs of creating a simple Broadway production, it was enough to mount a play handsomely in 1940. But the Depression was still on, and an institution like the Chase was more or less defined by its avoidance of risks like William Saroyan.

Saroyan poured out his anguish in a long, rambling letter, which *Variety* printed on the front page of the next issue:

> "If I can't borrow $15,000 from the Chase National Bank for the production of a play which I feel very strongly might lose money—which, nevertheless, I am eager to see on the stage as it should be seen—I feel quite confident that, if the worst came to the worst, I could win the money betting on the horses.
>
> And, on the other hand, in the event that I lost $15,000 betting on the horses instead of winning that much, I know I could write another play in a week, sell it, have it produced badly, and with the profits pay the people I had, one at a time, borrowed the money from.

Moving beyond the bankers, "the financiers, the real estate men, the tailors and the hangers-on," Saroyan went on to attack the audience itself.

> I have never been able to understand who the people are who go year after year to the plays that keep running on Broadway forever and then go on the road in five different directions.

The theatre now is obsolete. Watch what happens this year and know how obsolete it is. . . . A time of war, a time of confusion, of spiritual trauma, of despair—is he trying to tell us that that is the time, also, for art? That's exactly what he is trying to tell you. . . . A lot of collapsing is going on. A lot of restoring has got to take place. An excellent place to lick Hitler and other malignancies is in yourself. A most incredibly appropriate area in which to destroy assassins is in your own work if you are a writer.

It looked as though if anyone was going to save the American theatre Saroyan would have to be the one. This was the self-appointed task before him as he descended to his comfortable basement retreat on the night of December 30.

By then the first reviews had arrived for *My Name Is Aram*, and they were almost unqualified raves. As Depression America rattled and skidded toward the sickening war that already had sucked in all of Europe, Saroyan's semisweet dream sequence based on his boyhood was exactly the sort of escapism readers wanted. Sales were excellent. Combined with his guarantee from the Book-of-the-Month Club, the royalties eliminated the Shuberts and the Chase National Bank from Saroyan's theatrical accounts book. He was in a position now to produce his own play, to verify his unconventional wisdom by selling tickets to it.

Perhaps because it was his own money that he would be risking, neither *Sweeney in the Trees* nor any of the other unproduced plays seemed quite so attractive to him now.

Since he had bragged so often about the effortlessness of writing a play, he was obliged once more to prove it to himself. Six nights after he began *A Cup of Kindness*, his play about the eccentric family in the old house on the slopes of Red Rock Hill, he had finished it. It was midnight Sunday, January 5, 1941.

From a practical standpoint the play was in three acts, playable as two, and it required a cast of only nine. Finally—a producer's consideration—it used one simple setting.

His new title for it was *Pole Star and Pyramid*. The play lacked a plot in any usual sense of that word. It was, however, a gallery of pure Saroyan characters, and as opening night approached, he would finally name his new show for them: *The Beautiful People*.

CHAPTER TWO

IMPRESARIO

1. CALIFORNIA, 1941

Shortly after Labor Day, 1940, it had seemed as though Saroyan could deliver the whole new Broadway season single-handedly. Now, in January, 1941, the theatre year was half over and nothing of Saroyan's could be found on a New York stage. Far from collapsing, as Saroyan had predicted in his parting diatribe, the commercial theatre was moving from strength to strength. There was nothing mechanical about Lillian Hellman's *Watch on the Rhine*, no hint of music-hall nostalgia in the musical hit *Lady in the Dark*, and the new comedy *Arsenic and Old Lace* seemed capable of running forever. Saroyan bragged all his life that he performed best under pressure, but the rapidly dwindling season left him little chance to save face. He sent word east that he would personally produce and direct *Across the Board on Tomorrow Morning*, a play he had written and offered to Eddie Dowling, who had politely rejected it. Saroyan arranged now for a tryout production in Southern California, at the Pasadena Playhouse.

In the weeks until he joined rehearsals there as author and advisor, not director, he was free to polish *The Beautiful People* and to pursue his

San Francisco pleasures. If Saroyan had returned to San Francisco fearing that draft registration would mean early conscription for him, there was less to fear early in 1941. President Roosevelt had begun to use the phrase "arsenal of democracy" in his State of the Union speech and his fireside chats, and Congress was debating the new Lend-Lease legislation. Roosevelt's plan was to give Hitler's opponents everything they needed to fight except American troops.

While the draft board knew Saroyan's home address, there were few others who did, only the close friends he preferred to hear from by telegram. The phone number was altogether secret. But Saroyan was no recluse. Just as he wrote every day—a piece for the Armenian magazine *Hairenik* or letters and journal entries, if not a story or play—he walked every day. Sometimes the walk was a midnight ramble up steep Red Rock Hill, which rose above his mother's house. Sometimes it was a tour of the low life on Turk or Third Street downtown.

This is when Herb Caen, who already was San Francisco's star newspaper columnist, met Bill at Omar Khayyam's, the fancy and popular restaurant, which, despite its Persian name, was as Armenian as Saroyan himself. Saroyan was borrowing money from the proprietor, George Mardikian, when Caen was introduced.

"I soon discovered that Bill was always on the shorts, mainly from gambling," Caen recalled. "He bet on the horses at a bookie joint in Opera Alley . . . a dead-end off Third and Mission. When he wasn't losing there, he was playing idiotically bad poker behind New Joe's in North Beach. Not only did he not possess a poker face, in spades, he usually revealed his hand. In seven-card stud he'd say, 'Don't bet against me, I got aces back to back!' He was not lying."

Only in the past two years had Saroyan enjoyed a better-than-comfortable living from his writing, and he already had to answer rumors that he lost all of his royalties at the track or at poker. The current surge of money from his bestseller, *My Name Is Aram*, was pledged firmly to financing his return to Broadway under his own power. If the New York banks would not listen to him, no matter. The previous spring, as he had argued with his colleagues over the structural troubles with *Love's Old Sweet Song*, he had in a moment of exasperation offered to buy out Dowling and the other backers of the play, the Theatre Guild and the silent partner, Lee Shubert. Pat Duggan, Saroyan's play agent, had taken Lawrence Langner of the Guild aside to confide that Saroyan had no such money, adding, "and even if he had, I wouldn't let him." Now Saroyan did have the money. Did he have a play to bet it on?

The Los Angeles critics thought not. Saroyan had stepped in at the last moment with advice to the director, Frank Ferguson, and he was willing to make changes after opening night of *Across the Board on Tomorrow Morning*, but tinkering was not enough.

Perhaps stung by the New York critics who had accused him of dodging the great themes, Saroyan had packed birth, death, and the meaning of time itself into the fragile one-act fantasy. It opens with two of the main characters discovering the audience and addressing them directly—always an ominous sign. A baby born in the play's nightclub during the course of the action achieves maturity a few moments later through means of a poorly-explained wrinkle in the fabric of time. The Saroyanesque curtain speech about betting on a racehorse named Tomorrow Morning seemed to be stuck on. The point of the play, however, was the need for life to go on in the face of disaster. Specifically, although indirectly, he was writing about the war, about the way new generations of children would replace the victims of battle and genocide. At least one of the critics, the man from the Los Angeles *Times*, got the point, but still found the play "opaque."

In addition to being confusing, the play was too short to make a complete evening in the theatre. Trying to capitalize on both defects, Saroyan persuaded the Pasadena Playhouse to perform the play twice for each audience. There was an intermission, which gave reluctant ticket holders a chance to escape, and the plan was followed for five showings.

The bad news about the play appeared not to travel much beyond Pasadena itself. In New York the theatre columns dutifully continued to report the forthcoming Broadway production of *Across the Board . . .*, to be directed by Saroyan himself. And in California the whole affair was about to be forgotten, thanks to the arrival of Eddie Dowling, Julie Haydon, and the touring company of *The Time of Your Life*.

Before that play had won the twin awards, the Theatre Guild had been reluctant to tour it. Even after changing their minds, the Guild producers had hedged their bets on the warm-up period in New York, booking the play into the Guild's own theatre for a mere two weeks. But the New York run had been doubled to a month, and in cities like Chicago extra days were added to satisfy the demand for tickets from the general public. Instead of simply playing to the Guild's subscription audiences, *The Time of Your Life* was proving to have a broad appeal in each of the cities on the road. By the time the tour ended in a return engagement in Detroit in May, 1941, twelve weeks on the road had stretched into twenty-eight. The tour was one of the most successful of the season, and it allowed the Guild to claim its first and last profits from a Saroyan production. The experience may have satisfied Lee Shubert enough to pave the way for Saroyan's later dealings with him. The royalties certainly fortified Saroyan's own bank account as he set out to become his own producer.

But now, in March of 1941, as the road company neared San Francisco, the build-up was intense. Early that month, Saroyan's newspaper friend Herb Caen had sprinkled an item a day about the playwright into his column. As opening night drew near, entire columns celebrated Saroyan's eccentricities, and Saroyan's picture was published in all four local papers again and again. A restaurant announced a Saroyan cocktail, another invented a Saroyan salad, and there was even a Saroyan sandwich, their ingredients lost to history.

Then, as now, transcontinental train service to San Francisco reached only to Oakland, across the Bay from the city's isolated peninsula. Despite the new Bay Bridge, rail passengers still arrived by water.

JULIE HAYDON: When we got to San Francisco, the most beautiful thing happened. We arrived in Oakland, across the Bay, just before dawn. And in those days you crossed the beautiful bay in a ferryboat. And Saroyan, in the sunrise, was on the dock waiting for us. And he took us for breakfast to the counterpart of Nick's waterfront saloon, restaurant, and entertainment palace that he had put in the play.

The presumed inspiration for Nick's Saloon, by virtue of their shared location on Pacific Avenue, was the establishment run by Izzy Gomez, a self-made legend after Saroyan's own heart. Pacific Avenue is no avenue, but a relatively narrow street, and even in the darker, more realistic of the two sets built for *The Time of Your Life*—the set that retrieved the play from fantasy—Nick's was a splendid place compared to its real-world counterpart.

Izzy Gomez operated from a loft reached by a narrow, filthy stairway. Gomez himself was a pear-shaped man with heavy-lidded eyes, a snub nose with huge nostrils, and a salt-and-pepper toothbrush mus-

No one ever claimed to have seen Izzy Gomez without his hat. With the end of Prohibition, San Francisco's best-known speakeasy proprietor became celebrated, just like Jack and Charlie in New York, but his Pacific Street saloon (below left) remained a far cry from "21." But to San Francisco, he was immortal before Saroyan immortalized his joint as Nick's saloon. (San Francisco Archive)

tache. He wore baggy, dark clothing with waistcoat and gold watch chain, and the hat on Gomez's head was even more of a fixture than Saroyan's. It was a high-crowned, low-brimmed black fedora no one ever saw him take off. His joint was close to the city's old jail, and the reporters and writers who patronized Izzy's had been loyal since Prohibition, when the place was a speakeasy that offered food in a pinch. Both food and drink often got seasoned with ashes from Izzy's dangling cigarette.

Saroyan delighted in mixing people from the very different milieus he moved through, and the play's arrival provided rich opportunity for this exercise. A delegation of Fresno cousins arrived as an Armenian claque for opening night, and Saroyan, Dowling, and Julie Haydon were the guests of honor at a reception in the office of Mayor Angelo Rossi, who issued a proclamation.

On opening night at the Curran Theatre Mayor Rossi was sitting in a prominent box, and no tickets were to be had. The crowd was as packed with local bigwigs as an opera performance. Among Saroyan's friends and family the assumption was that Bill was backstage with Eddie Dowling and Julie Haydon. Backstage, it was assumed that Saroyan was in a box or aisle seat alongside his family or civic officials.

Saroyan's seat was on a side aisle by a fire door near the rear of the second balcony. Since his picture had been printed again and again in recent days, Bill kept the collar of his big overcoat turned up.

The performance was a triumph. The play drew curtain call after curtain call, until Dowling raised his hand and stepped forward to praise Saroyan. Dowling was a trouper with a magical ability to ad lib, and his feelings for the young playwright always had been warm. But his praise for Saroyan that night was so extravagant that, as one wag put it, it managed to match Saroyan's opinion of himself.

At the end of his speech Dowling called for Saroyan to rise from his seat and join the company on stage. The audience craned their necks for a look at him. Again, Dowling called for Saroyan to show himself. No Saroyan.

"He certainly can't be picking grapes at this hour of the night," Dowling cracked, and the laughter bought time for a quick thank-you and for the curtain to drop between the equally bewildered cast and audience.

Saroyan had left by the balcony fire stairs at the moment the curtain had fallen for the first time. His bags already were packed for his return to New York the next afternoon. Instead of celebrating that night with his old theatre friends, he was alone with his mother and sister at home. He wired Dowling and the cast, praising what he called the best performance he had ever seen from them.

Even at this late date, 1941, Saroyan liked to brag that he remained nobody special to his old friends in Fresno and that he could relax there knowing they had no idea of his complicated eastern incarnation. This was untrue, of course, as the advance planning for the play's tour had revealed to him. After San Francisco, the company's next stop was Fresno. The mayor of San Francisco had honored the actors with a reception and a proclamation, but the mayor of Fresno met them at the station with a band and was host at a banquet after the performance. Saroyan's young cousin Ross Bagdasarian, who had been in the cast from the very beginning, received star billing on the marquee that night and got to make the curtain speech afterward. This was long before an Armenian could dream of being mayor of Fresno, a time when Saroyan's old community remained isolated by prejudice and outright hatred. The Broadway stars, the overjoyed young cousin standing tongue-tied before the footlights, and the magic of the play itself all combined that night for a moment of triumph only slightly less sweet to Saroyan's cousins and their kind because Saroyan himself was absent.

It was true that if Saroyan wanted to produce anything on Broadway that season it was high time for his return to New York. But his explanation to the newspapers about his absence from the curtain calls at the Curran was entirely unlikely: that he had received a wire from his business agent during the performance itself, urging him to return to New York immediately to close a deal for a new show. Which new show? That he would not tell the reporter.

2. THE BEAUTIFUL PEOPLE

Late in March 1941, Saroyan began casting his personal production of *The Beautiful People*, the play he had started writing on the night of December 30 as *A Cup of Kindness*. His old directing collaborator Eddie Dowling would be of no use to him this time out, thanks to the continuing tour of *The Time of Your Life*. George Jean Nathan and Bill's other cronies might prove useful after there was something up on stage to criticize, but it is doubtful whether Saroyan was in a collaborative mood. He still had faith in *Across the Board on Tomorrow Morning*, for example, but he had just seen it fail in the hands of others. A year earlier, while working with Dowling on *Love's Old Sweet Song*, Saroyan had joked about the three requirements for a director: a pipe, an ability to make speeches, and a talk table, a known location in a theatre-district restaurant where the experts and well-wishers could sit down to offer counsel and consolation. Later, Saroyan would admit to listening to veteran producer-director Jed Harris and cutting away "considerable literary writing" in *The Beautiful People*. But he smoked no pipe, and he was unwilling to deliver a twenty-minute speech in order to evoke an eleven-word reading from an actor, to use Saroyan's own example. To his great credit as a novice director, he understood the importance of the line readings the actors offered at the beginning of work. The bulk of his energies went into casting.

In his earliest plays Saroyan's whims about casting had been tempered by the presence of colleagues. Eddie Dowling supposedly had been ignorant of the fact that Ross Bagdasarian was Bill's cousin when the boy tried out for *The Time of Your Life*. The youth's natural skill and a push from George Jean Nathan and Julie Haydon had won him the part. Angi O. Poulos, who played Demetrios, a lawn-mowing immigrant in *Love's Old Sweet Song*, had been discovered by Saroyan in a Greek coffeeshop in New York. In the same play the patriarch of the wandering Okie family was Arthur Hunnicutt, found working in the basement laundry room of the Algonquin Hotel. (It was the beginning of a long and successful career as a character actor for Hunnicutt.)

Perhaps Saroyan liked to work this way because of discomfort with open casting calls. Once, locked out of a rehearsal hall at the Theatre Guild building, he had been reluctant to walk through the Guild's main offices to get a key because it would have meant facing the crowd of unemployed actors who populated the Guild's lobby throughout the Depression. Early in his casting of *The Beautiful People* Saroyan had chosen Peter Xantho, then a part-time drama instructor at New York's City College, for a part that consisted of a single speech. The role was cut, but Xantho remained on as Saroyan's stage manager, and so, from the beginning, there was a guide to the folkways and protocol of the production process.

As the moony young Owen Webster, author of the one-word novel *Tree*, Saroyan chose a ballet dancer, Eugene Loring, for whom he had

"I'm not sure I've got anything confusing to say to actors. I'm not sure I've got anything more to say to them than, 'O.K., Joe, act.'" Saroyan was remarkably true to his word as he set out to produce and direct *The Beautiful People*, alone at last after the frustrating compromises of his previous Broadway efforts. (Courtesy Aram Saroyan)

written the title role in his scenario for Ballet Theatre's production *A Day in the Life of the Great American Goof* a season earlier. The allegorical ballet had resulted from a chance meeting at Sardi's between Loring and Saroyan, who confessed to having attended only one dance performance in his life. The idea of something happening onstage without dialogue was unbearable to Saroyan, and so *The Great American Goof* had included lines for the dancers. Saroyan, however, never saw it. He always happened to be in San Francisco whenever Ballet Theatre revived it. "George Jean Nathan saw it and told me it was the world's very worst ballet," Saroyan wrote. But Loring had been praised by critics, not simply as a dancer, but for his acting, too, and so Bill had found his Owen Webster.

>   JULIE HAYDON: Gene Kelly was engaged to a lovely young dancer, Betsy Blair. He told Saroyan he knew a girl who might be right for *The Beautiful People*. When Saroyan told the story at first, he said he was going by a restaurant, looked in a window and saw Gene sitting with Betsy Blair. She was a lovely dancer and she had no dream of being an actress.
>
>   Saroyan walked in, saw her, walked across the room, and said, "That's the girl!" He walks up to the table and says, "Would you like to play the leading role in my play *The Beautiful People*?"
>
>   Gene said, "Now, Bill, you know she has to read for it before you can give her the part."
>
>   He said, "No. No reason, no reason at all. But if you insist, come by tomorrow morning to my office."
>
>   Next morning, Betsy gets there with Gene, and she reads half a line. Bill says, "Fine, fine. That's it! Your contract."
>
>   And she was superb. No one could have been as beautiful as she played that.
>
>   Freshness! That's what George believed in, too.

Kelly, of course, knew the way the Saroyan lightning struck. He had been discovered beside the suburban swimming pool of the Theatre Guild's Lawrence Langner and Armina Marshall, was cast in *The Time of Your Life*, and since had graduated into the title role of Rodgers and Hart's *Pal Joey*, further fattening the legend of Saroyan as an idiot savant of casting. In another version of the Betsy Blair discovery legend, the audition takes place in the empty theater where Miss Blair has just

Betsy Blair, here with Curtis Cooksey as her father, was a 16-year-old chorus girl Saroyan selected for the key role as the most beautiful of *The Beautiful People*. Canadian writer Morley Callaghan attended *Panama Hattie* with Saroyan to see her and second Bill's opinion. (Vandamm)

finished dancing in the chorus supporting Ethel Merman. When Saroyan interrupts her after her first word of the reading, she bursts into tears, convinced that her voice is wrong. But, as in Julie Haydon's telling, the contract is hers. Contrary to the rumor that he had never seen her perform, however, Saroyan had attended *Panama Hattie* with friends to observe her fresh beauty. The Canadian writer Morley Callaghan was along on one such evening and seconded Saroyan's choice. None of Saroyan's friends were out of the running for roles. Al Hirschfeld recalls, "He wanted *me* to be in that thing," but Hirschfeld declined, just as he had done some years earlier when offered a part as one of the bearded religious fanatics in Hecht and MacArthur's *Twentieth Century.*

But the other newspaper artist who haunted Broadway was—reluctantly—willing to take a part. Don Freeman was a Californian whom Saroyan had met a couple of years earlier at the Art Students League, introduced by the Armenian painter Manuel Tolegian. Saroyan was enchanted with Freeman and his wife, Lydia, and had become a frequent caller at their Fourteenth Street studio.

While Hirschfeld's style was built on a sinuous ink line of unvarying thinness, a very hard and crisp look, Freeman worked in a warmer, looser way—a pencil and watercolor style with a softness that suggested lithography. While Hirschfeld's skill was consummate caricature and the ability to get down exactly that memory of the show or the star that the audience were likeliest to take away with them, Freeman was more interested in the show the audience never saw.

"Don couldn't get over the fact of a fellow dressed in a Roman costume reading *Variety,*" Hirschfeld says. "He just latched onto that, and he was intrigued and fascinated with everything that happened backstage. It was a fantasyland for Don. He never treated it as a form, or just a way of exploiting a craft, an art. It really was that to Don. He was a part of it."

Freeman had drawn the theatre from every conceivable point of view: the wings, the flies, the pit, the stagedoor alley. From everywhere, in short, except center stage itself. Saroyan's musical ideas about the role of the older brother in *The Beautiful People* would place Freeman at center stage at the end of each performance. Throughout the play, whenever one of the characters mentions Harold, the brother who has left San Francisco for New York, a cornet phrase from the song "Wonderful One" is to be heard in the distance. Freeman, who was a capable horn player, seemed just right for that offstage duty. In March, 1941, the Freemans had moved uptown to a studio at Columbus Circle. Don Freeman was a collaborator in Saroyan's current literary success, having illustrated *My Name Is Aram*. Some of the pencil drawings were made on location in central California. All of them captured Saroyan's tone of voice exactly, one of those lovely matches between artists in different media. Saroyan, then, was a welcome intruder when he burst in on a makeshift party while actor Eddie Mayehoff was at the piano and Freeman himself was playing the trumpet. According to Freeman's account, the tune was "Wonderful One," which explained its inclusion in the play. But the song is one Saroyan delighted in playing on the workroom phonograph, part of a limited background-music repertoire, which included Brahms's First Piano Concerto (whose last movement he called "the train music"). The morning after the party Saroyan phoned Freeman and asked him to come immediately to the Fifty-seventh Street Automat.

There, Saroyan explained his musical conception of the elder brother in the play, adding that he now had decided that the wandering brother would appear at the climax of the last act. Freeman was to play "Wonderful One" in the distance and then, after years of observing the stage from the wings, actually step in front of an audience. Freeman was uncertain, but Hirschfeld recognized a thwarted performer when he saw one and encouraged him to say yes. After all, Hirschfeld pointed out, being in a show only took a couple of hours a day. Freeman would have the rest of the time free for his usual work. Freeman agreed, but only after Saroyan cut the older brother's long speech down to a few lines.

In the same way that the song and Don Freeman's horn shaped the part of Harold Webster, Saroyan encouraged Eugene Loring to play music with which he was familiar during the brief scenes that placed him at the piano. One day Saroyan heard Curtis Cooksey, the veteran character actor playing patriarch Noah Webster, noodling at the onstage piano during a rehearsal break. "I hadn't played more than half a minute before Bill Saroyan came running down the aisle and asked, 'Can you play other songs?'" Cooksey said, "'If they're not too difficult.' 'Good. We'll have you play the piano.' Next day, I had piano passages added to my part."

Fredrica Slemons read for the part of an old flame of the father's whose main function in the play is to listen to exposition. "After I finished reading the part of Harmony Blueblossom, I was asked if I had good legs. Something they forgot to tell me was that in the final scene I was supposed to come forth in tennis shorts. My legs evidently passed muster, for I was given the role. The second day of rehearsal the tennis scene was out. About a week later I was told that I was to wear a long dress. 'Why so old-fashioned?' I asked. 'You don't want your legs to show.' 'Young man, I was hired for my legs.' I looked over at William Saroyan. I thought he would laugh himself sick. Nothing more was said about a trailing gown."

After an initial reading or two from his assembled cast, Saroyan backed away from them, asking only that they try to "find" the characters for themselves. He retreated to a bar across the street, leaving them entirely to their own devices. The Group Theatre had been dead for a year and the Actors Studio was not yet reality, but whether through instinct or dumb luck, Saroyan was working in a way that had yet to become accepted practice in the commercial theatre. As producer he could afford no out-of-town tryout. Opening night would be the only chance for a run. The tailoring of script to player and the extraordinary weight given to actors' initial readings are the hallmarks of the workshop-style productions that became popular thirty or so years later, but with *The Beautiful People* Saroyan made them work first.

Loring recalled an afternoon when Saroyan asked him to stay after the others had left. The playwright wanted to see how many different ways the dancer could sit in a chair. There was something of the puppeteer in Saroyan's behavior that afternoon. "Before Bill was through with me I was sitting, if you want to call it that, in every conceivable position. In more than half of them my feet were higher than my head. I'd get into a position and hold it while he walked through the theatre to see how it would look from different angles. What a workout!"

As the show came together Saroyan asked Xantho, his stage manager, to stagger the actors' calls. Some began arriving as early as ten in the morning, and the last would rehearse until midnight. Saroyan himself was putting in a fourteen-hour day to rehearse them as closely as possible, and even though the cast was small—nine—he sometimes lost track of the players.

"The afternoon he left me in the cellar for almost an hour I almost lost my patience," Fredrica Slemons said. "I had descended the trap leading below and was waiting for the cue to bring me up the stairs.

Fredrica Slemons was disappointed when Saroyan cut the scene in *The Beautiful People* where she was to appear in a short tennis outfit. Her character's main function was to listen to a full act of exposition delivered by Eugene Loring as the eccentric Webster son, author of the one-word novel *Tree*. (Vandamm)

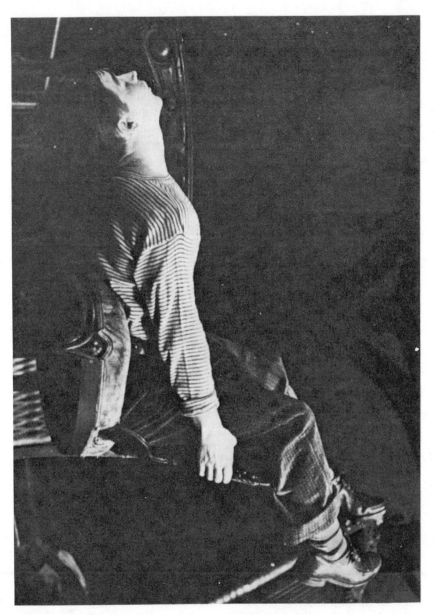

"How many ways can you sit in a chair?" Saroyan asked Eugene Loring. Saroyan thought of more ways than Loring did, even though the young actor was an accomplished ballet dancer, the choreographer and lead in Saroyan's dance-play for Ballet Theatre, *The Great American Goof*. (Vandamm)

There were no lights, and it was gloomy. I sat and waited and waited. No cue. Finally, I could stand it no longer and I marched up the stairs. Mr. Saroyan had started the rehearsal with the second scene and no one had informed me."

The early word-of-mouth about *The Beautiful People* was good—so good that Saroyan boasted of two late offers to co-produce with him, offers he was delighted to be able to turn down. The continued strong sales of *My Name Is Aram* and high grosses from the road company of *The Time of Your Life* made it much easier to say no. His total outlay for the new play barely passed $10,000.

For the physical production Saroyan set aside a grand $900 for materials, but the designer he chose to accomplish the job found him generous in other ways. He was Sam Leve, then at the threshold of his distinguished career.

SAM LEVE: Saroyan climbed up to my fifth-floor apartment. You know New York? On Fifty-first and Tenth Avenue then, in '41, was called Hell's Kitchen. He climbed up to the fifth-floor apartment to look at my drawing of [the set for] *The Beautiful People* with comments and changes and stuff. He *loved* it. Finally, he says, "Okay. Here." He accepted it. Not only was he the writer, but he was also the producer and director, so I had nobody to answer to but Saroyan. He loved it. Fine.

He looks down on the floor, though. He sees a mattress. "What's a mattress on the floor for, Sam?"

I said, "For sleeping."

"It's a double mattress. Are you married?"

"Yes. Last week."

"Why the hell aren't you away on a honeymoon?"

I said, "Bill, remember you were selling newspapers? *I* am still selling newspapers."

Next day at the theatre, he hands me a check for $1,000.

"I want you to buy yourself a car after we open the show a month hence and take your bride on a trip across the country, on a honeymoon."

Beautiful.

AL HIRSCHFELD: I remember going to a first run-through of *The Beautiful People*, sitting out in the audience. Bill had invited about

five people: Boris Aronson [the theatrical designer]. Myself. Bill
Zorach, who was a sculptor. Bill Cody, who used to draw
pictures on the sidewalk on Sixth Avenue dressed like a
cowboy—like Bill Cody, Buffalo Bill. And Pete the Piccolo Player,
a guy that played two piccolos at the same time.
    Now, that was the audience. And the play goes on, and at the
end of it, the house lights go up and Bill comes over to Bill Cody
and he says, "How did you like the play, Bill?"
    And Bill Cody is sitting there with tears streaming down his
face into his beard, and he says, "The greatest God-damned play
I ever *saw.*"
    Saroyan said, "Ever see a play before, Bill?"
    "Nope, first time."
    He attracted them somehow. There was a mutual-admiration
thing there. Any place that you went with Bill there was some
kind of a lunatic running around.

Saroyan thought it wise to build box office, so he hired a Broadway
veteran named Leo Freedman as his press agent. The job of Saroyan's
press agent was so charmingly redundant that Freedman immediately
was able to grant interviews in which he meditated upon his own
uselessness. This was far from the case, though. He had to sell tickets
on a tiny budget. It was Freedman who talked Saroyan out of wasting
a thousand or so on an art contest to solicit paintings that would have
served as the posters and lobby cards for the play. He also put the
quietus on a plan to costume a score or so of characters of the Buffalo
Bill/Piccolo Pete school and have them circulate around Times Square
as living billboards.
    But one idea Saroyan refused to drop was the free preview. He was
not the first producer forced to paper the house for an untried production, but he turned necessity to his advantage with the most micro-
scopic of advertising outlays, a notice in the classified advertisements
of the *Herald Tribune*:

> Wanted—750 persons who have never seen a Broadway play to be my
> guests at a rehearsal of "The Beautiful People" at the Lyceum Theater on
> Wednesday evening, April 16, and help me prepare my play for future
> paying audiences. Apply by letter only, inclosing stamped self-addressed
> envelope and tickets will be mailed you. . . .

Four thousand letters came, and there were only a thousand seats to give away. Saroyan himself plunged into the job of analyzing the letters, matching the sincerity of the plea to the appropriate location in the Lyceum.

"I am a truck driver who has always desired to see a play but has never seen a play." He got orchestra seats B7 and B9. A woman admitted, "To be honest with you, we have seen one Broadway show, and that was when our friends presented us with the tickets on our wedding anniversary." She received good seats, too.

As planned, the scheme was talked and written about, and when Saroyan announced that further free previews would be offered on a first-come, first-served basis, five policemen had to be called to handle the crowd, which reached west from the Lyceum box office on Forty-fifth Street all the way to the lobby of Loew's State on Broadway. The crowd was so big and so anxious that the nervous treasurer of the Lyceum opened the ticket windows early, and those at the head of the line quickly established an impromptu market, scalping and swapping the first tickets.

It was a publicity stunt, true, but it was more. At the same time that Saroyan was giving seats away (including a completely orderly free preview for schoolchildren), he was quarreling with his business people over a plan to charge a $6.60 top on opening night. As modest as the amount sounds, it would be equivalent to $60 or $70 a seat in terms of the present day. Just as he was prepared to help the poor see a play for the first time, he was eager to soak the rich, whose presence left him diffident. The four thousand letters proved that a large public wanted to see theatre, but felt disconnected from Broadway, or locked out by the prices. Even after the previews, the letters kept arriving.

"I would like to mention that Owen states that it is 3,733 miles from San Francisco to New York. The actual highway mileage is 3,056 miles and the rail mileage is about 3,100 miles." (Saroyan stuck with the prettier sound of the inaccurate figure.) Another man wrote to say he had been disturbed when the insurance investigator in the play tore up a photograph of his wife. "To me that was ugly and takes a lot of the beauty away." The bit was removed from the performance script.

The afternoon of the final run-through, Betsy Blair had gone to her dressing room for a lemonade and sat waiting to be called.

"Time went by but I thought nothing of it. I wasn't in the first scene and I thought they were going through it twice. Finally I went out. The theatre was dark. Everybody had gone. I went to the box office. They told me Mr. Saroyan had left for San Francisco.

"I felt very bad not having said goodbye to him and raced up to his hotel. He was still there. 'Why the sudden departure?' "'I decided that the final rehearsal was as fine a performance as I would ever see, so why should I hang around any longer?'"

Al Hirschfeld recalls that he did hang around for opening night.

AL HIRSCHFELD: I remember the opening night of *The Beautiful People* Bill came back, and the first guy he grabbed: "Greatest God-damned performance I ever saw! You were *marvelous.*" The guy's the *fireman.* He wasn't even in the play.

The reviews the next morning were surprisingly friendly, although even Saroyan's staunchest supporters admitted that *The Beautiful People* was less than the sum of its parts. Richard Watts wrote in the *Herald Tribune,* "There is so much humor, beauty, imagination and emotional richness about the play that its frailty, its slightness and its moments of excessive sentimentality seem of strange unimportance."

Burns Mantle had voted against Saroyan in the Critics Circle meeting the year before, but he now confessed himself surprised—surprised that Saroyan had the $10,000 with which to produce the play, surprised that Saroyan would dare to direct after watching three summer tryouts fail, and surprised that the play worked for its audiences. Mantle said Saroyan's new play was offering comfort, not escape (as though escape were the theatre's stock-in-trade), but that "humanity, God save it, stands more deeply in need of comfort today than it has ever stood before in our time."

A certain audience found comfort in the play immediately, returning again and again. Tallulah Bankhead was seen attending a dozen times, and she insisted on buying her own tickets. Saroyan urged the critics to come back, too: "It will be more casual and careless, and consequently more right and real."

The columnist Dorothy Kilgallen remained unmoved. It was her stubborn conceit that the new Saroyan play—indeed, the whole Saroyan phenomenon—was a conspiracy among critics to test their power by praising trash and watching to see if the public flocked to it. But Miss Kilgallen's was a lonely voice. Word was that Saroyan had a chance at the Critics Circle award for the second season in a row. And in the office at the Lyceum Theater the press agent Leo Freedman came across a copy of the letter Saroyan had sent to the trustees of Columbia University, advising them that, while his new play deserved the Pulitzer Prize, the cash award would go unclaimed, as it had the year before.

When the Critics Circle met for its awards voting, six ballots were conducted with no play getting a majority. By the seventh attempt, the vote was twelve in favor of Lillian Hellman's *Watch on the Rhine*, with six standing by Saroyan, including George Jean Nathan. Hellman won, and the Pulitzer went to Robert Sherwood's political drama *There Shall Be No Night*.

Saroyan was a good loser, attending the Critics Circle awards dinner, where he took pains to go over to Lillian Hellman and tell her how much he had liked *Watch on the Rhine*. He was quoted afterward as saying he was pleased that *The Beautiful People* had come in second, rather than winning. This could hardly have been true, but he had good reason to be satisfied with what he had accomplished.

After humiliating reversals on tryout stages and in the offices of producers and bankers, Saroyan had fought his way back to the top. If the summit belonged to Lillian Hellman at the moment, no one questioned that Bill Saroyan held high ground. More importantly, he had regained his reputation for being good-natured and a good investment.

"I am going to begin writing a new play in the next six or seven days," he announced at the end of May. "I am going to write the play to offer it to Eddie Dowling. In the whole American theater I know no other man with as fine an instinct for what is good.

"In the fall I will produce another play—maybe *Sweeney in the Trees*; maybe *Across the Board on Tomorrow Morning*; maybe another play, to be written after the one for Dowling.

"I'm not going to get rich. I'm going to put it all right back where it belongs."

3. FRESNO SUMMER

Back in San Francisco in the basement apartment at his mother's house, Saroyan spent the month of June writing a complicated allegorical play called *Jim Dandy, or, Fat Man in a Famine*. Lawrence Langner of the Theatre Guild was in San Francisco that month, not to see Saroyan, but to spend time with Eugene O'Neill, who was then living across San Francisco Bay in a remote corner of Contra Costa County. In Langner's brief meeting with Saroyan the two men discussed the new play intended for Dowling, and Saroyan came away with a $1,000 option from the Theatre Guild.

Jim Dandy appeared to well up from some deep subconscious need in Saroyan, and its themes of greed, inhumanity, the exploitation of art, and the sanctity of life all were notes that Saroyan had sounded before, but never in so curious a fashion. The setting was a giant broken eggshell containing cultural wreckage, which included, among many other props, a library desk, a revolving door, a cash register, and—most Saroyanesque of all mankind's inventions—a player piano. The characters included a pair of young lovers, a condemned man, an apelike creature with human aspirations, a magician perhaps willing to help the ape reach that goal, and the title character, an enormous fat man whose meaning is especially obscure. For the rest of his life, Saroyan took delight in teasing and hinting about the meaning of *Jim Dandy*.

Early in July, 1941, the play was complete, and Saroyan flew to Fresno to visit with cousins and old friends. His plan was to return to New York in September to produce and direct *Jim Dandy*.

The Beautiful People, meanwhile, had begun to suffer the typical summertime fate of all Broadway shows in that era. The July heat not only had sent New Yorkers hurrying out of town, but stay-at-homes and tourists were reluctant to spend an hour or two in a hot theater. Only smash hits tended to survive the summer doldrums, and *The Beautiful People*, while far from a flop, was not in that category.

The cast voted to accept salary cuts and, from Fresno, Saroyan tried to make up his mind whether to close and attempt returning in the fall or to try playing straight through until cool weather returned. A new gimmick was adopted, a money-back guarantee for customers who disliked the show. The first week, $139 was paid back. A couple quarreled in the lobby after a performance. "My husband liked the show and doesn't want his money back. I don't agree with him. There wasn't enough action in it for me." She got her $3.30. The money-back trick brought more free publicity, grosses climbed a little, and Equity approved the cast's scheme to cut their salaries. As a point of pride Saroyan insisted that he would rather close the show than pay actors less than scale. He announced the play would close, changed his mind briefly, then let the notice stand. By August the losses had become too great.

Saroyan had been warned about the summer heat, had ignored the warning, had lost. Perhaps if he had closed earlier he would have come away with a little profit. His dream had been for one production to follow another into what would have become known as the Saroyan Theatre. He had not tossed that dream away, but it would have to be postponed. There was no talk now of a new production in the fall. But, as *The Beautiful People* folded, Saroyan was in a relaxed and introspective mood. The trips to Fresno became more and more frequent, and each stay lasted a little longer. The job of writing the play for Eddie Dowling could wait.

Saroyan renewed his friendship with Young Corbett, who had peddled the Fresno *Herald* with him when the two were boys. Now Corbett ran a popular bar in Fresno, which left his daytime hours free, and so the two men went fishing day after day. Saroyan began to lose

the urban pallor which has become my normal complexion. The sun is very close to the earth in Fresno, its rays very direct and penetrating, the heat very great and magnificent, but if you expose yourself to all this suddenly, you are apt to get cooked. I know, because that is what happened to me every day until Corbett explained that you had to rub yourself with a mixture composed of two parts olive oil and one part vinegar. After that, instead of getting cooked every day and not being able to sleep all night and having the skin peel off after a week or so, taking the color with it and bringing out a fresh layer of pallor, the sun-color moved in slower and deeper and stayed there.

Writing about his weeks in the sun, fishing at Mendota or Friant (the fish were sparse), Saroyan catalogued all of the plans that had been pushed back indefinitely by the busy work of being himself: a winter in the woods, a summer working again in a vineyard, learning how to paint, discovering how to read and write Armenian.

I have planned to perfect my new theater—a globe device with the basic colors and forms capable of creating an inexhaustibly varied drama of objects and colors and relationships, accompanied by their related sounds—and have never done so.

I have planned to marry the most beautiful woman in the world and bring up a family, and have never done so; I have never met her—how could I do so?

CHAPTER THREE

MOVIEMAKER

1. M-G-M

By his own confession, Saroyan was not doing what he wished, whether that was to bicycle from San Francisco to New York or to "buy a hundred acres of fertile land with a stream running through it."

His writing had become filled with the life-or-death themes the critics had teased him, over the years, about avoiding, and perhaps he had discovered those themes in his own life. He was, after all, the child of a culture that measured its families in terms of tribe and clan, yet he was single and childless. And a genocidal war was under way, an affair that no Armenian really could ignore.

Saroyan did not return to New York at all in 1941. Giving life to *The Beautiful People*, only to see it fail, had been an exhausting affair. Instead of producing and directing the new allegorical play, *Jim Dandy*, he literally gave it away, to an organization of college drama companies and amateur playhouse groups all over the country, the National Theater Conference. Throughout the fall of 1941, dozens of versions of Saroyan's strange nightmare of a play would be presented for a night or two by unpaid actors. The play would then, like a dream, be quickly forgotten.

One further play needed to be written, however. The idea had struck him during his Fresno idyll, and the new script for Eddie Dowling came effortlessly. Although the play was born in the Central Valley sunshine, it was a dark affair, the story of a jailed man, a lynch mob, and the girl who tries to help the prisoner, but fails. An amateur company in Santa Barbara tested *Hello, Out There* for a few days early in September. Its future would lie with Dowling after that.

As Saroyan turned thirty-three on the last day of August, 1941, getting drafted seemed to be a distant prospect, although war in the Pacific was likely and Americans much younger than Saroyan had been getting conscripted for almost a year. Saroyan was frank about his feelings in the matter. "I think I would be wasted in the Army. It will probably work out that they'll find they'd rather not have me. I might get so bored as to disintegrate the whole morale. But, if I had to, I would accept the responsibility. I would play stud poker."

Some patriotic role was called for. In August he had spent $500 on a full-page ad in weekly *Variety* in which he offered to give away the movie rights to *The Time of Your Life* to any studio willing to donate the production costs and then hand the profits over to defense work. Fifteen years later, Saroyan's columnist friend Leonard Lyons would remember that "RKO wanted to buy the movie rights for $100,000, and I was with him when he refused it and, instead, offered to donate the film rights to the Red Cross." But the general understanding in 1941 was that *The Time of Your Life*, the action of which was confined to a single barroom setting, was especially ill-suited for translation to film. Saroyan's agents, Harold Matson and Pat Duggan, were at the top of their profession, and it is difficult to imagine either man permitting his client to decline a six-figure offer. When quizzed about why a Pulitzer Prize play hadn't been sold to the movies, Saroyan had explained that the price was $250,000, unheard-of in those days. Now the price was to be nothing.

Within a week after the offer, a producer at Columbia Studios, Lester Cowan, had pledged to make the picture. "We'll see whether Saroyan meant what he said," Cowan said, adding that bit players and technicians could ill afford to work for free, although he would expect his director and stars to do so. Saroyan replied by newspaper that he never meant for "humble people" to suffer under his proposal and suggested that the technicians and bit players be paid double. "I have chosen to challenge the rich because they have again failed to accept their share of sacrifice. Anything I have is the Government's, for the duration."

But by the end of August the talks with Columbia had gotten nowhere, and Saroyan announced that the offer was withdrawn. The public were left out of the further discussions, if any, between Saroyan and Columbia, but Bill had been, briefly, a dialogue doctor with the B. P. Schulberg studio in 1936, knew his way around Hollywood, and may have been reluctant to see his material in the hands of Harry Cohn's Columbia, then an opportunistic studio on the fringe of Poverty Row.

What was obvious was that Bill Saroyan was again thinking about the movies. In his first excursion to Hollywood, he had been a brilliant short-story writer pressed into duty patching up scripts. Now, in 1941, he was an award-winning dramatist and the author of a book that could easily be mistaken for a novel, *My Name Is Aram*. In a piece he dashed off for the Sunday *New York Times* Saroyan had, with no provocation, made the same kind of pointed comments about the movies that he had made a year earlier about the moribund theatre.

> The amusing thing about moving pictures is the enormous number of nonentities who work together to make something any normal half-wit would prefer not to make in the first place. I look forward to the day when Louis B. Mayer's bootblack, barber, chauffeur, gardener and garbage man will be given credit for helping to make a million-dollar movie. In my opinion these men are entitled to as much recognition as anybody else involved in the sweet miracle making.

Whether he knew it or not, and it appears that he did not, Saroyan had admirers inside L. B. Mayer's empire, a Metro-Goldwyn-Mayer then unmatched in power, in its roster of players and directors, in its technical support, and in its sheer output.

M-G-M's Arthur Freed had, by 1941, graduated from the music department, where he had worked as a songwriter, to his new post as head of his own production unit, the group that would turn out the most spectacular and successful musicals in film history. *The Wizard of Oz* already was behind Freed, and he had launched the Judy Garland–Mickey Rooney series known as "backyard musicals," the "let's-put-on-a-show" stories, which had begun with the adaptation of Rodgers and Hart's *Babes in Arms*. A great many of Freed's planned projects and future triumphs came from Broadway, as did some of his most successful collaborators, like director Vincente Minnelli. (A year or so earlier, Minnelli and Saroyan had toyed with an idea for the musical theatre, an all-black revue, but it had come to nothing.) Freed was a shrewd judge of talent and made regular raids on Broadway to spot it and sign it up.

He had seen *The Time of Your Life* and was impressed not only by Saroyan's script but by the young hoofer in the play, Gene Kelly. Freed tried to sign Kelly on the spot, but the young dancer had a good grasp on the momentum of his career, and he stayed on Broadway through his starring role in *Pal Joey*, eventually signing a Metro contract without a screen test, an unusual achievement. With Betsy Blair of *The Beautiful People*, now his wife, he had arrived in Hollywood in October, 1941, to begin work on his first M-G-M film, *For Me and My Gal* with Judy Garland.

Freed's link to Saroyan, however, was Stanley Rose, a Hollywood bookseller Saroyan had known since his earlier movie days. Budd Schulberg, son of mogul B. P. Schulberg and friend to both Rose and Saroyan, remembers Rose's haphazard business practices.

> BUDD SCHULBERG: He was a very poor businessman, but he sold a lot of books. Stars had accounts there, studios. He also took bags of books over to the studios and peddled them door to door down the corridors of the writers' buildings.
>
> He was about five foot six, five foot nine or so. Very ruddy-faced. He had a sort of outdoor, Texas complexion. Part of it was from the drinking. He was a very, very, *very* heavy drinker.
>
> He had a kind of—what I think of as a *Texas* face. Very un-West-Coast. Unintellectual.

One Saturday, Freed was browsing in Rose's Hollywood Boulevard bookshop, a weekly ritual, when Rose told him that he had just missed the famous Bill Saroyan. Freed asked Rose for Saroyan's Hollywood number, called him, and invited him to breakfast next morning at his mansion in Bel Air.

Freed told his biographer that Saroyan assumed the meeting was to be about making movies. The truth was that Freed was simply a fan, and the copy of *My Name Is Aram* was there to make that point, not to inspire negotiations. Saroyan, in turn, was a fan of one of Freed's song hits, "I Cried for You," and so the two men made friends quickly. Saroyan left their breakfast talk that day with an invitation to the studio to meet L. B. Mayer. It is an invitation Saroyan may have accepted in the spirit of an earlier pilgrimage to Jean Sibelius or his later one to the cottage of George Bernard Shaw: the visit to a living monument. At their first meeting Mayer was enchanted with Saroyan. He was familiar with Bill's reputation as best-selling author and Broadway playwright, and with the tone of the *Aram* stories, which matched his own sentimental tastes. Other writers brought to M-G-M by Mayer had looked down their noses at the tycoon, furious with the outside circumstances or inner flaws that had led them to sell out to Hollywood. Saroyan gave the impression of needing Hollywood less than Hollywood needed him, and his feisty egalitarianism sounded just like a Mickey Rooney speech from an Andy Hardy movie. Since Mayer preferred to have stories told to him rather than reading them in script or outline, Saroyan was in his element. A natural storyteller had met a natural listener.

Mayer was sold. The question is whether Saroyan was selling and the answer appears to be that, at first, he was not. Saroyan told Arthur Freed he was not interested in writing for M-G-M. In a late memoir Saroyan has described his financial situation in the fall of 1941 as exceptionally flush. He was staying at the Knickerbocker Hotel in Hollywood, "having four suits and two overcoats made to order, from being rich. . . . I wasn't spending anywhere near enough, though, because all of a sudden money had begun to rush in upon me, and I was using it mostly for sensible, family things. I was not banking a dollar of it. I was getting rid of it, because there was plenty more where that came from."

Suddenly, there was not. In that same spirit, that same season, Bill went to Las Vegas and dropped $3,000 in a single night.

> Very often, more often than not, whenever I gambled I lost all the money I had. . . . The reason I wrote *The Human Comedy* in eleven days, for instance, was that I had gone to Las Vegas and in one night had lost three thousand dollars, which at that time was a lot of money. Before I was broke, though, I made fifty-dollar bets at crap tables for men who were broke at three o'clock in the morning, and I won many of those bets and handed many of those men fifty silver dollars. I was showing my contempt for money and what it did to men.

Broke, Saroyan was willing to listen to Arthur Freed's offer of an office and $300 a week for expenses while he developed a story he would produce and direct himself.

On Thursday, December 4, word reached New York that Saroyan was under contract to M-G-M as a producer and that he would "spend some time at the studio studying film technique before he made a picture." The details came out on Monday the 8th, the morning after the Pearl Harbor attack. There was no contract at all, simply a handshake. For next to nothing, Louis Mayer had first option on an original screenplay by William Saroyan. He already realized that Saroyan would not attempt to adapt one of his plays, and Mayer had tried in vain to talk him into attempting a story called *The Rosary*, a Metro vault item with a high schmaltz count.

Whether it was discussed or not, Saroyan must have sensed that *My Name Is Aram* was wrong for the pictures. Too ethnic, for one thing, and it would require a child actor of uncommon skill, including the ability to age ten years. But that book was a near-miss for the movies, and Stanley Rose urged Saroyan to think about his Fresno days as a messenger for Postal Telegraph, Western Union's energetic rival, which had recently gone bankrupt.

Saroyan's idea of learning about the movies was to look at as many of them as he could. He commandeered a screening room and the popcorn that Metro executives were free to order and looked at dozens of films with Rose and other friends. In those days, in the dark and wandering the Metro lot, Saroyan must have realized that Louis B. Mayer's principal work of art was no single film, but a vision of small-town America that survived refraction through a variety of stories, actors, and directors. Mickey Rooney may have been a draft-eligible Hollywood sophisticate, but to moviegoers he was Judge Hardy's son, Andy.

Perhaps through the urging of Arthur Freed, the movie taking shape in Saroyan's mind was tailored for Rooney from the beginning. For all his spirited independence, Saroyan turned out a three-page outline tailor-made for Louis Mayer's small-town attitude, the juvenile star who embodied it, and the pressing need to make movies that said something about the war America was just entering.

The Human Comedy is set in Ithaca, California, an imaginary small town in the Central Valley, which is the same size in 1941 as Saroyan's Fresno had been twenty years earlier when Bill was a bicycle messenger. There is no sense of a special ethnic identity to the family of Homer Macauley, the telegraph boy Mickey Rooney would be playing. The name Homer for the hero and Ulysses for Homer's very young brother added to the classical aura generated by Saroyan's choice of an Ithaca for his setting, and the title borrowed from Balzac was a crafty bit of appropriation as well. Together, these touches would help convince Louis Mayer that he was dealing with an instant work of art. Teenaged Homer has a widowed mother, a beautiful sister, and an older brother away at war. There were a host of roles for Metro's stock company of character actors, including the part of a tippling old telegrapher for Frank Morgan, the accomplished character player now best remembered for creating the title role in *The Wizard of Oz*. The episodic plot allowed Saroyan to range freely throughout a town in a way he had been forbidden to try on stage. Here was his magic theatre where night or day occurred on command, where the audience could follow a racing bicycle or shrink to the size of four-year-old Ulysses, hunkering over a gopher hole or running in terror from the terrifying "mechanical man" peddling a tonic in the drugstore window.

Episodic though it is, there is a sure sense of movement to the story—toward Homer's loss of innocence. After delivering telegrams to the families of dead servicemen, Homer inevitably comes to the moment when he must carry the same kind of news to his own mother. But Saroyan was not content to leave matters there. He contrived for the elderly telegrapher to die at the shock of that message, and for a crippled compatriot of the dead brother to arrive in Ithaca at the same time. This second soldier is a foundling, mustered out of the Army now by virtue of his wounds, and he is to join Homer in the film's last moments—a new son and brother to temper the news of the real one's death.

Saroyan said afterward that he knew "Mayer likes a good cry," and *The Human Comedy* is full of them.

Impatient to hear what Saroyan had come up with, Mayer summoned Kate Corbaley, the one-time librarian who was the studio's dramaturge. She had two great abilities: skill at inhaling stories, novels, plays, finished scripts, and outlines in wholesale quantities and sniffing out the ones that smelled like possible hits for M-G-M—and an even greater skill at telling Mayer about them. Her nickname was "Mayer's Scheherazade," and she lived up to it. Mayer wept copiously as she recited the outline of *The Human Comedy*. He tried to reach Saroyan immediately to congratulate him.

But Saroyan was mysteriously absent from the Writers Building, and

Mickey Rooney delivers a flat and tuneless reading of "Happy Birthday" as Homer Macauley in *The Human Comedy*, the Saroyan story in which the telegraph messenger gets to star. Saroyan's brother, Henry, reported that Grogan, the old telegraph operator played by Frank Morgan, was a completely accurate portrait. (His real-life model in the Fresno offices of Postal Telegraph drank heavily, but did not die receiving a literally heartrending telegram.) (M-G-M)

"The most important thing to remember about the nose—is that it makes trouble, causes wars, breaks up old friendships, and wrecks many happy homes." Homer Macauley's speech was true to the spirit, if not the letter, of the digressions Saroyan himself indulged in as a high school student. (M-G-M)

The cast of *The Human Comedy* stare at a photo of Van Johnson, whose role as soldier brother Marcus Macauley was shamelessly padded for the shooting script. Left to right, Mickey Rooney, Jack Jenkins, Fay Bainter, Marsha Hunt as Diana, the society girl, and Donna Reed. (M-G-M)

the studio cashier had reported to Arthur Freed that he was holding checks Saroyan had not claimed.

"They gave me a crib of a room, a typewriter, a cell of a window, and told me to bang away," Saroyan would tell a friend years later, after his bitterness about Hollywood had hardened. "Finally, I saw that I wouldn't get anywhere at all if I were to remain in that city and that dungeon, and that I ought to return to civilization as soon as possible. So I just got up and left, not a word to anyone, and went directly to San Francisco, where I hired a room in a hotel on Powell Street and went to work."

Saroyan would say later that the studio dispatched a lawyer to the Powell Street hotel to warn him that he had broken an oral contract. "So he went, and, finally, I produced the scenario . . . in three weeks, between visits to the Kentucky Club."

So the old pressure Saroyan often said he needed in order to write was there: gambling debts, the threat of action over a broken contract, and a war that was getting worse quickly, so quickly that he sensed it might soon swallow him up.

The day after Christmas he sat in the house on Fifteenth Avenue with his Grandmother Lucy, his mother's mother. She was telling him a fable about a fruit tree: traveler after traveler would mysteriously toss its apples away and fall to their knees after a bite or two, groveling in the dirt. At the same time, Saroyan was trying to listen with the other ear while Winston Churchill addressed a joint session of Congress. Lucy, who could not understand English clearly, was oblivious of the history taking place on the radio. "What is this man saying?" "He is talking about the war." It was difficult for Saroyan to understand the point of his grandmother's parable. Why *had* the travelers fallen to the ground? They had seen gold beneath the tree. Saroyan himself was broke as he mailed away the incident of his grandmother's fable to *Hairenik*, the Armenian journal in Boston. The check he enclosed to help the enterprise was pitifully small, he confessed.

A month to think about it (December), a month to write (January). *The Human Comedy* took far longer than any of Saroyan's previous projects, and its bulk and complexity reflected the effort. The script was reported variously at 250 to 400 pages of character description and dialogue, but there were no camera instructions.

"I knew that what we had here was a fine piece of work—one of my best—so I decided that I would break my oath never to visit Holly-

wood again so that I could take the manuscript to Metro personally
and ask $50,000 for it—or nothing."

Early in February, 1942, Saroyan met with the powers-who-were at
M-G-M. One of the men alongside Mayer was Eddie Mannix, the
head-office middleman who mediated the sometimes open warfare
that broke out between talent and producers and among the executives
themselves. Benny Thau, also present, was the sub-czar who controlled the talent roster, "more stars than there are in heaven," as the
publicity department had put it. The final member of the panel, Bernie
Hyman, had been the right-hand man to Irving Thalberg, the brilliant
crown prince of M-G-M who had died five years earlier.

The conventional image of Louis Mayer is of a tyrant dosing his child
stars' gruel with Benzedrine, but there are reasons to believe that his
affection for Saroyan was authentic. In these negotiations and for the
remainder of their brief relationship, Saroyan would refer to the most
powerful man in Hollywood, an estimated twenty-five years his senior
(no one really knew), as Louie.

> BUDD SCHULBERG: It was definitely bravado. My mother and
> father, the inner group, would call him Louie, but basically it was
> L.B. or Mr. Mayer.
>
> He did, literally, charm Mayer at the time. It seemed as if he
> had Mayer eating out of his hand for a while. I was amazed by it.
> I was amazed because that man was so tough.

Even more unbelievably, Mayer permitted himself to be addressed
on a first-name basis by Saroyan's chosen agent, Stanley Rose.

> BUDD SCHULBERG: Stanley was an unlikely agent. Bill really made
> him the agent—and it was good of Bill—to pay him back for all
> the handout meals at Musso and Frank's and all the direct loans
> and general help.

> AL HIRSCHFELD: And Louis Mayer, who loved Bill—at least within
> his own way—rooked him completely.
>
> He said to Bill, "Who the hell is this loafer you bring in with
> you all the time?"
>
> Bill says, "That's my agent."
>
> And Louis Mayer, of course, with Stanley as an agent . . .

Bill said the only way he'd work out there was if he could use his own people. He wanted to use his own family, wants to put them in pictures as directors, as cameramen and so on, to learn the ropes.

Louis Mayer said, "Anything you want, Bill. The thing to do is try it out first, see how you like it, write a short. Work it out. I'll leave it up to you. You can take the studio—Studio Fourteen" (or whatever) "—do whatever the hell you want. Nobody's going to bother you. Write the script. You direct it, you hire the people, you produce it, you're the whole works on this short."

Saroyan had chosen Rose as his agent to thank him for making the introduction to Arthur Freed, for filling the windows of his bookshop over the years with displays of Saroyan's newest books, and simply for being a good friend. Rose's business was so poor that he was in danger of having to close the shop, and cutting him in on ten percent of a movie deal seemed a fair way to help an old pal, much in the spirit of his honeymoon check to a new pal, the designer Sam Leve.

But Rose was over his head in the plush-carpet precincts of Louis Mayer's executive suites. As Saroyan analyzed it later, Rose was side-tracked from the talks by the purposeful hospitality of Frank Orsatti, a one-time West Coast rumrunner who had become a Hollywood agent and then a close crony of Mayer's. Orsatti's alleged tactic against Stanley Rose was simple: generous doses of whiskey for Rose whenever he appeared for a meeting.

As for the money part of the deal, Saroyan's telling of that detail would vary, too. Sometimes the story was that he had wanted $50,000, raising the ante to $60,000 to cover the money to save Stanley Rose's bookshop. Press reports at the time had placed his asking price as high as $300,000. Metro's opening counter-offer of $25,000 sounds reasonable and real.

The deal was struck at $60,000, with an additional $1,000 a week to Saroyan for the period during which he would serve as a producing and directing "consultant." At the same time M-G-M announced that Mickey Rooney would star in *The Human Comedy*, the studio explained that Saroyan would work with a regular producer and director on the picture.

Was the short subject Mayer had promised a sort of screen test for Saroyan? A bonus? A diversionary tactic? Perhaps no aspect of the agreement between M-G-M and Saroyan got more publicity and attention than the handshakes and oral understandings. This was far from the usual way business was done in Hollywood. To Louis Mayer, Saroyan was a writer and contractual nitpicking was beneath his dignity. To Saroyan, Mayer was a tycoon with sense enough not to burden a genius with legalistic detail.

There were smiles and handshakes and drinks all around. In a hand as bold as his voice Saroyan inscribed the title page of Arthur Freed's copy of the script:

> On Wednesday, February 11, 1942, I, William Saroyan, joined up, officially and with happy heart, with the great organization of Metro-Goldwyn-Mayer with the kind help of my friend Arthur Freed & old Texas Stanley Rose—here's to good times and great pictures.

The ground had been made ready for a hateful misunderstanding.

2. CAROL

Saroyan was given the key to a richly-paneled office with a private bathroom, complete with bathtub. The significance of the office was hardly a matter of nuance. It was the office L. B. Mayer himself had just vacated in a remodeling, and it was far more splendid than the writer's hutch Saroyan had fled in the days before his signed contract. Saroyan immediately ordered the Remington "Noiseless" typewriter replaced with the noisy sort he preferred, and he complained aloud that there were no towels to go with his executive bathtub.

He also began to prowl the lot in search of a place to work with fewer vice-presidents and accountants than the Irving Thalberg Memorial Building. He settled on a loft-like space that had been used as a still photography studio and, before that, as a dressing room for the Marx Brothers. There was room enough to shoot baskets, so he had a hoop installed, and it was far enough off the beaten path for the player piano he ordered not to disturb anyone important.

Saroyan cheerfully agreed that it was up to others to cut and polish his overlength dialogue version of *The Human Comedy* into a shooting script. Mickey Rooney was at work on *A Yank at Eton* and was scheduled to play next in *Kim*. Saroyan's immediate task, then, was to write, produce, and direct the short subject that would establish his movie credentials in a matter of two reels. He chose his story "A Number of the Poor" for conversion into a comedy set in a fruitstand, and he began writing a script under the title *Jazz*.

Even after giving Stanley Rose more than an agent's percentage of the $60,000—$10,000 in all—Bill was comfortably off. There was the $1,000 studio salary piling up each week, and royalties were beginning to come in from a new Harcourt, Brace collection of accumulated playlets and sketches called *Razzle-Dazzle*.

His money problems of the previous fall were gone, and despite the occasional disaster at the track or the bookie's, his gambling was controlled by his busy schedule. Saroyan had entered Hollywood at a stratospheric social altitude, and he found old friends there to greet him.

One of them was Artie Shaw, the young clarinetist and bandleader whose fame was as great as any movie star's, and certainly the equal of Saroyan's. The columnist Herb Caen had introduced the two late in 1940 while Shaw was playing a series of engagements at San Francisco's Palace Hotel. Saroyan would drop by the hotel at the end of a night's work to listen to Shaw's band perform their leader's arrangements like the well-oiled machine that they were, and to hear Shaw's own inventive clarinet solos. Of all the big-band leaders, Shaw may have been the most accomplished in his own right as a jazz soloist, a role he would pursue in later years in small-group work before abandoning the clarinet altogether in favor of farming and writing. In San Francisco, the two men often had wound up their evenings at Sally Stanford's, where both were fond of the society madam's Chinese cook and his way with a scrambled egg. In Hollywood, Shaw played himself in musical pictures such as *Second Chorus* with Rita Hayworth and Fred Astaire, and he already had left Lana Turner behind in his complicated roundelay of marriages.

Shaw was indeed a complicated man, whose immense popularity and highly public love life obscured his seriousness. He was as interested in being a writer as in playing music, and his taste in music was not limited to "Star Dust." Saroyan had asked him to compose incidental music for solo clarinet to accompany the play *Jim Dandy*, but nothing had come of the proposal, and Shaw had been amused at Saroyan's halting attempts to write lyrics for popular songs.

Shaw's Hollywood entourage in 1942 included a very serious young composer, David Diamond, who was at home not only with Shaw and his performing friends, but with expatriate composers in Hollywood such as Schoenberg and Stravinsky, and with alumni of the old Group Theatre, including John Garfield and Clifford Odets.

Diamond remembers Saroyan's tirades that winter over the Japanese attack, which had left America no choice about entering World War II. And he also recalls several social occasions at which the intellectuals in the Group Theatre's West Coast circle revealed their friendly feelings for Saroyan and his work.

> DAVID DIAMOND: Once Cliff Odets, I remember, said, *apropos* of *My Name Is Aram*, "By God, I wish I had been able to write stories as well as that."
>
> Cliff Odets and Bill were good together, like listening to two great men—not trying to outdo each other—but they finally got to boring each other. One would shout and the other would shout the first one down. And Artie in the middle with his nonstop high voice. It was really something—a "Concerto for Three Solo Males." Impossible.
>
> Artie with his theories on Dostoevsky, the novelist, and out would come, every three minutes, "*De gustibus non disputandum.*" That was one of his great statements when anyone disagreed. "*De gustibus non disputandum.*" But he always had strong statements.
>
> And then Cliff would walk right over him with rather extraordinary, romantic, Goethe-like statements, you see.
>
> And then Bill Saroyan, *pomposo*, with that voice, that rabble-rouser kind of thing: "Ah, yeah. It's all a lot of bullshit!"
>
> Now, one night we go out and we go to Julie Garfield's—*John* Garfield's (Julie to all of us in the old Group Theatre days)—and it was a nightmare of an evening because Frances Farmer was sort of in her manic phase—drunk as a lord, but absolutely okay. But miserable in the arms of Harold Clurman, crying herself into a terrible stupor because Cliff Odets wouldn't marry her and wouldn't live with her and God knows what else.
>
> And then started one of those evenings which I shall never forget. In came Bill Saroyan yelling, "Come on, we all gotta go get laid! What the hell's going on here?"
>
> It was unbelievable, the sophomoric carrying-on of all the males there except Harold Clurman. Movie stars, people like Garfield, so successful, and they have to go around screaming,

"We gotta get laid!" And the result was, watching poor Frances Farmer in such a state of agony, I thought, "What a bunch of really, really bastards all these guys are, thinking only about getting laid."

The previous fall, when he had been staying at the Hollywood Knickerbocker Hotel, Saroyan had had an experience that lingered in his memory, an encounter at the elevator bank with "a voluptuous woman of about forty-four, absolutely stacked, who had come to Hollywood to get her daughter into films." Watching them walk down the corridor in high heels, Saroyan had thought, "Lord, lord, there are these monuments of glory, are there not?" and was startled a little later when the daughter knocked on his door to say, "If there's anything we can bring you, please let us know." Saroyan declined the kind offer, suspecting blackmail.

Aside from utilitarian visits to Sally Stanford's establishment or dates with a starlet whose name no one could recall later, Saroyan's love life was empty for a man so attractive, famous and, from time to time, well-to-do. He occasionally was asked what kind of woman he was looking for, and he answered once, "Women were meant to be beautiful. I admire women who are brilliant and beautiful like Clare Boothe." There was a story, half true, about Grandmother Lucy taking him to visit a nice Armenian girl who danced and made thick black coffee for him, but Saroyan liked to joke that any girl he married "will become Armenian." Perhaps the best clues to what he was looking for lay with the girls and women of his stories and plays. The husky-voiced Kitty Duval of *The Time of Your Life*, who is really a frightened little Polish farmgirl; the young Betsy Blair with her fresh-faced virginal beauty; the charming mixture of child star and Broadway sophisticate in Joan Castle, his latest real romance.

Joan Castle was in Hollywood early in 1942, married now to a Broadway actor with a new studio contract. Both Joan and Artie Shaw knew a girl there who was, without their suspecting it, precisely the woman of Bill Saroyan's dreams.

Her name was Carol Marcus, and she was in Hollywood that winter more or less by accident. Her true venue was Park Avenue, the New York society pages, the special room at the Stork Club that was reserved and lighted as a jewel case to display Manhattan's loveliest— and wealthiest—debutantes.

ARTIE SHAW: When Sherman Billingsley had the Stork Club he recognized the publicity value of having people like that in the Cub Room. The Cub Room was the hangout. I used to go there, and I'll tell you the basic reason to go there when you're a star. People don't ask for your autograph. People don't bother you. You're among peers, so nobody looks at you askance. I mean, if I'm sitting there and Charlie Chaplin's over there and the Prince of Wales is over there and Judy Garland is here, who the hell cares? You don't go among common folk.

Upton Sinclair quotes a Scottish proverb: "Don't marry for money, go where money is." That's the advice of a Scottish father to his son. And you will automatically marry a rich girl, because that's where they are, and one of them will be prettier than the others, and you might as well marry her because you like her. Rich ain't gonna hurt.

So I was around where *beautiful* people were. People ask me, "Why did you marry so many beautiful girls?" I said, "Well, what would you say if I married *ugly* ones? Wouldn't you think that's weird?"

When she left the Dalton School in New York in the summer of 1941, Carol had decided against college and in favor of an acting career, and her cool blond beauty helped to win her parts at summer playhouses in Maine, Pennsylvania, and New Jersey. She was seen in magazines, endorsing Woodbury Soap alongside Maury Paul, the man who chronicled and to some degree controlled café society in his role as Cholly Knickerbocker, columnist for the New York *Journal-American* and Hearst papers everywhere. Carol's endorsement fee for the soap advertisement went to one of her charities, and she worked hard at the theatre parties, at the evenings at El Morocco for refugee children, at the whole complex calendar of good times and good works in which all debutantes and pre-debs were expected to participate.

Her father, Charles Marcus, was a senior vice-president of Bendix Aviation and was deeply involved in war preparations as were, in their own way, Carol and her debutante friends. In the summer of 1941 Carol was recording secretary of the Gloom Chasers, a group of debs headquartered at the Stork Club and dedicated to providing dates for servicemen, a completely wholesome and acceptable work of charity in those days. "Miss Marcus is a grand bet for blind dates because of the fact that she has had stock company experience, and thus is able to make a soldier think she likes him, even if she draws zero in the raffle," one of the columns reported.

As grown-up as her public world was, there was a girlish side to it as well. Her two closest chums—Carol had introduced them to each other—were Oona O'Neill and Gloria Vanderbilt. Oona was playwright Eugene O'Neill's second child by his second wife, Agnes. The third Mrs. O'Neill, Carlotta, disapproved of Oona's circle and fretted that she would arrive for visits from New York "covered in red fingernail polish." Gloria was a child of the society pages. Her mother, Gloria Morgan, was a gorgeous twin Cholly Knickerbocker had starred in his columns as he launched the very idea of café society early in the twenties. "Big" Gloria's marriage to Reggie Vanderbilt, Reggie's death, and his sister Gertrude Vanderbilt Whitney's custody battle for "Little" Gloria were a tabloid circus of the twenties and thirties. "Little" Gloria's aunt, Mrs. Whitney, had won the fight in court, but the de facto victory went to "Big" Gloria. As Cholly Knickerbocker had written, "A gay, sophisticated and cosmopolitan world lies before little Gloria if she is given into the custody of her mother." Although custody went to the aunt, it was the mother's world the girl chose for herself as she reached an independent age.

Carol and her two close chums all looked striking, but Carol was arguably the loveliest. Gloria and Oona had dark hair and Carol's was the most glamorous of blond shades, but all three followed fashions in clothing and makeup that advertised their *milieu*.

JOAN CASTLE: They looked like all the little debutantes of New York—dead-white faces. They looked like they dipped them all in a flour bin. And black—purpley black lipstick. (I've never seen Carol's skin.)

This is a girl who used to take her lipstick off with $50 lace handkerchiefs. The first time I saw her do it, I said, "Carol, why don't you use a piece of Kleenex?"

"Oh," she said, "the laundry will get it out." I mean, these handkerchiefs were little museum pieces.

ARTIE SHAW: I remember playing the Strand Theater one day, first show, 10 A.M. I get out there with my eyes half closed, and I look

The fresh beauty of Carol Marcus
needed no studio lighting or special filters to shine through. This is
a candid newspaper flash photo.
(Wide World)

out and there in the first row: Carol and Gloria with their
grinning teeth shining up at me. Gloria . . .
  Poor little rich girl. I remember the first time I had a date with
her, she was living in River House, and so I went to her
apartment, and we were sitting on the couch and doing what kids
do. I mean, I was twenty-nine, and I was still very naïve at
twenty-nine. I had been playing music most of my life.
  Fabulous God-damned apartment. River House is a pretty
hincty place. High ceilings, not like a New York place. I found
out why. She had a two-story apartment, and part of it, they'd
gone right through the ceiling to make what they call a cathedral
ceiling. In New York, that's unheard-of. And in River House, to
have a *duplex*. Holy Shit!
  Anyway, so we're making out a little bit on the couch, like kids
do, and at a certain point, I heard some noise.
  I said, "What's that? Is somebody here?"
  She said, "That's Nanny."
  I said, "What?"
  Her childhood nurse was living with her.
  God.

Artie Shaw was the dream of every teenaged girl in 1941 and 1942,
including teenaged girls like Carol, Gloria, and Oona. But these three
had bigger ambitions, too. Gloria confided to Artie that the three of
them had sworn a pact that each would hold out for a special kind of
Mr. Right—a certified genius, recognized as such by all the world. In
Oona's case, it would be Charlie Chaplin. (Joan Castle remembers sitting with Chaplin between sets of tennis in Hollywood in 1943: "He
said, 'Oh, I wish I'd met Oona twenty years ago,' and I said, 'You
couldn't have. She wasn't born.'") Gloria dated actors older than she—
Franchot Tone, Errol Flynn, Bruce Cabot, Van Heflin. Some of them
were old enough to be her father, and Howard Hughes was more of a
contemporary, but not in the true genius category. Four years ahead
lay marriage with a genius old enough to be her grandfather, the con-
ductor Leopold Stokowski. But in 1941 her man was neither far older
nor terribly famous. He was Pat di Cicco, a one-time Hollywood agent
who had gone to work for Howard Hughes. The engagement stories
late in 1941 that portrayed di Cicco as a film executive overstated the
case somewhat. He was a young beginner, an attractive one. Gloria

planned the wedding for Hollywood, not New York, another expression of her growing independence.

In November, 1941, Carol was cast in a role that helped prepare the way for her meeting with Saroyan. Geoffrey M. T. Jones, an old boyfriend of Gloria's, was acting in the Princeton campus production of Saroyan's *Jim Dandy*, and he arranged for Carol to play Flora, the prissy librarian. Carol had gone to see *The Time of Your Life* the year before, and she had toyed with making Saroyan the subject of her class paper during her last semester at the Dalton School, although she finally wrote about T. S. Eliot instead. The Princeton production of *Jim Dandy* was the one Brooks Atkinson of the *Times* and other New York critics chose to view. Al Hirschfeld joined Atkinson on the excursion to New Jersey, and met Carol for the first time there, even before their old friend Saroyan had heard of her.

Carol's biggest role late in 1941 was as the star of her own debut. The principal organizer was her mother, Rosheen, a beauty in her thirties who was capable of being mistaken for a debutante herself. (People would ask Carol, "How old were you when your mother was born?")

ROSHEEN MARCUS: Carol's debut was just unbelievable. The papers just took over the whole story. Errol Flynn was to come out in a coach and present her. He was going to be Prince Charming. It was going to be done at the St. Regis Hotel, the St. Regis Roof, and they were in the process of repainting the whole top of the St. Regis Roof and getting busy finding a theatrical coach. The invitations were—I *think* they were—already sent out.

And war broke out. My husband said, "No way is my daughter going to be presented like that during wartime. We're at war." December 7, 1941. We had to cancel it. The most heartbreaking thing, and we lost a lot of money because we'd paid for a lot of things.

Carol's role as a bridesmaid in Gloria Vanderbilt's wedding to Pat di Cicco was something of a consolation prize. It was a Christmas-season wedding, December 28, 1941, in the chapel of the old mission in Santa Barbara. Little Gloria's Aunt Gertrude was opposed to the match and was not on the scene. Her nanny, Dodo, was there, and so was "Big" Gloria. While there was nothing of Cinderella about Gloria Vanderbilt, her first wedding was a teenaged girl's fantasy, mixing Hollywood with a few envoys from New York society, such as the Marcuses.

ROSHEEN MARCUS: I came to California with a whole entourage. My secretary came and my daughter Carol and myself. And I think Gloria's mother was on the same plane with us.

That was the night my husband brought me a box wrapped in brown paper, and as I got on the plane he handed it to me and he said, "That's for you." I said, "Well, thank you," and as soon as I got on the plane, either I said it to my secretary or I said it to Gloria Morgan, Gloria's mother, I said, "He brought me a box of candy. I don't know why Daddy gave me a box. I don't eat candy." I decided, "Well, I'll give this to the stewardess," so somebody said, "Well, open it first and see what it is. You can always give up a box of candy."

So I took off the brown paper, and it's a black jewel case, and I open it up, and it was a diamond necklace like you have never seen in your life. I almost gave it away. I might have left it on the plane. That's how spoiled I was.

Children. We were all spoiled in those days.

After Gloria's wedding, Rosheen decided to stay in California for a month or so. Charles Marcus had war business at his company's Long Beach facility, and the weather was far preferable to the New York winter. Mrs. Marcus rented a fancy penthouse at Sunset Towers, a brand-new garden-apartment complex dotted with swimming pools, and she established a salon where bright young people could enjoy drinks, good food, and talk.

One of Rosheen's close friends was the jazz singer Lee Wiley, who also was a friend, but not a romance, of Artie Shaw's.

ARTIE SHAW: Lee—we used to laugh a lot at people like Eddie Condon and Josh Billings and all these guys, and we'd have jokes. We'd say something about the *blues*, and we'd both fall over flat. She had a musician's humor. She was a real musician. She was like Mildred Bailey or Billie Holiday. She was a real jazz singer, very understated.

Somehow I was invited or found myself in an apartment with Rosheen and Lee and her daughter Carol. I don't know whether I was supposed to be coming on with them or whether they were coming on with me.

The fact of the matter is, my particular sexual sensibilities were not triggered by people like Rosheen. She was too worldly, too grasping.

But her little daughter was coming on to me in a peculiar way. And she was cute. Little, white-faced, looked like Lewis Carroll's White Rabbit. I used to call her the White Rabbit, and she even had a nose like the White Rabbit.

So I was kidding around with her, and somehow she— Rosheen and her girlfriend went to the door, the girlfriend was leaving, and Carol said, "Let's see each other sometime." So I said, "I'm staying at the Chateau Marmont across the street." So she said, "I'll call you." I said, "Okay." It was a joke. This is a little kid.

But she wasn't so little. She was—she was *ripe*.

Next God-damned day, the phone rang and it was Carol. Breathy little voice: "Mommy is going to Palm Springs for the weekend. What're you going to do on the weekend?"

So I said, "Well, nothing specific."

"Why don't we get together?"

So I thought, "Well, it should be amusing. Take her out. Have dinner. Lunch. Whatever the hell." Well, we did.

I realized that, "Christ's sake, this is ridiculous," this whole aberration with this little girl was nutty.

I said to her one day—she was becoming kind of infatuated—I said, "Look, Carol, this is a waste of time. I mean, I've got my life to live." Twenty-nine seemed as old as hell. I was *thirty* almost, and she was sixteen. I said, "This is silly, and we're not going to go anywhere. If you're really interested in meeting a nice guy, I'll introduce you to a guy who's a very lonely man, and you've probably heard of him."

"Who?"

I said, "Bill Saroyan."

She said, "Do you know *him*?"

I said, "Yeah, we're good friends. He's coming out, wrote me that he was coming out." Called me. Something.

So I introduced her to Bill, and that went on, immediately, like a house on fire. I think she was looking for an out to get away from Mother-Hen.

Well, of course, that was her career—Rosheen. That marvelous line of Flaubert's, somebody saying to Flaubert (they're walking along and he says), "I did this terrible thing and I hope God will forgive me." Flaubert said, "*Pourquoi non? C'est son métier.*" Isn't that a nice line? That was Rosheen's scene. It was her *métier*—the daughter.

JOAN CASTLE: Hollywood in those days . . . it was one big, glamorous factory with a lot of palm trees. If you like that, fine. And the money was very good.

I went to the lot, had lunch with Bill, and he came to my house several times—and then the birthday party where I introduced him to Carol.

It was my birthday, and I decided to give a party and invite my chums, and I talked to Carol almost daily, and she said, "Oh, I'd love to meet Bill Saroyan. You know him."

I said, "Arranged!"

But she said, "And I also want to see Artie Shaw."

I said, "Well, I don't know Artie Shaw, but I'll get to him somehow," and I did, and invited him, and he brought Betty Kern, whom he eventually married, so Carol's nose was out of joint—for about two minutes—and Saroyan came in, and that was it.

They never looked back.

ROSHEEN MARCUS: I know the true version of how they met. What happened was, there was a club called the Players Club at the time. Preston Sturges owned it. It was across the street from that hotel we stayed at, Sunset Towers. Lee had a date with Artie Shaw, and she said to me, "Rosheen, please come with me. I've got to meet Artie Shaw, and you come on with me." That's when I first met Artie Shaw.

And so, when we got there, Artie Shaw was there, but he had Bill Saroyan with him. So we sat down and we all had dinner together. Carol was home, with my secretary. When we finished dinner, I said, "Well, let's go back. I have my daughter there." And Artie said, "Yeah, let's go back to her place. She's got this apartment there, Bill."

And Bill was very nice and we talked generalities and whatever it was. We came back to the hotel and he said, "Where's your daughter? You said you had a daughter."

And I said, "Oh, I'll have her come out," and I went in and I said to my secretary, "Bring Carol out. He wants to meet her— Bill Saroyan."

And Carol says, "Bill *Saroyan*. Oh, my God! Mother!" And starts combing her hair, all excited.

Walked out, came out, and he took one look at her and went out of his ever-loving mind. He said, "God, what a beauty!" He said, "Sit down here. Sit down here." And he just went crazy.

That evening when they left, they all left, he said to me, "Please. Please let me take her out to the studio tomorrow. Don't worry. She'll be all right. I want to show her some of the studios. Has she seen Twentieth? Has she seen Paramount?" (Or whatever it was.)

And Carol said, "Oh, Mother, I'd love to go. Yes, Mother. Can I go? Please?"

I said, "Okay, fine." I figured, "Look, Bill Saroyan, a big-shot writer," and he knew we were not some people from the hillbillies. So I figured, why not? Why not let her go and see the studios?

He said, "She doesn't need a chaperone. Don't worry. I'll just take her to the studio."

And he took her to the studio, and when she came back, that was the end of it, as far as I knew.

But, "Mother, he's so wonderful, so brilliant. Such a poet." And all that business.

I said, "Well, I don't know. He's a good writer." I knew that, and that was it.

After that, everybody claimed that they introduced them. The Harry Careys said that they introduced them—everybody, everybody in California.

CAROL MATTHAU: I was very—the fact that no one had greater social charm, in a way, than Bill in certain situations.

He was very handsome and very romantic-looking, very intense-looking. Oh, I thought he was wonderful because he looked like a gangster or something. Very handsome. I loved the way he dressed.

I really got a big, crazy crush on him instantly. And he said such beautiful things, and I believed every word. There's nothing more wonderful than a man who loves you and knows how to *tell* you that he loves you.

Words are things to some people. I'm a word person. They were always ringing in my ears, all the sweet things he said— "Pink rose petals and vanilla ice cream," and all sorts of things— when all you've known before are very young, shy boys.

I loved the fact that he was a man. I thought he was very old. And I knew nothing about him. I never knew the dark side of Bill until after we were married.

ROSHEEN MARCUS: She was so taken with Bill because he'd look at her and say—he said to *me* once—"She's a cherub. She's a *cherub*. I've never seen anything as lovely as this. Look at her hair. Her hair is like wheat."

And then Carol after that wanted to go to hairdressers—she was a natural blonde—and the fact that he said her hair was like wheat made her feel, "Oh, Mother, it isn't *really* like wheat. I've got to go to a hairdresser and tell him to fix my hair like wheat."

She was a *baby*.

CAROL MATTHAU: When I first knew him, I was a little worried about it: I didn't really want him to realize how young I was. I remember one day later, in New York, he came unexpectedly and I was in my regular clothes, a sweater and a skirt and I think bobby sox and a raincoat. I was so upset.

I didn't know at the time that that's what he really liked. I was nervous about it, but I needn't have been.

She was sixteen, he was thirty-three.

3. THE FEUD, THE FLOP

The affair was immediate, intense, passionate, physical, and it was soon interrupted when Rosheen took Carol back east. On March 19, 1942, Saroyan began four days of photography on his short subject, now retitled *Corner Store*, and the month of April was devoted to cutting the film. Although old friends and the occasional cousin had been welcome in his Metro loft and as visitors on the set, he had not packed his payroll with cronies and favorites.

Those who saw it (it never was released to theatres) recall workmanlike performances by the contract players and an unforgettable moment when a woman drops a watermelon down her decolletage for safekeeping. *The Good Job*, as it was finally called, leaned heavily on talk, including the crutch of narration, and it lacked visual texture. This latter problem may have been a result of the short shooting schedule, but the absence of satisfying close-ups or dialogue reverse shots made the little movie look stiff and stagy.

> AL HIRSCHFELD: Well, the short having been made, then comes along *The Human Comedy*, which was the big property. And Bill said he wanted to direct it. And Louis Mayer said, "No, that's not for you, Bill. We have directors here."
>
> "But I have a contract with you that I am to direct my own film."
> He says, "Well, you've directed your own film."
> "What are you talking about?"
> "The film that you've just directed."

> ARTIE SHAW: That's when that mania began, that obsessive thing when they screwed him. Well, they didn't screw him, but they made a deal with him in which he assumed that if he did this short, *The Good Job* (I saw the thing three or four times; he'd run it, you know), he assumed that if it worked . . .
>
> He was thinking of *merit*. He didn't understand that they were thinking the bottom line: how much money does something make? And a short is just something that they throw away.
>
> So they gave him the short in order to get rights to *The Human Comedy*. And he signed over that, assuming they would give him the directorship. Of course, they couldn't take the chance. It was a big cast, a lot of money, and they couldn't let an untried guy with all his ebullience and all his verve and enthusiasm, they couldn't take that shot. It was understandable to anybody who knows the film business. I can't say it was ethical. Anybody who gets in the film business looking for ethics is like a guy who goes into court looking for justice. Dumb.
>
> I was astounded by his reaction. He was so bitter.

*   *   *

Having heard directly from L. B. Mayer that he was not "experienced enough" to direct one of M-G-M's A-pictures, Saroyan walked out on Metro, even though he likely could have remained there, drawing $1,000 a week, until *The Human Comedy*, directed by someone else, was ready to be released. Mayer had writers far less famous than William Saroyan who earned twice that much.

As his parting shot Saroyan wrote an allegorical letter about California shore-birds that lay their eggs on the beach sand—"very pretty, but not commercial." The piece also contained plain anger, undisguised by metaphor: "Sooner or later a man gets bored with bores, finaglers, and jitney politicians. A man just naturally gets fed up with the baloney. He gets tired of witnessing the continuous and disgraceful crying, trembling and shaking. In three months I made a neat profit of one million for Metro. That is enough for any shore-bird in the world, orphan or otherwise." Daily *Variety* printed the outburst word for word.

BUDD SCHULBERG: It was unheard-of. It was heresy. Like attacking Jimmy Carter in Athens, Georgia, something on that order.

It was dangerous to attack L. B. Part of my father's downfall was that he would confront L. B. so openly, with so much hostility, and some of my own troubles probably came from the same thing. There's anger at him, and my rebellion. L. B. was not the sort of fellow whom you could easily cross. He was very much bigger than just *a* tycoon. It was considered way, way out.

In terms of being in the industry, it was like writing your own exit, your pass out of there. Mayer's power was so great it went way beyond M-G-M. It wasn't just M-G-M, which was the most flourishing of the studios. If Mayer called one of the others and said of Bill, "He's a troublemaker, he's no good, he's a Communist," or whatever, Bill was pretty much washed up.

DAVID DIAMOND: I think Bill made one mistake, which was to think that M-G-M was simply going to stop and let him do everything he wanted to do. I always had a feeling that Bill never figured out there were many, many things going on at M-G-M, and that even Garbo—I believe that Garbo's last picture was still being made—and that things just didn't stop because Bill Saroyan had come to the studio.

It was discussed a lot by a mutual friend, a woman who was at Warner Brothers. There was much talk about Bill and his problems over at Metro. She thought he was extremely courageous and that because of it, Mayer just might give in and do the things that were really up Bill's alley.

But I remember one night at the Players, Preston Sturges' place, where everybody used to come, all the directors and actors, and I remember there was a big discussion, [which] was: "*Why* does Bill think that he is the most important thing that hit M-G-M?" There was a lot of that feeling: "Where the hell does this guy get off?"

Behaving like a ship deserted by a sinking rat, M-G-M counterattacked royally, assigning Howard Dietz, its vice-president of publicity, to the task. Dietz was the lyrical half of the songwriting team of Schwartz and Dietz, and he was a class act whose reply to Saroyan was calm and believable. He pointed out that *The Good Job* was the most expensive short subject Metro had filmed in two years, but that no one could determine whether the finished product represented simply exposed film or, as *Variety* paraphrased him, "just what the public subconsciously wants."

"At any rate," Dietz said, "the esteemed dramatist got a chance to write that farewell-to-Hollywood piece, which has almost gone out of fashion with authors who flop."

Saroyan wrote more than his letter about the shore-birds. Back home in San Francisco he set to work on a new play called *Get Away, Old Man,* and announced that Metro could buy it for $250,000 if they acted by noon the following Monday, May 11.

"I sincerely recommend immediate purchase, sight unseen, as I believe this play is my greatest, perhaps one of the greatest ever to appear in this country, and in all probability my second play to win both the Pulitzer Prize and the Drama Critics Award."

The old man of the title was Louis Mayer himself, and the play pits an idealistic young writer against the tycoon, who urges him to write a script called *Ave Maria* (shades of *The Rosary*). The offer naturally went unclaimed.

In later years the story grew that Saroyan had attempted to buy back *The Human Comedy* that May by returning, unspent, the $60,000. Budd Schulberg remembers a trip to San Francisco with Collier Young, a producer interested in negotiating a buy-out with Saroyan. "Bill's demands—at least to Colly—were outrageous. Not only the money, but he wanted to produce it, and he wanted to have complete control. I don't know whether he said *direct* it or not, but that was the feeling, just that he would do it only if there was an Orson Welles attitude toward it." After the war, however, Saroyan did attempt to retrieve the remake rights, but M-G-M would not negotiate.

Saroyan had ideas about whom Mayer should use for *The Human Comedy*, now that the would-be *auteur* was out of the picture: "The only man other than myself who is qualified to transfer the story to the screen, Victor Fleming," who had completed *Gone With the Wind* and directed *The Wizard of Oz*. "For producer, I would like to recommend Arthur Freed. If for any reason these men are not available, I would like to recommend for director William Wyler and for producer, Sam Zimbalist."

The director Mayer chose was a close personal friend, Clarence Brown, who had directed Garbo's first talkie, *Anna Christie*, and Gable's movie debut in *A Free Soul*. Mayer had turned to Brown before with problem assignments, such as the screen test of Marion Davies, mistress of Mayer's crony William Randolph Hearst. Brown also had a successful track record with Mickey Rooney, who often was difficult to control on screen, but who had shone under his direction in O'Neill's *Ah, Wilderness!* Howard Estabrook reworked the screenplay of *The Human Comedy*, trimming half a dozen episodes and adding narration from the Macauley family's dead father. Saroyan's screen credit became "from the story by."

Now the story struck Saroyan as something worth preserving in its original form as a benchmark against which to measure M-G-M's depredation. Robert Giroux, the young editor at Harcourt, Brace who had been the first to learn of Saroyan's rejection of the Pulitzer Prize, was summoned by his boss and mentor, Frank Morley, who "handed me a new Saroyan manuscript which he called a headache," Giroux recalled.

It was a movie scenario Saroyan had written for M-G-M; he wanted us to publish it in a spiral binding, with all the boring technical directions. It was called *The Human Comedy*, and, aside from the technical directions, I liked it.

I reported to Morley that Saroyan, whether he knew it or not, had more or less written his first novel. The characters were there, so was the dialogue, and the story was excellent. It lacked only the trimmings, the furniture of a novel, and not much of that was needed. Morley felt that Bill would never agree that what he wrote as a scenario was actually a novel, and wondered how we could get him to admit to himself that a novel is what he intended. After thinking about it a day or so, I retyped the opening scene in narrative style, under the heading Chapter One, using only Bill's words, and sent it off with a letter which said, "As you can see from my rough transcription of the first scene, Bill, you've actually written your first novel."

This provoked an instant response in telegraphed form: "Your approach is all wrong. Am airmailing the new version showing how it should be done."

"I was amused that M-G-M's ads for the movie carried the line "based on the novel by William Saroyan."

Illustrated by Don Freeman, *The Human Comedy* would be Saroyan's second Book-of-the-Month Club selection and an even bigger bestseller than *My Name Is Aram*. Like *Aram*, it never has gone out of print.

But, even before that windfall was in hand, Saroyan realized that he was wealthy enough for another run at Broadway.

He announced plans for the Saroyan Theatre, his scheme for a New York showcase where the playwright-producer-director would remain constant: himself. The actors would change according to the needs of his new scripts, rather like a repertory company in reverse. The idea was to bury the commercial theatre, which, he said, had died during the just ended 1941–42 season, a season without a single new Saroyan play. At first, he appeared to be preparing to bury Broadway simply through his massive output, boasting five or six full-length plays, six or seven shorter ones, and eighteen one-acters in the inventory.

Three months at Metro at $1,000 a week. The screenplay rights to *The Human Comedy*, $60,000. Royalties from the *Razzle-Dazzle* collection, and now the novel version of *The Human Comedy*. Saroyan was almost dangerously well-off. Realizing that he could lose this small fortune at gambling or on Broadway, he decided to make over the bulk of it to his mother, Takoohi, and his maiden sister, Cosette. (He also paid off the mortgages on the houses of his brother, Henry, and his sister Zabel and her husband.)

This act of prudence quickly proved to have been terribly rash, because his poor relations were all that stood between him and the draft board. By elevating his mother and sister into the comfortable middle class, he had eliminated the official reason why he was not serving in the military. His San Francisco draft board on Taraval Street took immediate notice and reclassified him 1-A.

A few days before the draft board's action, Saroyan had been confronted, briefly, with the reality of the war and had fallen uncharacteristically silent. Paramount had asked him to write the text of a prologue to that studio's movie about Wake Island. In the earliest days of the war in the Pacific, the surrender of 450 Marines on Wake had left America stricken. Admiral Halsey's heroic attempt to recapture it in February, 1942, had been one of the earliest battles worth enshrining in celluloid. Saroyan had replied, "The factual story by itself is so eloquent. I am sure I could never write anything half so effective. Won't you put one of the Paramount writers on the job and I'll see if I can't say something worthwhile about something not quite so impressive by itself."

Leaving San Francisco could not spare him from the draft, but it could delay proceedings if and when they began. Saroyan now went east to begin the Saroyan Theatre. Eddie Dowling had looked at *Get Away, Old Man* and had turned it down, and so Saroyan decided that *Across the Board on Tomorrow Morning* should open the new theatre, and the house he rented for the experiment was the Belasco. This theatre was named for David Belasco, the San Francisco impresario who had built it, complete with a rococo velvet-and-gilt office with a tiny peephole for keeping an eye on the stage. It was now the property of the Shuberts.

The cross-country move required him to transfer from Selective Service Board No. 84 in San Francisco to Board No. 31 in New York, which immediately ordered him to report to St. Luke's Hospital on the morning of July 29 for his draft physical.

Saroyan appeared with cocked hat, broad smile, and brightly-striped suspenders. He was waiting for the reporters and used the occasion to plug the new bill at the Belasco. "If such plays don't come out, it will be not only damaging to the theatre, but also to all American reality.

"If I were drafted or given a commission to do writing, it couldn't be one bit as effective as the writing I am doing as a civilian. I'm 1-A, and if they want me as a person, as a body, and they think I can do better service as a soldier, the responsibility is theirs.

"However, I'll insist on one thing, and that is that I be a soldier and no more, that I will not be required to write. I have been the best American propagandist this country ever had, and I can't do more than I am doing by writing."

Saroyan's written plea for deferment made this same argument, but it was a narrow argument at this stage of the war. In Fresno the newspaper called editorially for Saroyan to be drafted, joking that he should be ordered to write plays and forced to serve KP every time a GI in the audience walked out of the theatre. "A touch of regimentation and discipline might even improve the writer's unquestioned talent."

Saroyan's "neighbors," the conservative businessmen on the Taraval Street draft board, were bound to find it impossible to exempt a healthy young man from a raging war on the ground that he wanted to produce plays.

The boastful, wisecracking persona Saroyan had invented and amplified so skillfully was ripe for a comedown. As a professional dramatist, he could see the next turn of the plot coming.

He renewed his affair with Carol, and he cast her in *Across the Board on Tomorrow Morning* in the role of a lovely girl who enters the play's nightclub on the arm of a distinguished older gentleman. Carol was mentioned as Saroyan's "discovery," but because of her age, the seriousness of their affair was not for public consumption. Her mother was wary. Her father was acutely distrustful.

A double bill at the Saroyan Theatre opened the Broadway season of 1942–43. It was a sweltering August night when the curtain rose on *Across the Board* . . . with the distinguished black actor Canada Lee in the role of Piper, the waiter who explains events in Saroyan's metaphysical supper club. The ancient evaporative cooling system in the Belasco had been loaded with too little ice, and the muggy weather reduced its efficiency. Lee's long speeches put some of the audience to sleep right away. Others were amused, as they were not meant to be, by the participation of harpist Lois Bannerman, who had been placed in an alcove overlooking the action. Her spasmodic musical punctuation did not have the desired dramatic effect.

Late in the first of the evening's plays, Bill's promotion of street characters to stage roles took a disturbing turn with the entrance of Maxwell Bodenheim. For decades the quintessential Greenwich Village Bohemian, but now a raving piece of human wreckage, Bodenheim's ad-libbed poetry only made the audience more fidgety, and those who tried to escape the Belasco at this point were greeted by a wall of rain.

CAROL MATTHAU: It was embarrassing. I'd been in summer stock, but I didn't really belong in a Broadway play. But I wasn't really thinking about it.

But I knew that it was wrong to see that man in that state on the stage. It only ran for a week, but there was just something very terrible about his doing that. Bill was very rich then. If he wanted to give him some money, he could have given him some money and not had him do that. Bodenheim wasn't there anymore. He was like a derelict you thought you'd see in some gutter.

I also remember at that time Canada Lee asked him if he would take him [Lee] to the Stork Club. It could have been done by Bill, but Bill was very harassed by that request and very upset by it.

"Well, what the hell does he want to go there for? Why would you want to go where you're not wanted?" And that was his attitude about it.

But Canada Lee didn't want to go to the Stork Club. Canada Lee wanted to break a little ground.

Saroyan's production assistant had resigned even before opening night, and Canada Lee would not speak of Saroyan at all after the closing, thirteen performances later. Lee was praised for his work as the prizefighter in the evening's second Saroyan one-act play, *Talking to You*, but the damage had been done. Even friendly critics like Brooks Atkinson of the *Times* said flatly that Saroyan's only real successes on the stage were a result of collaboration with professionals such as Bobby Lewis or Eddie Dowling. "On the whole, Bill is O.K. But he knows very little about the theatre," said Atkinson.

Saroyan begged the critics to return, promising that the air conditioning and the plays would be fixed. None did. Ticket sales were so low they fell below the house minimum specified in the Shuberts' contract. Lee Shubert had come to the theatre to wish Saroyan luck when the lease was signed. "Go in there with a free heart. Don't worry about business matters," Saroyan heard him say. Now Saroyan had to clear out and send the production to the warehouse. Lee Shubert was not interested in subsidizing a flop with free rent. He now joined Louis Mayer on Saroyan's list of unforgivable enemies.

Saroyan's plan had been for one of his productions to follow another, but he was unready for instantaneous disaster. He announced that the experiment was at an end, explaining that he had surrounded himself with "inept people."

A month later Eddie Dowling and Julie Haydon were onstage at the Belasco in *Hello, Out There,* Saroyan's one-act play about the jailed man, the young girl, and the lynch mob. It shared the bill with a bit of fluff by G. K. Chesterton, *Magic,* and the producer-director was Dowling himself. Now and ever after, Saroyan's plays would reach the stage in the hands of others.

George Jean Nathan was disappointed by Saroyan's misadventure, but he retained faith in Bill as a playwright, and soon set to work attempting to repair his young friend's fortunes. Within days after the Saroyan Theatre folded, Nathan was entertaining Bill and the producer Mike Todd at the critic's personal corner table at "21." For all his dedication to art, Nathan had a healthy respect for the simpler and more direct forms of show business, and he heartily approved of Todd's current production, *Star and Garter,* a burlesque revue starring Gypsy Rose Lee. Sitting at Nathan's table was something of an honor, and Mike Todd returned the favor by sending the critic a case of the whiskey he had seen Nathan order at "21." He also optioned Saroyan's *Get Away, Old Man* for Broadway production. But that production must have seemed terribly distant to Saroyan. Indeed, he and Todd would quarrel and the option would be dropped.

Saroyan's draft notice went unpublicized, but it arrived at about this time, the early fall of 1943, when Saroyan already had been counted down and out of a Broadway season hardly begun.

Like a messenger of the personal war that lay ahead, Bill's young cousin Ross Bagdasarian materialized in New York, in uniform. He was a soldier now, a private headed for Army motorcycle school in Rhode Island. Gypsy Rose Lee had invited Bill and Carol to a lobster feast at her townhouse, and they asked Ross to join them.

Miss Lee was the intellectual stripper Lorenz Hart had satirized in *Pal Joey* by quoting her as singing, while undressing:

"Zip!
Walter Lippmann wasn't brilliant today,
Zip!
Will Saroyan ever write a great play?"

Of course Saroyan had; the Pulitzer committee said so. But at her party that evening, the real-life Gypsy Rose Lee, whose intellectual leanings were entirely in earnest, preferred the calm company of Mark Van Doren, the poet who gratefully accepted his Pulitzer the same morning that Saroyan refused one.

Carol sat in near silence while Bill and Ross shared private jokes in loud, public voices, oblivious of Miss Lee's embarrassment, or Carol's own.

She had suffered worse than this—when he directed at her his anger over his series of bad breaks. In a memoir published as a novel many years later, Saroyan described the morning that fall when the two of them awakened in his suite at the swanky Hampshire House. The bedroom was decorated in candy stripes and bright cabbage roses, a motif Carol would use later, as though by duplicating the room she could recapture the emotions they had shared there.

But on this morning they quarreled. He told her to go home, "to go back to the boys who didn't have work to do." When he left the suite an hour later he found her crumpled on a bench in the hallway, sobbing uncontrollably.

"I don't want to go home. . . . I never want to go home again. I want to stay here the rest of my life."

"This apartment's twenty-five dollars a day. I'm leaving it in a few days to go into the Army."

"I want to go with you."

He would not permit that, not just then, but in a few weeks he would be on the telephone to her, begging her to join him, to prove herself worthy of marriage, to show that she could bear the child who could carry his line and his name through the perils of a war.

CHAPTER FOUR

SOLDIER

1. DRAFTED

Now Saroyan could no longer simply raise his voice and let the world know exactly how he felt about everything. His sense of publicity was accurate enough to censor his true feelings about the war. Opinions such as his would not play.

At the draft physical one of the reporters asked him, "How do you feel?" and there was every good reason to expect a Saroyan monologue on war from the dawn of time.

"I feel fine, how are you?" Saroyan had answered. Banter like that was effortless for him, and he would invent it for the rest of the war. Beginning now, late in 1942, there would be a difference between the public Saroyan and Army Private Saroyan, and that difference would become greater and greater. Only those closest to him would hear and feel his rage and heartsickness.

Artie Shaw had become a sailor, emerging from boot camp on Staten Island just before Saroyan set out to drive to California and the Army.

ARTIE SHAW: I had one of those monkey suits on, and I was embarrassed to come into New York. I was living at the Gainsborough Apartments, a studio facing on Central Park West. I was a pretty sophisticated kid. I knew everybody in New York and everybody knew me. Walking around in this God-damned suit with a little hat, I felt foolish, so I called Bill.

I said, "Listen, I'm coming out of boot training, and the only place I can wear this God-damned suit and not look conspicuous is Coney Island, so let's go to Coney Island."

So we all got in the car and went out to Coney Island and I bought a little balloon and walked around the street carrying a balloon—you know, that's what a little kid in a sailor suit does.

And there was Bill carrying on, acting like a lunatic. They were going to draft him. "What do they want me for? They don't need me!"

"Christ almighty!" I said. "Bill, they don't give a shit about plays. This is a big thing going on. There's a fellow there rampaging around the world, and whether we helped put him there or not is beside the point. He's got to be stopped. And I don't know whether you can do it or I can do it, but the more the merrier."

CAROL MATTHAU: He was absolutely violated by the fact that he had been drafted. It was an agony for him, and he was determined to get out of the Army.

He did not believe in the war, and even if he had, he wouldn't want to be in that position. He felt that Hitler was a great zealot and that we should mind our own business.

You didn't have to *believe* in it. It was right there.

But it wasn't really so much his point of view about it, it was his personal discomfort at being a private in the Army, or being in any Army. Or having any regimented life of any kind. There's a Shaw play—I forget the name of it offhand—which names the army that you're in as the real enemy, and that's what he felt.

It was just something that made him feel that he had been violated, and I think he was never the same again.

If Saroyan feared ending up as a foot soldier, as he once had claimed he would prefer, there were legitimate reasons to worry. On the day he was sworn in, October 18, 1942, the battles of Guadalcanal and

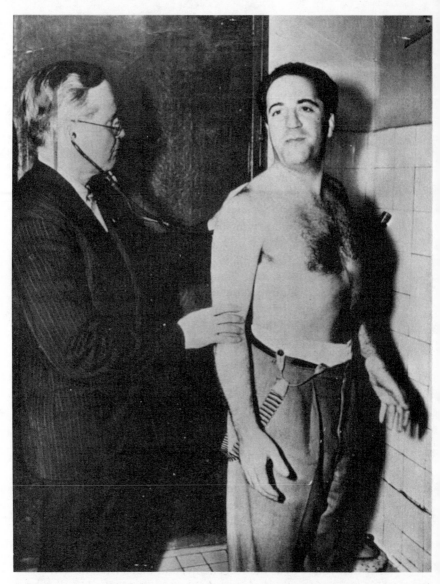

Dr. H. Lawrence Dowd found Saroyan fit for active duty at his draft physical in the summer of 1942, but Saroyan said, "If I were drafted or given a commission to do writing, it couldn't be one bit as effective as the writing I am doing as a civilian . . . if they want me as a person, as a body, and they think I can do better service as a soldier, the responsibility is theirs." (Wide World)

Stalingrad were raging. He was granted the usual two-week furlough to settle his affairs, and when reporters called his mother's, Takoohi's, house in San Francisco to see how Saroyan was spending his time, they were told that he was duck hunting. "He wants to see how it feels to shoot things," an unnamed family member was quoted as saying. Saroyan was no hunter, and undoubtedly was the source of the cynical remark.

When it came time to leave for enlistment at the Monterey Presidio, Saroyan got his own GI haircut, which made his hat seem even bigger, and he packed a portable typewriter and portable radio for the trip. He also wore an identification bracelet, a gold one, and fingered it nervously as he glanced around the Southern Pacific station at all the other recruits waiting for the Monterey train.

"They're all scared," he told his friend Carolyn Anspacher. "I'm scared, too. That's what makes a good army. You have to be scared. Fear is an integrating force. It's terrific apprehension that makes all this reality.

"For once I'm relieved of fumbling," he said. "I'm turning over to other people complete control of some areas. But I'll get adjusted to things. I'll get adjusted to saluting, for instance. It's a silly gesture. It lacks intimacy. But then handshakes are silly, too. You have to learn the gesture. You know, of course, that there are only a couple of gestures that really mean anything—like kissing. That's something you don't have to learn."

As he boarded the train he was plugging *The Human Comedy*, still unreleased as a film, and promising to write "the greatest war novel from the inside. We're going to win this war while I'm writing it and fighting it."

The prospect of fighting evidently had led Saroyan to another decision, one he withheld from Carolyn Anspacher and the newspapermen at the station. He had resolved to marry. It was unthinkable that he could be killed in a war without leaving heirs.

ROSHEEN MARCUS: He called me from San Francisco and he said— he spoke to Carol first, and then she called me in her room and she said, "Mother, it's Bill Saroyan and he wants to talk to you."

And he said, "Look, I want to marry your daughter." And he said, "But I want to introduce her to my mother first." And he said, "Won't you please send her to San Francisco?"

And I said, "I can't do that, Bill. She's a *child*." And I said, "Remember that she's a virgin child."

And he said, "I promise. I'll send her back exactly as you send her to me. Send her with a chaperone. Send her with anybody. I wanted my mother to meet her before we get married."

I said, "I'll have to discuss this with my husband." (My husband kept calling him a bum, and I didn't know what a bum was. To me, a bum was somebody on the streets who didn't have enough to eat. "He's a bum," he said. "He's a bum.")

Finally, I acquiesced. I said, "I'll send her with a chaperone."

He said, "Send Oona with her."

I said, "Oona is also a young girl. What kind of chaperone is that?"

And he said, "Well, she's older, and she'll know how to take care of Carol. And please remember, I'll send her back to you exactly as you send her to me. I won't touch her. I won't *anything*. You're not dealing with just anybody," and so on and so forth.

After a long spiel on the telephone and telling him how my husband would take offense and so on, I said, "Well, all right. I'll try to arrange it."

And Carol is there, "Please, please. You've *got* to, Mother," carrying on.

I acquiesced, and the last thing he said to me on the phone was, "You know, Rosheen, you really are a great woman."

Carol and Oona arrived by train, and Bill took them to the house on Fifteenth Avenue for a welcoming dinner. Most of the conversation that evening was in Armenian, which left Carol acutely uncomfortable as she was appraised by Bill's sister and by his mother Takoohi, with her deep voice and her stony expression. "His mother was a man, there was no question about it," Carol recalls. Only Grandmother Lucy was warm toward the two girls.

Time was terribly short before Saroyan had to move on to Signal Corps basic training near Sacramento, and he was direct with Carol about what he wanted—proof that she could bear his children. He told her she must become pregnant before they could marry. Carol was startled by this demand, never having doubted that she could bear children, but she was incapable of persuading him to accept this on faith, and so she reluctantly agreed to his plan, which brought an air of urgency and distrust to their lovemaking.

When Saroyan left San Francisco for Camp Kohler at Sacramento, the girls went, too, and he established them in rooms at the Hotel Senator for the two weeks while he could neither leave the base nor receive visitors or telephone calls. Oona had her own private reasons for coming to California with Carol. Her meetings with her father had been few and far between over the sixteen years since Eugene O'Neill had left his first family, and she wanted to visit him again at Tor House, his hideaway home between San Francisco and Sacramento. But she waited until she was in Sacramento to write him, and this was a mistake. O'Neill was outraged that she had turned down the chance to attend Vassar and continued to be seen at the Stork Club and to play in summer-stock productions, like her friend Carol. O'Neill wrote,

> All I know of what you have become since you blossomed into the night club racket is derived from newspaper clippings of your interviews. . . .[A]ll the publicity you have is the wrong kind, unless your ambition is to be a second-rate movie actress of the floosie variety—the sort who have their pictures in the papers for a couple of years and then sink back into the obscurity of their naturally silly, talentless lives. . . . I don't want to see the kind of daughter you have become in this past year.

This letter, which Oona received at the Sacramento hotel, was the final break with her father.

All three of the young people were under extraordinary pressure: Oona now totally and shockingly estranged from her father, who had been little more than a stranger to begin with; Carol reduced from the role of fiancée to that of candidate mother; and Bill undergoing the everyday humiliations of the buck private. Even though he could not see or telephone Carol, he was obliged to meet the press on his first day in camp.

"They got me up at 5:30 and the first thing they made me do was make my bed. Then they made me tear it up because it was not right. I made it again and tore it up and made it again. For a while all I did was make my bed. I got quite good at making beds."

Saroyan had asked Carol to write him every day, and she was paralyzed by having to write something that would satisfy his sophisticated eye. The beau Oona had left behind in New York was J. D. Salinger—Jerry to his friends—and his long love letters to Oona were filled with easygoing fantasy such as, "I've just sent my typewriter to the laundry." With Oona's help, Carol cribbed the best lines from Salinger's letters for her daily page to Bill, and when the two weeks were up and she finally was admitted to the base to meet him, she found him cool and distant. Saroyan was disturbed by the letters—shocked to find that she was not a simple young girl but a complicated, clever one. He long had told interviewers quizzing him about his future wife that the "comic" woman, however lovely, was the type to be avoided. When Carol fearfully confessed that she had borrowed the clever passages to please him, he grew angry and accused her of lying—a sin even worse than cleverness.

Nor was she pregnant—at least so far as they knew—and on this tense note they parted, with the prospective marriage hinging on whether or not she was carrying Saroyan's child. The two girls caught a train for Los Angeles, where old friends waited.

> CAROL MATTHAU: Oona liked Bill, but thought he was absolutely impossible. She saw him, of course, more clearly than I, but she understood how I felt. And by this time we had had an affair, and I wanted to marry him. I was in love with him.
>
> Gloria was by that time married to Pat di Cicco, and she would just say, "He's too difficult, Carol. You have so many beaus, so many people who love you, and he's so difficult. But if you love him . . ."

Carol stayed in Hollywood only a few days, returning to New York. Oona, who had confessed to being very deeply hurt by her father's harsh rejection, now met and would soon marry the older man she had dreamed of, Charlie Chaplin.

Carol proved not to be pregnant from the California lovemaking, but the affair of the purloined letters was forgiven, and during a holiday furlough in December 1942, Bill telephoned her. He was in New York. Was she still interested in getting married? This time, she conceived.

Bill had been assigned to duty with the Signal Corps in the Army's film center at the old Astoria Studios in Queens. Now, two of his nightmares converged: the rules and regimentation of the Army joined with the sickening internal politics of the movie business.

> ARTIE SHAW: What irked his ass was what irked a lot of us. The guys we knew who wouldn't be office boys in our own business

were being admirals and generals. I ran into a few fracases like that, but what were you going to do?

By late February, 1943, the wedding was absolutely necessary. Carol was two months pregnant, but by now Bill had been transferred away from New York. While he was serving at the Army film studio in Queens, Saroyan was free to spend his off-duty hours with old friends like columnist Leonard Lyons, and when occasional wisecracks about easy duty reached print, they embarrassed and angered his commanding officers. Advance publicity had begun for the première of *The Human Comedy*, which was to open at Radio City Music Hall in New York, and the buck private who saluted on his own terms found himself at the mercy of men who perhaps were his artistic inferiors. His mistake was reminding them of it. The public-relations officer at Astoria telephoned Saroyan every time his name showed up in the press, warning him that the Army was handling his publicity now, not M-G-M. He was sent to a remote outpost already scheduled to be closed down, the Signal Corps film laboratory at the Army Air Force's Wright Field near Dayton, Ohio. His arrival there was witnessed by someone who snitched to *The New Yorker* that Saroyan "strode into the barracks as if it were Sardi's. Trailing along behind, with Saroyan's luggage, was a starry-eyed sergeant."

Rosheen decided to accompany Carol to Ohio to supervise a wedding which, all agreed, was best kept private for the time being.

ROSHEEN MARCUS: My husband and I were very much opposed to that marriage. Very much opposed to it, because we didn't think he was a feather in our cap. Carol had been brought up a particular way. She was young, a baby, and my husband was just livid about the whole thing.

I was a bit more cautious, but when Carol said, "Mother, please, I love him—" And she was so—she *did* love him. It was just a terrific thing for her. And I, being a romanticist—and I had also married when I was very, very young, so I understood that feeling that she had—and I just said okay.

When I got there, I had to arrange for blood tests and everything, and I remember going to the governor and to the City Hall and arranging it, expediting it. And I remember—only certain things I remember—that they finally married in a courthouse, late at night, with—I don't know whether it was the janitress or somebody and his wife in the courthouse that took care of it. Whatever it was, they were witnesses, and I arranged for that wedding to take place in a hurry.

I was very unhappy that my little baby, Carol, was to get married this way. Every mother always lives in hopes that it's going to be a white gown in a church wedding, and it's going to be beautiful, but anyway, it didn't turn out to be that.

After they were married in this courthouse late at night, we all walked back to the hotel, and I had arranged at the hotel to have champagne in the room where I stayed and all kinds of foodstuffs and everything, just for the three of us. I had it all planned.

And they walked me back to the hotel and Bill said, "Well, I got to get back now. Let's go, Carol," and he just took her by the arm and they left me standing in front of the hotel.

And Carol, like a little infant angel, "Mother, I'm sorry, but Bill has to get back, and I just have to go." And off they went. And I stood there in front of that hotel and I thought I would die. The next morning, I took the train and came back. They went back to the base, and that was all. That was the most horrible experience I've ever had in my life, leaving my child there like that.

The wedding had taken place at midnight on a Saturday, and by the following Wednesday the word was on the front page of the New York newspapers. The justice of the peace had confirmed what reporters heard rumored along Broadway and from Wright Field. Saroyan refused to speak to the press, and Carol would do no more than say that her plan was to stay beside her husband in Dayton, in the hotel suite, which he was free to visit on weekends.

At the Army base, Saroyan was accomplishing very little for the Army, which he was discovering to be a disorganized and mean-spirited institution. One of Saroyan's fellow writers there was a veteran of the educational film business, Ralph White, a newlywed and a buck private like Saroyan himself.

RALPH WHITE: Our companions were a congenial assortment of Hollywood executives, directors, artists, cameramen, editors, writers, office boys, and party-girl procurers. Those who had enlisted received direct commissions as colonels, majors, and

The justice of the peace in Dayton leaked word of their marriage, but since Saroyan believed he had been reassigned to Ohio for turning up in New York gossip columns, he and Carol greatly restricted coverage of their wedding, with absolutely no interviews.

captains. Draftees, like Bill and I, were privates. When the workload was not burdensome, we could request the screening of any movie produced in the U.S.A. and hold a critical discussion of the writing, directing, camera technique, editing, special effects, and musical score—an opportunity unmatched by any university.

After work, the military caste system took over. Common soldiers were warehoused by National Guard and Reserve officers, who ordered us to have our uniforms recut by Dayton tailors, graded us on shoeshines, bounced coins on our tightly-tucked blankets, maintained charts on lavatory walls to record our bowel movements, and supervised early evening activities that included scraping windows with razor blades and polishing stovepipes that poked through barracks roofs.

Several members of our company had rented apartments for the Saturday-night companionship of wives who had come east from California. My recent bride had arrived from Maine. Bachelors rented apartments to get closer-acquainted with new friends. (One bachelor had his authentic Louis XVI velvet-curtained, mirror-domed bed shipped from Hollywood.)

A perpetual war of nerves was played out between the draftees and the enlisted officers and their regular-Army allies. There were midnight drills with one of the lieutenants shouting, as White recalls, "I'll learn you sons-of-bitches you don't have to go to college to be a God-damned soldier!" One Friday, the company captain suspended all weekend passes indefinitely, and the off-base wives and girlfriends learned what happened only when they received Monday's mail. There were forbidden meetings of enlisted men to plot strategy against the captain, threats of court-martial from above. But by the time Carol was on the scene peace had been restored, and the announcement had been made that the unit was being disbanded.

Saroyan was returned now to New York City, to the film center in Astoria. But as a married man he was free to live wherever he pleased, and royalties from *The Human Comedy* made it possible to live in style. He rented a penthouse at Number 2 Sutton Place South, which Carol decorated with the cabbage roses and candy stripes she remembered from the suite they had shared the year before at the Hampshire House.

Reviews of the movie version of *The Human Comedy* had been cordial, praising its slickness and effectiveness, but faulting its overemphasized sentimentality. The novel was something else. The ghosts of the dead father and son were missing from the book, and so were the sweet violin passages of the score. Saroyan's tone of voice retrieved the story from stickiness. Don Freeman's illustrations, less literal than the images of the movie, managed at the same time to be more realistic. The reviewers were delighted with the volume, which went immediately onto the bestseller lists.

Saroyan commuted to the war by subway, and whenever he was late for first formation, men who lived in the barracks would answer his name. Most days he was there for rollcall, but instead of heading to the mess hall with the other men he went instead to a nearby coffeepot restaurant run by an elderly couple. Sometimes he was joined by another soldier, the comedian David Burns.

Elihu Winer, then a struggling writer, later became a successful playwright and an executive of the Writers Guild. He recalls Saroyan and Astoria vividly.

ELIHU WINER: When I say that he was the worst soldier in the world, I don't literally mean that he looked lousy, not a *schlump*. His clothes were very neat and he made a good appearance as a soldier. It was just that he had no interest in being there, and that's the only way I can express it.

For example, we would have classes in New York because there were not a lot of classrooms at Astoria, and they'd get down a bunch of guys—about thirty of them, a whole platoon down there—and you'd line up and march to the subway and go into Manhattan. And Bill would always run around to be the last in line. And Hunt Stromberg, Jr., whose father had been a Metro producer. They would run around to the back, and then some smart-ass sergeant would say "Left face!" instead of "Right face!" and they were up in front.

He paid no attention whatever to the lectures on Army organization and map reading. We had a lecture on map reading, and whenever there was a test he never did anything. He always flunked the test down to zero, but he really wasn't paying any attention. We were talking about azimuths—north azimuth, that kind of thing, and he whispered in my ear, "What's the difference between a north azimuth and a horse's azimuth?"

The sergeants and the very junior officers who tormented privates like Saroyan were, in turn, at the mercy of a cadre of senior officers who commuted by limousine from quarters the Army rented them in an Eighth Avenue hotel. Many of them only nominally lived there, preferring their own suites at the Plaza or the Waldorf-Astoria. The Hollywood character actor who had been cast as the star in the series of standard training films about the M-1 rifle lost that assignment after appearing on a radio program during the shooting. The host asked him what he did in the Army, and he identified himself as a "subway commando," an innocent-sounding small joke that infuriated the Army's studio bosses at Astoria. The actor was on the next train to duty in Denver, and the first of the M-1 films was reshot with a replacement.

At 3:30 each afternoon, the giant sound stage was put to the use intended, filming, and men without specific duties, "casuals," as the Army calls them, were recruited as extras. The huge stage, which rivals the largest in Hollywood, sheltered some of the all-time Army classics, including *VD Hygiene* and *How to Wash*, and the big studio also claimed genuine talent, men who created their own hierarchy of achievement, whatever their actual rank. A general, Brehon Somerville, reportedly was furious when a private first class at the film center dared to tell him how to behave during his brief appearance in a training film. The PFC was George Cukor. Irving Wallace, Irwin Shaw, and John Huston were among those who served there, in most cases only briefly before moving along to more rewarding assignments in the European theatre of war.

Irwin Shaw was a private and Budd Schulberg a Navy ensign when they joined Saroyan for lunch at Manny Wolf's one day in the summer of 1943.

BUDD SCHULBERG: Bill was talking rather loudly, and I had an impression of people listening to us, and we were obvious fakes—these kind of fake, toy soldiers.

Bill's attitude seemed rather cavalier. I wasn't delighted with it because it was sort of a messy thing. It wasn't really like standing up and saying, "Fuck 'em, I'm going to burn my draft card, burn my uniform." No act of real defiance.

It was just kind of, "We're artists, we're poets. War—we shouldn't be concerned with this."

Schulberg recalls Shaw rather gently admonishing Saroyan about his attitude and Saroyan complaining about the training film he had been assigned to write. The subject was how to load a boxcar with military supplies.

ELIHU WINER: And he kept stalling and stalling and not delivering any material. And two or three weeks, or months, went by and he finally turned in a script, and it was one line and said, "It is very easy to load a boxcar." That was the whole thing.

AL HIRSCHFELD: They sent him around the country to every camp, because there is some sort of logistics to loading a truck: the last thing in is the first thing out, and so on. It's not that easy. Well, Bill tried to latch onto that, and he came back to Astoria after the government had sent him out all these months, paying all his fares around the country, and he sat down at the typewriter and he handed in a script, one page, that said, "It is very difficult to load a truck."

That kind of joke didn't go in the Army.

They had him cleaning latrines for *months*. And they broke him. They broke his spirit.

Difficult, easy, truck, boxcar. The story is alive in the oral tradition of Saroyan's friends, although he himself rarely referred to it afterward. In some versions the assignment comes from a commanding officer, a lieutenant colonel who had been a doorman at the Laemmle Studios before the war. A more credible account has Saroyan threatened with court-martial by an officer on the writing staff, a writer who went on after the war to write scripts for several of the most successful spy thrillers ever filmed, and who bore no particular personal grudge against Saroyan. Hirschfeld is correct, however, that filling a military truck or boxcar requires considerable forethought and skill, and Saroyan was being asked to create nothing more than a useful short film in the same genre as another Astoria classic, *How to Build a Timber Trestle Bridge*.

What is certain is that, by the late summer of 1943, Saroyan's obstinate attitude had gotten him into serious trouble with the Army. From the beginning, for ten months now, Saroyan had experienced his discomfort with the Army as physical pain, lower-back trouble. He referred to it sometimes as an upper-leg condition, a description of sciatic nerve pain.

"One morning at five I couldn't get out of bed: the slipped disc of the lower spine was out of place, and I was in terrible trouble. I telephoned the sergeant at the Astoria Army Post, and after a little chat he said, 'Well, come in when you can.'"

When Saroyan finally made it to the film center that afternoon, he believed that the sergeant was hinting to him that a bribe was in order, just as "one thousand dollars under the table" was sufficient, Saroyan believed, for a medical discharge from certain Army doctors.

"A month later, I couldn't get out of bed again, so again I phoned, and I believed the situation was the same as last time, but around eleven two military police, two medical corps sergeants, and two privates all came up to the penthouse at 2 Sutton Place South."

Saroyan was invited to lie on the stretcher the medical corpsmen had brought, but he left on foot, escorted by M.P.s past his wealthy neighbors and his doorman. He was taken to the military hospital on Roosevelt Island for a week of observation before transfer to a bigger hospital on Staten Island. There he was placed in a Section 8 ward for further observation before a hearing on whether he should be discharged as mentally unfit. Confinement to such a ward was no permanent blot on a man's record. Many returned to active duty at the front after such an experience. Artie Shaw, who suffered migraines, had his own encounter with military psychiatry.

ARTIE SHAW: They put me in Oak Knoll Hospital under psychiatric examination, and a guy would ask me the God-damnedest questions you ever heard, and I would look at him in utter astonishment.

"Do you hear voices?"

I said, "Yeah, I do."

"Whose?"

"Mine, yours, kids out there in the yard hollering at each other. I hear all those voices. What do you expect. You mean like Joan of Arc?"

He said, "You hear Joan of Arc?"

Some young, earnest fellow. Probably a proctologist they made
a psychiatrist. It was abysmal. You're talking to dumb people,
so I can understand Section 8.

CAROL MATTHAU: In fact, when Aram was born, Bill was in a
Section 8 ward. Halloran Hospital in New York. But then the
board met and decided he was just pretending to be crazy.
I mean, he was there—but no crazier than I'd seen him all the
time. They said he was pretending to be crazy, and he said, "Can
you be any crazier than someone who's *pretending* to be crazy?"
And he was outraged that they wouldn't let him out of the
Army. He was totally outraged and very quickly after that went
overseas.

AL HIRSCHFELD: They broke his spirit. He was in the hospital,
psychiatric, and they just knocked him out. They knocked him
out of the box, and he never quite recovered from it.
He tried to figure it out. He became philosophical and he
became cerebral. It didn't work.

When their son Aram was born on September 25, 1943, Bill was
furloughed from the hospital and was at Carol's side within two hours.
After his Section 8 hearing, his duties were light enough and his supe-
rior officers lenient enough for him to attend both New York rehearsals
and the Baltimore tryout of *Get Away, Old Man*, which finally was
about to reach Broadway, produced and directed by George Abbott.

After Eddie Dowling had rejected the play, it had bounced from Billy
Rose to Mike Todd to Michael Myerberg. One of the last-named three
had visited Saroyan while he was in Dayton, ostensibly for a pre-pro-
duction conference, but had been satisfied to leave with no discussion
at all after Bill let him drop the option and sent him on his way with a
$1,000 check.

Abbott had failed in 1940 with *The White-Haired Boy*, the play that
satirized Saroyan. Now, for the first time, he was working with a
Saroyan script, and he found it a far cry from the rigorous craftsmanship he was accustomed to. He cast Ed Begley in the role of the can-
tankerous tycoon and a young Richard Widmark as the Saroyan
counterpart. One of Dowling's objections had been the scene in which
a dense starlet had appeared in nun's costume. Abbott had qualms,

too, and dressed her in a vaguely Shakespearean outfit, which eliminated Saroyan's joke entirely. He also added comedy business freely, including bits that George Jean Nathan identified as stolen from *The Front Page* and a stuck-on ending intended to produce a belly laugh for the final curtain. This calculated stagecraft was the exact opposite of the benign anarchy Saroyan used in staging a play. Now Saroyan became convinced that Abbott was destroying his play as purposefully as the Army was toying with his sanity, and while he expressed this opinion over and over to Carol, he kept his silence to the press.

When *Get Away, Old Man* opened late in November, the other critics agreed with George Jean Nathan that it was not worth seeing. But the other critics did not agree with Nathan in laying the blame at George Abbott's feet. It was dismissed as ineffective satire, inspired by a grudge, and Abbott closed it after thirteen performances.

Despite his anger about the production, Saroyan attended every performance he could, often watching from the balcony with Carol at his side. He told her that he was interested in Glenn Anders's performance in the role of Sam. But after a solid year of bewilderment and humiliation, after recently having been escorted from his penthouse to a prisonlike hospital ward, it is possible that he simply wanted to sit in a theatre and be reminded that he was, indeed, Saroyan. There on the stage below him, an actor playing Saroyan was getting the better of an actor playing L. B. Mayer. Life had been satisfyingly rearranged for a couple of hours, even if box office was poor. It would be fourteen years before his next play opened on Broadway.

Word of his troubles could not be contained. He told the boxcar story on himself, but friends in the old haunts also had heard by now of his promotion to private first class. This was no great honor, simply a matter of time, but it was a promotion Saroyan determined to decline, the same way he had refused the Pulitzer Prize. As with the Pulitzer, he had little choice in the matter, but he decided to make his point by leaving his PFC stripe off his uniforms, and for this transgression he again was threatened with court-martial.

A vague echo of his hospitalization surfaced as a gossip item in the *New York Times*: "Rumors that William Saroyan will receive a medical discharge from the Army are, at this writing, more vigorously and authoritatively denied than affirmed. A tentmate of Saroyan usually is given as the source of the story that Saroyan is to be discharged. Harold Matson, Saroyan's literary agent, says that the report is false."

The law said draftees would serve for the duration of the war plus six months. The end of the war was nowhere in sight. True, the allies had gained a foothold in Italy, and air operations against Germany were at their peak, but the island-to-island fighting in the Pacific was inconclusive. Early in December, 1943, after long congressional debate, Roosevelt signed the law granting fathers the lowest priority for military service, but the law protected only undrafted men who had been fathers before December 7, 1941. It was clear to Saroyan now that he was in for the duration plus six months, and that seemed an eternity to him.

Carol now had more than an occasional glimpse of what a bitter and touchy man he was becoming.

CAROL MATTHAU: It was all like a nervous breakdown. It was all—very, very hard to explain. He lived by his own gut. If he had the slightest discomfort, he felt like killing someone.

In a rage. He was always that way. When I say "always that way," of course, in between, he wasn't. When we'd get in bed he was loving, and as he would go to sleep, he would sort of change.

He had a young Armenian boy come to the apartment to photograph Aram and me with him. I forget his name. He was just a kid, in the Army, Armenian.

He came to *Saroyan's* apartment, and he wanted to talk.

And Bill wanted him to take pictures. And in between each shot, the boy would want to talk and have a conversation with him. And Bill went into a rage and threw him out. It was like that.

It was always embarrassing to live with Bill—not so much for what he did with me, but how he was with the world around him.

Even though the end of the war could not be forecast, the next step in Europe was clear to everyone on both sides. The Allies were obliged to attempt an invasion of the mainland from Great Britain, and late in December, 1943, Eisenhower was revealed as the chosen Supreme Commander for that effort. For soldiers in the Astoria film unit, documentation of the fighting itself was the big assignment, and it was convenient for Saroyan's officers to send their problem soldier along with all the others heading for London.

Saroyan sailed on a snowy day in February, 1944. The photograph of Carol and four-month-old Aram was in his pocket. Death was on his mind, but with Aram safely arrived, the worst prospect no longer was intolerable. The essential thing had been achieved: "The family line had been moved forward again, to another generation: and Petrus begat Armenak and Armenak begat William and William begat Aram, and so there was a chance that this might go on for some time to come."

2. EUROPEAN THEATRE

The London where Saroyan arrived late in the winter of 1944 was a city ruled by war. The pace of life there and even the altered makeup of its populace were factors in the planning for the big invasion. Despite the Blitz, the terrible air attacks of 1940, London resolutely had remained a capital. The government was there, the King was there, and so were the theatre and ballet and music and publishing. When Russia drew Germany's attention east from 1941 through 1943, London had come fully alive in that special atmosphere that accompanies warfare the way ozone accompanies a thunderstorm.

Throughout the winter of 1943–44, Allied air attacks from England had begun to do Germany serious damage, and now, in February, Hitler was retaliating with attacks on London, raids that immediately became known as the "little Blitz." These bombings pulled the opening curtain at London's theatres ahead to five o'clock, and they brought back the blackouts, whose silence was as remarkable as their darkness—at least until the bombing and ack-ack began. "The scenic effects are terrific," George Orwell wrote that season. "The orange-coloured flares dropped by the German planes drift slowly down, making everything almost as light as day, and carmine-colored tracer shells sail up to meet them: and as the flares get lower the shadows on the window pane move slowly upwards." Orwell noticed that men were once more wearing evening clothes and that titled ladies were advertising once more for servants.

Germany's innovation this winter was the introduction of the long-range, unmanned missiles—the buzz bombs, which were most terrifying when the buzzing stopped and they began their arcs down to their random targets. Saroyan could, and did, watch attacks like this from hotel rooftops, chatting with friends, with a drink in his hand. He was as near the killing as he ever would be, and it was death you read about in the morning newspaper, an incident in a suburb.

The weather was mild all winter, and on fair days when the streets filled, the Americans in uniforms seemed to outnumber everyone else. British troops were forbidden to go to London on leave unless London was their home, and the city was becoming the adoptive home not only of the brains of the invasion force, but of the second army of journalists who followed them. Reporter Mary Welsh, soon to become Mary Hemingway, was greeting old friends that spring, including the movie director Henry Hathaway and Corporal Irwin Shaw, who introduced her to Private Saroyan. Welsh belonged to several private drinking clubs, but their rules barred anyone below officer rank, and in order to entertain friends like Saroyan and Shaw, she and her friend Connie Ernst improvised a salon, which met for Friday lunches at a cozy restaurant.

Saroyan returned her hospitality by calling at seven-thirty one morning to take her to breakfast in Park Lane, in the U.S. Army mess hall in the basement of Grosvenor House.

As they walked, Mary Welsh noticed that Saroyan was picky about whom he saluted.

"How come you don't salute them all?" she asked.

"I salute the looks on their faces," Saroyan answered.

The hubbub of D-Day preparations worked to Saroyan's advantage from his arrival in London. He was exempted from barracks if he so chose, and he was delighted to be able to live with Irwin Shaw, whom he first had met five years earlier when the Group Theatre was producing plays both men had written. Shaw had won success and praise with *Bury the Dead*, his play in which the bodies of men killed in war return to life to confront those who have taken warfare for granted. *Bury the Dead* is not topical. It remains a strong antiwar statement to this day. But that did not mean that its young author was categorically opposed to warfare.

> IRWIN SHAW: I wrote, in fact, for the *New York Sunday Times*
> drama section, right after the play's run, that it was *not* a pacifist
> play. There's a line there that says, "A man can die contented,

allow himself to be buried, for a cause that's his own, not Pharaoh's or Caesar's or Rome's." And, when the war came, I knew it was my cause, and so I went, and I did as much as I could to help win the war.

I went through Monmouth and then the film center at Astoria. They called us draft dodgers in uniform. I was working with a British film unit to do a picture about D-Day, and because of that, I had to represent the American Army at high-level meetings, even though I was a PFC and everybody else was a colonel. But I represented the American Army, and we did shoot three reels preparatory to D-Day. The Americans backed out of the first picture I was making with the British because they said I was hornswoggled by the British and made to put too much emphasis on the British. Since it was all taking place in the British Isles, I couldn't pretend it was taking place in North Dakota.

But, when I got back to London, I had a lot of free time. Nobody bothered me. I checked in. I was busy preparing the schedule of the equipment that we were going to use for our outfit, so George Stevens, who was our lieutenant colonel, could make his requisitions. I was also talking to Stevens all the time about the kind of pictures we should be taking. Unfortunately, none of the things that I wanted to do panned out.

And by pulling wires, by using pull even though I was just a PFC, I didn't live in billets. I lived in some rented places, and when Bill came, he and Captain Reese, who was with our outfit, and I took a flat at Pall Mall together. The flat had three bedrooms, a big living room where we used to play poker. And we lived there until we had to go to Normandy.

Although, actually, I was living there with Reese before, and we saw Bill, who had come over on a boat, and he was a sorry-looking soldier, as you can well imagine, and the Army had no right to take him. He was of no use to the Army, and he hated the Army. They just took him because he was well-known and because he was very antiwar—completely—and anti-Army.

He just hated all organization, and it happened that this huge, clumsy sort of organization just ground him down. And he just should not have been taken. It was a mistake on the part of the Army to have taken him. He should not have been taken because he was more trouble than he was worth. I mean, if a guy has a trigger finger missing, you don't take him in.

Well, rather than anything *missing* in Bill, he was too much of an anarchist—not in any philosophical terms, but in personal terms—to be able to work for any organization. For example, even in the theatre—all the plays he had that people wanted to put on that he wouldn't let them put on because he can't stand organization, can't stand being told, "You've got to do it this way because that's the way the theatre is built." So, rather than compromise with those things, rather willfully he said, "Nothing doing," and he didn't have the plays put on. That was his attitude toward the Army, and the Army psychiatrists should have known that. Anybody who ever read one of his books should have known to leave him alone and let the war go on without him. We'd have won without him.

Of course, he was a most amusing man to have living in the same house with you. We did have a good time.

The Armenian community in England kept showering him with gifts—with wine, with brandies, with melons, with fruits. They'd come and they'd sort of bow down to him in the living room of our place.

We used to have big poker games with George Stevens and [Bob] Capa. Stevens was absolutely deadpan, cold. You never could figure out what he was playing. Bill—no-good gambler. Wild. Reckless.

One night I won a lot, and I had a lot of Bill's I.O.U.'s We were playing at somebody else's place—Bob Capa's girl's, their apartment.

We got back to our place and Bill said, "You've got a lot of my I.O.U's. I'm not going to pay you."

I said, "What do you mean you're not going to pay me?"

He said, "I'm going to play you double-or-nothing until I win."

I said, "Tear the God-damned things up."

Movie director George Stevens was, in fact, a legendary poker player. Saroyan recalled attempting to pay an $800 gambling debt to him. The check never went through.

"Colonel Stevens, permission to talk, please."

"Private Saroyan, permission denied."

"I always pay my gambling debts. I'd sooner not pay the grocer. That check for eight hundred dollars hasn't gone through."

"Willie, you don't play poker, you play art, you play religion, you play comedy, and any man who takes your money is a son-of-a-bitch, that's all. You know *how* to play to win, but you refuse to bother."

Saroyan had far less work to do than Shaw and his other acquaintances. He spent a great deal of time behaving as he might have done on a peacetime visit. He lunched at the Ritz with Geoffrey Faber of Faber and Faber, his British publisher. He lunched at the Connaught with T. S. Eliot, Faber's best-known employee. He lunched at Claridge's with Herbert Read, the Faber author who was an acknowledged master of English prose style, although his book on that subject still lay in the future. There was a dinner at which Saroyan sat beside Anthony Eden, Churchill's heir-apparent. The conversation at that table turned to Dikran Kouymjian, son of an Armenian mercantile family in Manchester and a world-famous author of popular novels under the *nom de plume* Michael Arlen. Saroyan was struck by the warmth and respect that the wealthy creator of *The Green Hat* commanded from England's ruling class.

Wartime London also gave Saroyan the opportunity to reopen hostilities with Ernest Hemingway, with whom he had quarreled a decade earlier, but only in print. In war, Hemingway was in his element, equally the master whether the conversation was literature or military strategy. Saroyan had lunch one day at a Greek restaurant with a group of American writers who were guests of Cyril Connolly, the British critic, and Arthur Koestler, the novelist and journalist. Saroyan squirmed while the tart-tongued critic and his Hungarian-born disciple talked—in Bill's view—above the heads of their American colleagues. Hemingway was not at that luncheon, but a few weeks later he did attend a party at Connolly's, where Koestler hung on his every word.

Saroyan's most memorable London encounter was with George Bernard Shaw at the elderly playwright's suburban home in Ayot St. Lawrence. An Australian newspaperwoman arranged the meeting, and the invitation came in a letter to Saroyan from Shaw himself. Saroyan visited Fortnum and Mason and bought appropriate tribute: grapes, figs, peaches, a melon—costly wartime luxuries.

Shaw was in a deliberately provocative mood when the younger man arrived: "Armenian? But didn't the Turks *kill* all of the Armenians?" Saroyan was impressed by his piping voice, his knickers, and his evident worry that the American guest would consider him some sort of saint, a notion he was at pains to correct. "But he couldn't fool me, and he remained the gentlest, kindest, the most decent fellow in

England, and possibly in the world." Shaw said he felt that he was dying, and Saroyan reassured him—correctly, as it turned out—that he had productive years remaining. Shaw also said that if he were as young as Saroyan he would forget the stage altogether and turn his career toward film.

That spring, Saroyan was writing little except his journal and a letter a day to Carol. He was making revisions on the stories and short pieces Harcourt would publish in the fall of 1944 as *Dear Baby*, but there was no new play. The wartime novel he had boasted about writing remained on his mind, and as D-Day approached, Saroyan decided that producing that book would be preferable to taking part in the invasion. Saroyan stayed behind in London.

His nominal duties were writing press releases and speeches, and there was scant need for either as the invasion began. Irwin Shaw and others in the film unit were preparing to follow Operation Anvil, the landings in southern France later in the summer. With his apartment mates gone, Saroyan was billeted now in the Savoy Hotel. He continued to attend the theatre and the movies. (An old lady sitting beside him at a film one afternoon that summer introduced herself to him as the mother of Noël Coward. She had no idea whom she was talking to.)

Saroyan now set out to strike a bargain with the Army—a full-length William Saroyan novel in exchange for a furlough to New York to see his wife and baby son. The job was to be done for Herbert Agar, head of the London section of the U.S. Office of War Information. Agar was a distinguished critic and historian who had a Pulitzer Prize of his own, for a scholarly work. He also was a hard-headed editor and diplomat. From the time of Hitler's first threats, he had urged America to join the fight against Germany, and he had left the editorship of the Louisville *Courier-Journal* to serve in the war. Perhaps Agar's literary leanings led him to listen charitably to Saroyan's plea for a trip home in exchange for work completed. Perhaps there was an element of a wager involved, and Saroyan was betting that Agar was unfamiliar with the speed with which he wrote. The challenge was to write the book in one month, August, and the purpose of the resulting work was to help celebrate and cement the Anglo-American alliance.

At five minutes before eleven on the morning of Tuesday, August 8, 1944, Saroyan began work on not one but two books. The first was the novel, which he was toying with entitling *London Immortal* or *The Eagle and the Lion.* The other book was his journal of the novel's creation, which he at first called *Captured by the U.S.A.* The first book was for the government, as he put it, and the second, "for God."

The book for the government quickly turned into a picaresque novel featuring an innocent-in-uniform, Wesley Jackson, whose Army assignments include Wright Field, the film center at Astoria, and London. The book for God became a minute accounting of the days of a driven man. Saroyan guessed within the pages of his journal that it would prove useful to psychiatrists, to his biographers, to chroniclers of failure.

Other writers have used journals to track their creative process, but in the droning tally of meals and pages completed and self-imposed deadlines met or missed, little is revealed of how the novel's characters or incidents were born. These matters are taken for granted, unexplained. But there are pages and pages of embarrassing passages that reveal Saroyan, at the height of the war, haranguing secretarial help at headquarters about typewriter ribbons and the availability of stenographers to copy his work, pleading at the hotel for new furniture and better room service, suffering nostalgia for his basement workroom. At the Savoy there was no pianola, only a phonograph, whose erratic mechanism made "Wonderful One" sound more doleful than ever as Saroyan wrote to its strains.

And there are many passages of worry and complaint about his health. He suffered backaches again, and both the common cold and the uncommon malaise the war had inspired in him from the beginning:

> My health becomes very poor when I am not left alone. I have been sick all the time I've been in the Army—my saying so now is part of the sickness. I ought never need to say such a thing, but as it's the truth I must say it—for I am in the Army, I am sick, I got sick when I began to be in the Army, I was sick when I was in the Army—sometimes very sick, sometimes less sick than at other times, but always sick. . . . The disease is this war. It is the vilest, the deadliest disease there is. . . . I enjoy no part of it, I cherish no part of it, I loathe all of it and always will. I despise the heroism it brings out of people; I despise the courage, the gentility, the kindliness and all the other good things it brings out of them, for I cannot understand why a war is required to bring these natural and common-place things out of them. . . . There are better reasons for being human than inhumanity.

Saroyan himself speaks and moves in many guises through his novel

The Adventures of Wesley Jackson. He is Wesley himself, spared from carrying a gun when a heartfelt letter to his missing father ends up in the pages of *The New Republic*, making him famous, an episode similar to Saroyan's own literary discovery. Saroyan also is on hand as The Writer, a more cynical and realistic self-portrait. Although Wesley's adventures take him beyond London to capture by the Germans, even the Nazis are lovable and kind. And there is a meeting with a gorgeous blonde teenager like Carol. There is next to nothing of the required message material about the Anglo-American alliance. There is a great deal of satire directed at the Army bureaucracy, some of it quite bitter. Saroyan must have known the book could not be published with the government's imprimatur, at least not as written, but he was working under the assumption, or delusion, that he could say what he said under the aegis of art. After Saroyan had been in the Army almost two years, *The Adventures of Wesley Jackson* was his first opportunity to reach inside himself and produce a work that expressed his anger and pain about the war.

As he neared the end of his task early in September of 1944, the entries in the journal came faster and faster. He was working hard, but not so hard as to miss a performance of *Cosi fan Tutte* or a matinée of *Madame Butterfly*. He rehearsed his cover letter to Agar: "Here it is. I think it's great—or will be when I get through with it—and I hope you think so, too. I'm very tired now and would be very grateful if you would get me home as soon as possible, as you promised to do if I wrote this story."

But Agar was out of town for ten days when the manuscript was ready. Saroyan polished, added chapters, supervised the retyping, made a note that he had spent more time on the Wesley Jackson book than on anything he had ever written. The daily love letters to Carol continued, promising his early return to America. Sometimes they would pile up before he mailed them, but there was one for each day, and usually a letter from Carol each day in return.

One morning there was a letter from the *New York Times*: "Will you comment on the rumor we have heard that the War has fundamentally changed your attitude toward life and that we may expect evidence of that change in your future works?" It went unanswered.

The bitterness that clouds *The Adventures of Wesley Jackson* was plain to the Office of War Information when Agar or his second read the novel in manuscript and rejected it. Saroyan never revealed what the

OWI's plans for the book were to have been, but the office's reaction was immediate and unambiguous. Copies of the manuscript circulated among the brass as evidence of scandal. If there had been any question about Saroyan's out-of-step attitude toward the war, here his military enemies could point to hard proof. One of the Hollywood colonels wrote a memorandum that called the book treasonous. The promised furlough—if, indeed, there ever was such a promise—was denied. There was loud shouting on Saroyan's part, but no court-martial.

As he was writing the book, he turned thirty-six and the Allies liberated Paris, and Paris now became his next Army assignment. He was to write routine hackwork, such as a speech for General Eisenhower about conserving tires, and an occasional piece in his own name and style for consumption by the troops in Yank or Stars & Stripes, the Army publications.

In Paris he moved naturally into the circle at the Hotel Scribe, whose writerly name appealed to him as much as the crowd of American journalists who made it their unofficial headquarters. Hemingway and his entourage had chosen the Ritz as center of their post-liberation activities, but there were sorties to the Scribe. One such reconnaissance resulted in an unpleasant confrontation between Hemingway and Saroyan. Saroyan was standing outside the Scribe bar when a correspondent drinking with Hemingway saw him and waved him over, saying, "Here's Bill Saroyan."

"Where's Bill Saroyan?" Hemingway asked, and Saroyan said, "In London you had a beard, but even without it I haven't forgotten you. Did shaving it off make you forget me?" Saroyan was embarrassed and angry at the way the newspapermen were playing up to Hemingway, just as he had seen Koestler do in London.

A few evenings later, Hemingway spotted Saroyan while both were dining in a basement room of the Hotel George V. According to his companion that evening, Group Captain—later Air Marshal—Peter Wykeham-Barnes, Hemingway had been drinking heavily and opened hostilities by saying in a loud voice, "Well, for God's sake, what's that lousy Armenian son-of-a-bitch doing here?" There were retorts from Saroyan's companion if not from Saroyan himself, and soon there was a brawl, engaging utter strangers, hotel management, and police, and ending in ejection. Saroyan denied to Hemingway biographer Carlos Baker that the incident happened, but Sir Peter was adamant that it did, while admitting that Saroyan might have extricated himself before the fisticuffs broke out.

As miserable and out of place as Saroyan was among the men who seemed to delight in the war, he was not without friends among the officers, and one of them was Colonel Lawrence Colt, a West Pointer from New England who was willing to listen to Saroyan's tirades against the Army without threatening discipline. In fact, Colt had suffered as the target of one such tantrum, writing it off as something Saroyan needed to get off his chest. In London, Colt had agreed that Saroyan should be furloughed back to America, at least for a time. In Paris, he took Saroyan along on a venture by jeep beyond Verdun and all the way into Germany itself, late in the long, cold winter of 1944–45. The trip ended in Luxembourg, and there Saroyan was hospitalized with lower back trouble. By mid-March, he was back in the United States, at an Army hospital in Auburn, California, near Sacramento.

From Southern California, his Uncle Aram, his mother's younger brother, announced to the press that Saroyan was undergoing treatment for an old back injury he had suffered in a fall from a bicycle as a Postal Telegraph messenger. The job had been real, but the accident Uncle Aram described was a fabrication. By July, when Saroyan was in Madigan Army Convalescent Hospital at Tacoma, Washington, he was said by the hospital to be suffering a leg injury. But while the injury was not so great that the Army was willing to release Saroyan, neither was it so serious that he could not accept the long-deferred furlough to join his wife.

Carol and Aram boarded a train for California and took up residence in Takoohi's house on Fifteenth Avenue in San Francisco. After the reunion, Carol was pregnant with their second child. But she still could not command the respect of her mother-in-law, and Bill was unhappy and often unreasonable, she felt, during his time with her.

CAROL MATTHAU: While he had been overseas I had taken Armenian lessons to surprise him. A terribly sweet older woman used to come, five days a week at four o'clock, for about an hour, and I learned to write. I thought it would be a wonderful surprise for him.

I wrote him a letter in Armenian and he couldn't read it because he couldn't read the Armenian alphabet. But I had learned a lot of things from her. So now, when we got back and were staying with his mother and sister, every night at dinner they spoke *nothing* but Armenian.

They both spoke English, but it was as though I wasn't there. And I, at the beginning, I thought, "Well, it's easier for them. They haven't seen him in a long time, and it's okay." And I thought, too, that of course they would never say terrible things about me in Armenian *while* I was sitting there. I thought no one would do that, but that's exactly what they were doing.

I knew what they were saying, and I was stunned. They were sitting there, talking about me. "She doesn't know how to do anything," and "What are you doing with her?" and "She doesn't know," and "She's a baby and she doesn't know anything."

And he would argue with them, "Mind your own business," and "None of your business," and "This is my girl and I'm happy."

But the mother would keep haggling, and Cosette would keep agreeing with the mother.

So finally one night they were at it, and I just said something to them—in Armenian. Something like "I understand what you're saying, and it's very upsetting and please don't."

The reaction was the perfect Saroyan reaction. *I* could not be trusted because I could understand everything they were saying about me.

Although he was free at last from the grinding day-to-day military bureaucracy, Saroyan remained at the mercy of Army doctors, technically still a private first class, not a private citizen. The duration, plus six months. This twilight private war shadowed his relationship with Carol, and the quarrels occasionally became intense, as did the one on the night of August 15, V-J Day.

CAROL MATTHAU: I was at the square in San Francisco near the St. Francis Hotel. We had had a terrible, terrible fight, and I had to get away, so I went—I took the bus or the trolley, or whatever, I don't remember. And I got there, and I wasn't even aware of what was going on.

Sailors—it was like Times Square on New Year's Eve. It was like that. I was in such a daze.

This young sailor suddenly turned and smiled at me, and then he threw up all over me. I started to cry, it was so silly. And he was so sweet, and I felt so sorry. I said, "Oh, no. It's all right.

Please, please. It's okay, it's okay." And I managed to go into the ladies' room at the hotel and clean off, and I got back and Bill had forgotten everything.

He said, "How are ya, kid? What's going on?"

And I said, "Nothing."

One month later, September 14, 1945, now aged thirty-seven, Saroyan was released from the Army. The discharge papers were issued at Fort Lewis, Washington, along with $300 in mustering-out pay.

The press remained intensely interested in the story of Saroyan's personal war with the Army, but the public-relations officers at Madigan Hospital found Saroyan totally unwilling to help them deal with the reporters. "Saroyan's become afraid of the public, I'm afraid," a young lieutenant told the woman from United Press. "Private Saroyan is not well. He is suffering from a boil."

"Where?" the reporter asked.

"Private Saroyan is now lying in his bed on his stomach." If Saroyan no longer could be counted on for funny copy, the Army would invent it on his behalf. He was, in fact, in an eight-dollar-a-day hotel room with Carol, waiting for the day the discharge papers would become effective.

Two years and eleven months had passed since he had taken the Army oath. He had served with no distinction, failing even in his parting promise at the train station to write an important book that made the best of war by turning it into art. *The Adventures of Wesley Jackson* fails as a war novel because the war it is so closely based upon, Saroyan's war, is too distant from the common experience of that conflict.

He had watched Metro-Goldwyn-Mayer make money on their over-sentimentalized version of *The Human Comedy*, and he had suffered the bittersweet indignity of sharing an Academy Award for its screenplay. But the award, in his mind, had only increased the reprisals and enmity from the men he despised the most, those who had planned their war better, who had secured commissions. Saroyan hated cleverness, a trait he attacked throughout his life, but in this war cleverness could, indeed, buy comfort—or at least exemption from grief. Putting on the uniform of a buck private, a draftee, he had trusted some basic American spirit of fairness to protect or rescue him.

His trust, he decided, had been misplaced. In his own mind William

Saroyan had become as certain a casualty of the United States Army as Hitler or the people of Hiroshima. The door to Hollywood was closed, perhaps forever. His one ready manuscript had received advance word-of-mouth as an act of treason. Broadway seemed impossibly distant.

It was time to retreat to the workroom, put on a piano roll and start something new.

And now there were a wife and child—*children*—to think of.

CHAPTER FIVE

MARRIED MAN

1. STALLED

CAROL MATTHAU: We were driving up to Seattle or Tacoma. He was getting out of the Army, and I was now pregnant with Lucy, and he would drive and drive and drive, for ten hours without stopping. If I had to go to the loo, I was afraid to tell him, afraid he'd be enraged. Any small annoyance—I knew if I was hungry when he wasn't, I knew to forget it. Finally, it was nighttime and we ended up in a big diner somewhere. Eugene, Salem—I don't know.

There was a jukebox, soldiers. We ordered steaks and he had a drink. I was looking at him, and I saw a man at the bar and I said, softly, "Bill, I just saw Lon Chaney, Jr."

"*What?*"

I said, "I think I just saw Lon Chaney, Jr."

He said, "*Christ!*"

I said, "No, no. Really. That's Lon Chaney, Jr."

"*Jesus Christ!*"

I didn't get it. I was dense or something. He went into a total rage. I said, "Why are you so angry? I just saw him at the bar. Turn around and look."

Finally, he was exploding. Exploding. He said, "Jesus Christ, I'm coming out of this hell-hole, the Army. I've been in the *Army*, and there's a war on and *you* see Lon Chaney, Jr.! That's all you're thinking about."

I said, "Bill, it wasn't—"

"I can't stand it."

He was mad, and he stayed mad. And we left and never ate. And I ran after him, and we got in the car, and he drove like a fiend. And finally even he got tired.

There was nothing open, nothing around, and he wouldn't speak to me. He saw an empty orange on the roadside—one of those big oranges they have in the summertime, where you go and have orange juice—and he parked the car by the orange.

We went in there, and it was empty. Around the inside of the orange there was a board bench, and that's where we slept. In the orange. He wouldn't speak to me. I couldn't understand what I'd done. I saw Lon Chaney, Jr. I thought I'd mention it.

Bill and Carol were hardly strangers. They had lived as man and wife for almost a year before Saroyan left for Europe. But in the months just after the war they had much to discover about each other.

With a second child on the way, it made sense for them to set up a household of their own now, away from Saroyan's disapproving mother and his sister, Cosette. Perhaps Saroyan had realized that he never could coax his mother to accept Carol fully. Carol's pregnancy made the move at once more necessary and entirely diplomatic. When the baby was born on January 17, 1946, she was named Lucy, to honor Bill's beloved grandmother.

The new house they bought was a plain clapboard two-story, two-flat affair, which fronted directly on busy Taraval Street, one of the alphabetical streets that sweep across San Francisco's Sunset District and down to cold, bleak Ocean Beach. It was a practical investment for Saroyan. In a pinch, the upper flat could provide rental income. For now, it would be his work space. Here, however, the view was different from the paneled basement apartment at Takoohi's—a clothes-line, not the Pacific Ocean. But the main thing had been to have their own, separate house, and the Taraval Street flats were only to be tem-

Bill and a pigtailed Carol at Fresno, 1945, while she was pregnant with Lucy. Saroyan recalled weenie roasts with his cousins and their wives by the river at Piedra, calling them "the best fun in the world. I ate thirty hot dogs and drank two dozen bottles of soda." The waistband of his civilian trousers appears tight. (Courtesy Aram Saroyan)

porary. At the same time, Saroyan had bought a vacant lot in the fashionable Sea-Cliff district and had commissioned blueprints for a splendid residence befitting an author and his growing family.

The work itself was understood to be a novel, but for many months after the war Saroyan's writing seems to have been confined to his journals and his correspondence. The letters paint him as busy and full of plans and optimism. The later confessional books—and by implication the journals upon which they rely—describe Saroyan as bewildered and defeated by the war, and recovering slowly, if at all.

He remained angry, too, and anger was the mainspring of *The Adventures of Wesley Jackson*. The war was over, Saroyan was a civilian, and no official displeasure could stand in the way of the book's publication now. It appeared in June, 1946, and Saroyan immediately learned he would win little or no sympathy for his attitude about the war and the Army.

The most telling attack on *The Adventures of Wesley Jackson* came from Saroyan's sympathetic ally in the months before D-Day, his old roommate Irwin Shaw. Shaw would later work out his own attitudes about the war in *The Young Lions*, a vast success that helped to reshape his career as short-story writer and playwright into that of a best-selling novelist. Shaw's novel conveys the ironies and complexities of warfare without ever wrapping itself in patriotism or sentimentality, and it even contains an understanding portrait of a reluctant German officer as one of its main characters. In 1946, however, Shaw was handling the war in brilliant short stories in *The New Yorker*. It was the *New York Times* that approached Saroyan's old friend about the review.

IRWIN SHAW: I didn't want to do it, but I felt that somebody who knew Bill well, who knew what kind of war he'd had, ought somehow to defend the Army against what *I* considered unnecessary and untrue attacks.

Shaw wrote an article that filled the front page of the *New York Times Book Review* and did its work in a straightforward way:

. . .[I]n 285 closely printed pages, the sweet singer of Fresno has not one good word to say about the forces that liberated Europe and lifted the Japanese hand from the East. . . . In this book he uses fantasy and sentimentality for a dangerous and sinful purpose—to discredit the causes in which we fought and the men who did the fighting. . . . Once more

Saroyan is full of love for the entire world. He loves the Germans, he loves the Japs, he loves the Bulgarians and Finns and Rumanians. The only people he can find to hate are the Americans. He forgives the Germans Dachau and Belsen without blinking an eye, but he cannot forgive the sergeant who assigned him to KP in New York City. He goes through the entire American Army without finding a single officer who is worthy of any but the most savage satire and derision. The only decent and pleasant officer in the entire book is the German officer who shoots Jackson's friend and takes Jackson prisoner.

Shaw went on to relate the episode in which the German guard goes all the way to Paris to buy a straw hat for the American prisoner who cannot play his trombone without one. He contrasted Saroyan's fantasy about the hat with the reality of Germans who lynched Allied pilots and machine-gunned whole companies of American prisoners.

Just why Saroyan feels that a world being murdered by fascism is merely "sad" and a world saved, even momentarily, from fascism is "hideous" is a matter between him and his conscience. Certainly, the people of France who greeted us when we drove the Germans out of their villages, the people of Belgium and Holland, Denmark and Poland, China and Mindanao, who had held a more immediate view of the matter, would at least reverse the phrase. I am certain that they consider it quite a fair bargain—Saroyan on KP, Hitler dead.

Shaw sympathized to some degree with Saroyan's attacks on Army politics and confessed that he himself had wished aloud that some of his Signal Corps colleagues could be made to suffer combat duty. But he decided, he wrote, that they had done their job, and had done it well.

Many other reviewers noticed, as Shaw did, that Saroyan's skill at creating pleasant characters slightly at odds with the world remained undiminished, that his comic invention was more or less intact. *The Adventures of Wesley Jackson* is, in fact, a far richer work, technically, than the retouched screenplay of *The Human Comedy*, and in a few years a new edition would give the critics a chance to appraise it with a cooler eye.

The same day that Irwin Shaw's highly critical review was published in New York, one of the San Francisco papers featured Saroyan's prewar face on the cover of the Sunday rotogravure section. The old friend from the newspaper who had gone to interview him on the occasion of his first postwar book was startled to find a new face— Saroyan with a bushy black mustache identical to those worn by the

Armenian elders of the Fresno backgammon parlors. Saroyan refused to be photographed looking like this, however, explaining that the facial hair allowed him some degree of anonymity in moving around town. His new reticence was as newsworthy as the mustache or the new book, and the only subject Saroyan was ready to be quoted on was the Army.

> From the beginning they scare you to death in the Army. They begin scaring you with the Articles of War. They don't mean to be human about any of the difficulties a fellow is apt to get into, they just naturally threaten to kill you, that's all. They tell you before your arm is down, before you're in the Army, '—the punishment is Death.' . . . You get six or seven months of that kind of law and order and if you aren't scared to death, or full of confusion and anger you're a better man than I am because even though I'm easy-going about all things, and by rights shouldn't be scared or confused or angry, I am scared, I am confused, I am angry. I don't like it, but I just can't help it.

One of his old Broadway newspaper cronies, Earl Wilson, gossip columnist of the New York *Post*, visited the West Coast in the summer of 1946 and made a special trip from Hollywood to talk with Bill. Wilson had trouble taking notes as Saroyan chain-smoked and paced in his living room.

"Right now, there's no healthy protest against conscription. Controllers of our destiny are continually coming to situations they can't cope with when they say 'Call in the boys. Get 10,000 troops.' Why not get volunteers? Pay them $10 or $15 a day."

"Are you doing anything about it?" Wilson asked.

"Except for writing about it, not a blessed thing."

Saroyan was correct in believing that anything he chose to write would command an audience, at least for the moment. Harcourt, Brace had sold more than 32,000 copies of *The Adventures of Wesley Jackson* before publication date. It was no bestseller on the scale of *The Human Comedy*, but neither was it a neglected minor work from a major author. But, in crystallizing Saroyan's reputation as a reluctant soldier, a stand Bill amplified every time a newspaperman called, the book separated him from the way most Americans thought and felt.

The country's view of the returning veterans was exemplified by *The Best Years of Our Lives*, a long movie directed by William Wyler. It swept the Academy Awards with its story of wartime heroes (including a young sailor whose hands have been amputated) struggling to readjust to civilian life and to the women they had left behind.

Like most other American women, Carol wanted to see the picture, and she asked Bill to take her. He did so reluctantly, and what he saw on the screen infuriated him: "the most preposterously phoney damned job of expert belittlement of both the truth and people, in the Army, or home waiting for the return of people in the Army." Saroyan wanted to leave the theatre, and the movie provided him many exit cues. In one scene, two of the veterans beat up a late-blooming America Firster, whose isolationist views closely matched Saroyan's more bitter outbursts. There is a heroic young Air Force officer who is a nobody in private life, precisely the reverse of Bill's situation—the somebody swallowed into khaki anonymity. And there is a gorgeous blonde wife who prefers a good time in nightclubs to the hard job of making her new marriage work. This is the stock description of Carol that Saroyan adopted in later years.

In his work of that period, however, it is the loving half of his love-hate feelings toward Carol that was in the ascendant. Over the years she would walk through his work in the guise of various women characters. In *The Adventures of Wesley Jackson* she is the little London streetwalker Wesley marries before she can score her first trick. In the novelized memoir *Boys and Girls Together*, withheld until the 1960s, Saroyan offered a frank portrait of their life together on Taraval Street. His writing was coming hard, angry words coming easily. Gambling was a temptation. Carol's old friends were enemies or, at best, rivals.

CAROL MATTHAU: We're settled, living in San Francisco, and he reads a story called "My Side of the Matter," Truman Capote's first published story. Bill is laughing as he's reading it, really enjoying it.

He says, "Ah, there's this divine story"—whatever he said—and he said, "It's some kid I've never heard of, Truman Ca*pott*," he said. "Ca*pott*."

And I said, "Oh, no! That's Truman Capote! He's an old friend of mine."

He goes crazy again.

He said, "You don't have to know him, just because I said I loved his—what are you talking about?"

I said, "I *know* him. He's a great friend of my sister's and a friend of mine. I've known him since I was in grade school."

"Jesus Christ, you're a congenital liar!"

Total exasperation. Finally, having learned from Lon Chaney, Jr., I just sort of gave up and didn't mention it again. But it was very interesting because, something like seven or eight months after that, Truman came through San Francisco and got in touch with us, and we went out with him.

He forgot his reaction entirely. Truman was talking about my sister—this, that, the other thing. But, as far as Bill was concerned, Truman had gotten in touch with him because he was William Saroyan. It had nothing to do with me. (Which he might have done.) But he was really confronted with it, because of the conversation.

Once in a while he'd like to "go out on the town" as he put it. I'd get all gussied up, and we went to that bar at Vanessi's. The bartender would say, "What'll it be, you guys?" I was so dressed up.

But you see that exhausted him. He could do an evening, and he could go to a party and be a star, but he had to go to bed for four days afterward. He'd say, "It's my back, it's my sacroiliac," and he would go to bed. He'd have to refuel, have to get filled up again. He found the social thing a great drain.

We were very, very isolated.

Carol turned twenty-two in the fall of 1946 and Bill was thirty-eight now, older than his father, Armenak, had ever lived to be. Having been raised without the presence of a father, Saroyan was ad-libbing marriage and fatherhood to a certain degree. In his writings about the marriage completed before the period when rage at Carol overtook him, Saroyan described two things at the center of the relationship. First, the children. He had told Carol he wanted multitudes of them. Her pregnancy had been a prerequisite to any marriage at all, and now he was rehearsing the role of mustachioed Armenian patriarch. So far, there were only two: the son and heir and his treasure, blue-eyed Lucy. He wished for many more, said so aloud. The other thing that bound him to Carol was his joy in physical lovemaking with her, and his delight in her unique beauty and charm—the quality of "roses and snow," which he had written about, of her light against his darkness. Her gamine-like manners and high-key beauty placed her a universe away from the dark kitchen-bound women of Saroyan's childhood. Carol's smile, her husky little-girl voice, her movie-star figure—these were elements in a fantasy romance that obsessed William Saroyan for almost forty years, from his first glimpse of her until his death. It was the reality that was harder to manage.

Saroyan's working day took him up a short front staircase to the flat, where music—the phonograph or the radio—drowned out the sounds of Carol and the household below. Money was abundant and help was cheap, but there was no servant. Bill felt that he had Carol's promise that she would metamorphose into an old-country wife, like a butterfly turning into a caterpillar.

AL HIRSCHFELD: Bill had, like all artists, limitations, and one of Bill's limitations was that he wanted his wife to be Armenian.

He wanted her to be his mother.

He didn't want her to socialize, didn't want her to be the life of the party, didn't want everybody to say, "How lovely! How funny! She can write!" and "She's amusing, she's witty!" He didn't want any of that.

He wanted somebody who would be in the kitchen with grape leaves, and everybody who came in, they could have a bite to eat and they'd leave and he would go out and come in at four o'clock in the morning and— He was not, he should *never* have married. He was not the marrying kind.

He was just a hopeless Bohemian. Always had been. Bill was not a worldly figure.

I don't mean by that he was provincial. He was a poet. He made his own rules, his own laws. They don't work all the time, and he had his limitations, and one of his limitations was that.

He never understood Carol's great qualities.

Never.

ROSHEEN MARCUS: I went to visit them in San Francisco, and I found her sitting on a player piano down in the basement with laundry going, and the player piano was going like crazy. He had her doing laundry. I will never forget that scene. . . . She was sitting, cross-legged. She was a little *girl*. She didn't know anything about *laundry*.

Carol was raised like a queen. She would ring bells for a glass of water. I lost more God-damned butlers and maids on account of her. They'd say, "Well, she's a young girl and this is our rest period, and why can't she go get her own glass of water?" She was very spoiled, to some degree.

But my plans for her, as far as domestic science and all that—I thought that would come in time. She had just finished high school. So I had intentions of teaching her things, and I had no idea she was going to be married at such an early age. So she wasn't trained for anything domestically.

(His mother *adored* me. She said, "You, you, you—why not *you* marry Bill? Your daughter—she thinks she *queen.*" Oh, she just adored me.)

How could Carol be a proper parent, having that to go through, to go through what she went through with Saroyan? They heard nothing but four-letter words, screaming all over the place.

If Carol didn't know how to make a pot of food, which she didn't know, he would say, "Don't you know how to cook? Don't you know how to do anything?" instead of saying, "Look, honey, do it like this," or "Why don't you take a course or something?"

There was no reason for that. He was making a lot of money. They could have had a cook. They could have had a maid.

Why not? What is money for? When you make it, you want to live well, you want to do what you can. Why not? Get the most out of life with your money. You're not going to take it with you.

There was money in 1946, but less than either Bill or Carol would have liked. *The Adventures of Wesley Jackson* had performed capably and Harcourt faithfully published what Saroyan gave them. The puzzling allegory *Jim Dandy* would appear in 1947, for example. And there were royalties from the continuous stock productions of *The Time of Your Life* and the other early plays.

But there was gambling, too. In addition to the classical music filtering down from Saroyan's workroom, his wife could hear racing reports on the radio. He made his bets by phone, and his luck was no better than it ever had been. He remained an impetuous gambler incapable of holding on to any winnings, and his depression inspired wilder bets.

For a year, this was the pattern of their married life: Carol downstairs running the washing machine, diapering Lucy, playing with three-year-old Aram; Bill upstairs, typewriter clattering, occasionally phoning out to his bookie or vanishing for an all-night card session.

For periods of the marriage Bill had forbidden Carol to reveal their unlisted telephone number to Rosheen. Carol got letters from her old friends and even an occasional visit. Oona and Charlie Chaplin came to town and came to dinner. Saroyan later would paint Chaplin cruelly, as an aged, impotent has-been. At the time of their first meetings, Bill was cordial, evidently undisturbed that Carol's friendship with Oona, not his own reputation, accounted for his acquaintance with the world's most famous comedian.

But no epic was emerging from the upstairs workroom. The perpetual fog in San Francisco's western reaches is at its worst in high summer, and the weather had come to irritate Saroyan. By the end of 1946, when the prospect arose, Saroyan was willing to return to New York and the faces of old friends like George Jean Nathan and Julie Haydon, Al and Dolly Hirschfeld, even Irwin Shaw, whose friendship Saroyan had been at pains to retain despite the *Wesley Jackson* review.

Rosheen had found an out-of-season summer place at Millneck, near Oyster Bay on Long Island. It was close enough to Manhattan for forays into town by train, but isolated enough for Saroyan to work uninterrupted if he preferred. The retired Navy officer who owned the house would be returning the next summer, so the lease was short— the first half of 1947. The swimming pool was empty, the tennis court was snowed in, and Saroyan was appalled by the heating bills and the cost of the servants who came with the house.

One guest at Millneck that winter remembers Saroyan squirming at the head of the table as a formal dinner was brought by the servants. He stared with a mixture of curiosity and disdain at the dollop of sour cream floating in his clear soup. Gloria Vanderbilt di Cicco had by now become Gloria Stokowski, and she was among the guests that evening. She and Carol were at their most glamorous and most animated. Bill always was discomfited by seeing Carol perform brilliantly in her own social element, as though she were insulting her husband's peasant upbringing. But on this occasion two of Bill's young Armenian cousins were among the guests, and they and their dates were made to feel at home. Ross Bagdasarian and Chesley Saroyan were as sophisticated as any of Carol's friends that evening, but in later years Saroyan would censor out memories of anyone at Millneck except for Carol and her friends.

"Everybody knew that after three years in the Army and two years back in society, so to put it, I was broke and in debt, but this reality was acknowledged only now and then when far gone in alcohol and pushing to another orgasm with the little woman she said, 'What are we going to do?'

"We?

"Well, of course she and her little mother always believed—why, for that boy money is the easiest thing in the world to make, by the hundreds of thousands of dollars. They were both not unlike literary agents, or more accurately Hollywood agents. They put packages together, even in idle social conversation."

There was a package that winter, but it was James Cagney who put it together. Cagney's long relationship with Warner Brothers was over, and with his brother William he had founded Cagney Productions, a company designed to make personal pictures for release by United Artists. The Cagneys now were willing to do what no studio had risked, to bring *The Time of Your Life* to the screen, and to film it intact. Cagney would play Joe, the barroom philosopher and fixer. His roots in vaudeville matched Eddie Dowling's quite closely and helped to make him right for the part. Cagney's sister, Jeanne, would get the plum Julie Haydon role of Kitty Duval.

Cagney telephoned Saroyan in Millneck to arrange a lunch in the city, and he was puzzled by the long wait before Saroyan came on the line, baffled even further when Saroyan professed unfamiliarity with the Players Club. The next day Saroyan ventured from Oyster Bay to Gramercy Park, and Cagney was startled by his appearance: "jet-black hair in high pompadour, a complexion white as bleached parchment, and strong, dark, protruding eyes."

When Cagney introduced himself, Saroyan said nothing, but stood at the bar and listened to the sounds of the Players Club: billiards, a card game, a cocktail shaker.

"It's kind of a symphony, isn't it?" he said, and Cagney agreed. Then, as Cagney and Saroyan began their talk, an imposing figure materialized beside them. It was Allan Reagan, an ex-vaudevillean who delighted in one-upping Cagney with obscure song lyrics. As Cagney recalled the incident in his autobiography, "This day he stood before our table, drew himself up to his full six foot two, pointed his finger at Saroyan, and sang very loudly and solemnly:

> "If you don't like your Uncle Sammy,
> Then go back to your home o'er the sea
> To the land from where you came

Jeanne and James Cagney were Kitty and Joe in the film of *The Time of Your Life* produced by their brother, William. Bosley Crowther of the *New York Times* praised them for trying hard, adding that the film "sinks very slowly in its own sand right up to its cauliflower ears . . . to no discredit of the people who made the film." (Cagney Productions)

Left to right, Tom Powers, William Bendix, James Barton, and James Cagney in Cagney's movie version of *The Time of Your Life*, 1948. The crooked vice cop could not be shot to death in the film, thanks to the Hollywood code. (Cagney Productions)

> Whatever be its name;
> But don't be ungrateful to me—
> I said, to me—
> And if you don't like the stars in Old Glory,
> And have no use for the Red, White and Blue
> Then don't act like the cur in the story,
> And bite the—'My Country 'tis of thee!'—
> And bite the hand that's feeding you!"

Saroyan was appalled by this outburst, turning even paler.

"I asked Bill what disturbed him so much," Cagney recalled. "'I thought he was accusing me of being un-American,' he said." Cagney, not a bookish man, apparently was unfamiliar with *The Adventures of Wesley Jackson* or its recent effect on Saroyan's reputation.

The money deal was struck separately by the men's agents, evidently at a point somewhere in the comfortable five figures, because Saroyan's money worries eased somewhat, even if his displeasure with Carol and her mother had not.

"I just happened to be married to the little woman, and she just happened to be who she was, which she knew and I didn't."

On occasion, Carol coaxed Bill into the city, for a dinner with the Chaplins, for example. Artie Shaw was married at the moment to Kathleen Winsor, author of *Forever Amber*, a huge romantic bestseller, and they lived across Long Island Sound from the Saroyans, dropping in occasionally by cabin cruiser.

Before the six-month lease was up, Carol miscarried early in her third pregnancy. Later, in conversations with friends or in the shadowplay of his fictions, Saroyan would accuse her of having sought and received an abortion. Since Bill wanted more children, many more, very badly, his anger showed more than his sadness, deepening Carol's own grief over the incident.

When the Saroyans and their children returned to San Francisco late in the spring of 1947, the work Bill began was not the promised "epic" novel, but more playwriting. The theatre he wrote for now was the theatre of his own mind. He would always identify 1944 as the year he gave up on the idea of producing and directing his own material, but Harcourt was willing to publish plays that had never reached the stage, and Saroyan invited his readers to join him in a playhouse of their conjoined imaginations. The new allegories he seemed to prefer writing were not, in fact, ideal evenings for the real theatre. In the bizarre *Slaughter of the Innocents*, Saroyan's familiar barroom setting has metamorphosed into a kangaroo courtroom where a variety of minor offenders are sentenced to an offstage firing squad. George Jean Nathan was sent a copy because he and Julie Haydon were portrayed as victims who escape the tribunal by taxicab, but the play so dismayed Nathan that he pretended not to have read it.

"I wish I had an enormous idea signifying fun and money, but the very truth is that I haven't," Bill wrote to Artie Shaw that summer. Back in 1941, Saroyan had asked Artie for a little clarinet music for *Jim Dandy*. During Bill's Long Island winter, they had fantasized about a musical together, and one of the ideas Saroyan proposed was based on a real incident from his Fresno boyhood. A rich man had been ruined and his house sold and moved across town from the ritziest neighborhood to the poorest; there an immigrant shoemaker had installed his family. In addition to the powerful image of the empty mansion returning to bustling life, Saroyan was fascinated by the house-moving operation itself, the notion of the empty rooms as stages for visitors and stowaways. Soon after returning to San Francisco, Saroyan sat down and dashed off *Sam Ego's House* in one of his two-week bursts of creativity.

Saroyan later wrote a preface for the play claiming that it stood in the tradition of Near Eastern storytelling, but its real resemblance was to his other allegorical works, like *Jim Dandy* or *The Slaughter of the Innocents*. He also tossed in a funny parody of pompous sermons and of war movies, such as *The Best Years of Our Lives*. (The house buyer in the play is a junkman, whose three sons manage to represent Army, Navy, and Marines in every possible theatre of conflict.) But the dull private barbs aimed at draft boards and Carol's cooking clearly were out of place, and the rich man's surprise victory in a sanity hearing was an unconvincingly happy ending.

ARTIE SHAW: It was a very disorganized idea, but the idea was marvelous. I said, "Bill, you know there's a musical in this. There's a hell of a musical in this. I don't know what yet, but it needs work."

He said, "What do you mean, work?"

I said, "Bill, a musical isn't written, it's rewritten. And rewritten. And rewritten." (I was looking for something to do at that time because the thing with Kay and me wasn't going that well.)

So we both went out to San Francisco. Bill and Carol were living on a little street—a series of little houses looking all alike. And a funny thing happened that night. We were supposed to have dinner, and Carol was going to cook a chicken. We were sitting in the living room and talking, and the God-damned chicken is cooking, and suddenly the room begins to stink. I mean, a stench like you can't believe. I've never smelled anything like it again in my life—or before.

And we all ran into the kitchen. The chicken was burning, the stove was in flames. What was it? We looked at it, everything was fine. She said, "Oh, my God. I'll bet I've made a mistake." She forgot to take the entrails out.

We started to work, and I began to see that Bill's type of lack of discipline, or whatever you want to call it—he had his own discipline, an inner thing that made him sit down and get those words to spill out, and sometimes I'd envy him that. I said, "Look, Bill, if we're going to do this, we have to get a schematic. A musical play requires some kind of approach. You've got to know where act one is, where we are and where we close the curtain. And I can only write music to a specific situation. I can't write music from the blue and then say, 'Go write words.' Besides which, you keep saying you don't want to rewrite this."

"Well, what do you want to do?"

I said, "I just told you. Any time you write a scene that you think is right and that we both agree will work, I'll go to work on the music. Very simple. And when we get enough words and music together, we'll take it to New York, get it produced, and then we will have to rewrite it anyway, a dozen times."

"Oh," he said. "Jesus, I don't think I can do that."

So it's a little over two weeks. During that time we got to talking and talking and talking. Got nowhere. And then there was episode after episode—he'd write me, call me and talk, talk, talk. Finally, one day I said, "For Christ's sake, Bill, I get the feeling your typewriter is a kind of sexual symbol: you're an autoerotic."

He loved that word, autoerotic. "Oh, auto-ee-*row*-tic! Auto-ee-*row*-tic!"

I said, "Oh, shit, don't hold me up on a word. I'm making a point. I think what you're doing is jerking off with the typewriter, if you want it in plain language."

Well, he hated that, hated me for saying it. It never got resolved, this question of what we were going to do. I'm at the Hotel St. Francis and I'm waiting for him to make up his mind whether or not we're going to do this. This is the resolution of the whole question: "Dear Artie, I have started to work at last on a long novel which I have wanted to start for many months, but have put off starting because I enjoy loafing so much. I'll be lucky if I finish the novel by the end of this year, but that is what I hope to do. . . . I'm boring you with all this on the chance that you are still thinking about the musical idea."

(The night before, I was.)

"If you get back to Frisco one of these days, let's see if I can get away from my work for a short session of drinking. In the meantime, all the best."

Charlie Chaplin had politely asked to see a copy of *Sam Ego's House*, which he passed on to his son Sydney, who was working with the Circle Players of Hollywood, a company he would manage until he moved east for a Broadway career. The younger Chaplin's company tested the play for a few performances late in 1947. Oona, Charlie, Carol, and Bill were on hand to make an occasion of opening night, but the play got a far cooler reception than the company's earlier production of *The Time of Your Life*.

There had been snags with the movie version of *The Time of Your Life*. Cagney had wanted to treat the stage script like holy writ, and had granted his director, Henry Potter, and the cameraman, James Wong Howe, two weeks of rehearsal time to plot every angle, light, and camera move. But, according to Cagney, they changed their minds once filming began, and the picture was over budget before the second problem arose. This was the matter of the ending. The climax of *The Time of Your Life* is the offstage killing of the sadistic vice cop, Blick, by the old-timer, Kit Carson, who has spun tall tales for most of the evening. The shots are heard and the old man steps into the bar and explains what just happened in the language of one of his yarns: "I shot a man once. In San Francisco. Shot him two times. . . . In 1939, I think it was." It is a satisfying, large laugh in the theatre, a magical bit of plotting, which focused and finished Saroyan's impressionistic play. But, no matter how cruel the policeman was, Hollywood's production code would not permit a happy ending based on the unpunished shooting of a law officer. Saroyan was asked to help with a new ending that would satisfy the industry censors in the Johnston Office, but it was work he was unsuited for, and he escaped it by demanding a fee the Cagneys were unwilling to pay.

Despite these professional false starts and setbacks, Bill and Carol and the children appeared to enjoy days of genuine happiness together in 1947. They left Lucy with Takoohi and took Aram on a trip to Fresno for his first meeting with his multitude of Armenian cousins. They also visited the state fair in Sacramento, where Saroyan concluded that the exhibits and entries from Fresno were by far the finest.

Earlier that summer, before Artie Shaw and his wife came west, Saroyan had written his old friend, "Life out here is as nearly perfect as I could ever imagine it could be anywhere, and I am not harassed by any need for money. Result: everybody in the household sings all the time."

But what Artie Shaw observed was different, a strained marriage and a change in his old friend. The experimental mustache had been shaved off. The voice was as loud as ever, but the sureness was gone, and the isolation of the workroom seemed to be an essential requirement for his well-being, not just a matter of convenience. Saroyan showed Artie Shaw the red-bound journals he kept in that room. They contained drawings that exhibited, Bill explained, the aleatory—or chance—nature of creation. He proposed to Shaw a stage play in which magic-lantern projections represented "the imagined interiors of such things as fire, water, clouds, rocks, grapes, figs, roses, fish eyes . . ." and a plot in which a sick, daydreaming child in a charity ward refuses her boiled potato and "instead went inside of it into a world of potato-like people who believe the potato is God, and so on."

The typing continued in the upstairs flat, but the epic did not emerge. There were letters, long letters, advising his old friends at the Armenian journals in Boston about every aspect of publication, from graphics to appropriate acknowledgment to financial backers. The new play he was working on was spun from the slenderest of impulses, to use the name four-year-old Aram had made up for an imaginary playmate, but that play quickly turned into a grim allegory about men dying in a cancer ward.

The windows were closed against the fog, and the air in his workroom was stale from the smoke of his Chesterfields. Scattered in the workroom were unopened letters, unread magazines, dozens of publishers' free copies of books, many of them still wrapped or crated.

There were twisted, bleached bits of driftwood and hundreds of rocks and pebbles, which reminded him of the places where he had collected them. Some of them he kept in bowls of water, which restored the colors that had caught his eye beside the sea.

He wrote of himself:

> He had no heart for the work, he had been fighting the idea of abandoning it for days, and now he knew it was abandoned. He'd worked eight days for nothing. It was the tenth or eleventh job he had abandoned in ten or eleven weeks. Well, he would have to start again and this time see that it was not a false start. But when he tried to think what would not be a false start, he could think of nothing that wouldn't, everything would be a false start, anything anybody might do would be a false start, there was no such thing as a true start.

2. THE REVELATION

At first, the gambling had come as a surprise to Carol. During the courtship, the months in Dayton, and the year in New York, the betting was light, or else lost in the crowd of events like the enforced hospitalization, the birth of Aram.

But the relative idleness of the first postwar months on Taraval Street and the royalties that had kept piling up from *The Human Comedy*, the short stories, and the stock productions left Saroyan free to indulge his dangerous pastime. The long-deferred servant was hired, a nurse for the children so that Carol could be by his side.

"All of a sudden, every night, we went to a place called Russian Mike's," Carol recalls. "And they gambled all night. They had a wheel. And he lost.

"In the afternoon, he would call a bookie, and he would gamble six races, five thousand a race. And finally lost all of his money and got some advances from Harcourt.

"He said, 'I need a handicap. I've never written without a handicap. I need to *have* to make money, or I won't be able to write.'

"And so I thought, if he isn't able to write, he won't love me, and it's very important, and so on. I just went along. I never said a word.

"We went out every night to this place and he lost everything, including the advances."

Saroyan lost the very house they were living in. It was to be a tem-

porary home to begin with. Bill had promised Carol a new house in
Sea-Cliff, the very fashionable district perched on high bluffs above the
Pacific outside the Golden Gate. The lot had been purchased and an
architect had drawn plans.

But when the gambling began to go wrong, badly wrong, Saroyan
turned for help to George Mardikian, the restaurateur who had introduced him to the columnist Herb Caen. Saroyan was putting the touch
on Mardikian as that introduction was made, but now the borrowing
had escalated wildly, as high as $30,000, a very considerable sum in
1947. Mardikian was willing to help, but he was not so foolish as to
risk the well-being of his business and his own family on his friend's
uncontrollable gambling habit, so he demanded security. By mid-1947,
it was apparent that he would have to call in the debt by claiming the
Taraval Street house and the Sea-Cliff property.

> CAROL MATTHAU: And finally, we had to give him the lot and the
> drawings and the house we were in, including an enormous
> amount of books, paintings I'd had as a child. We left with a
> suitcase for each of us.
>
> And Bill said, "Well, no man can write with a handicap like
> this."
>
> And I very stupidly said, "Oh, Bill, I thought you said you had
> to have a handicap." And he went into an absolute ice rage. He
> said, "You're not a real person. You're not a real woman. Any
> other woman in the world would have stopped her husband from
> doing this. You never said a word. You saw me losing all that
> money."
>
> So I said, "No, but you said—"
>
> "You're crazy. You—you should have stopped me."
>
> And now it was all my fault.

During their last weeks on Taraval, the movie version of *The Time of
Your Life* had opened to light box office and mixed reviews. Even further tampering had been necessary. Cagney's long speech about the
evils of money had hit the floor, but Saroyan was used to that. Eddie
Dowling had refused to speak it in the play, despite promises to
Saroyan that he would restore it once critics and producers were out of
earshot. And the final scene, as rewritten for the censors, had left audiences baffled in sneak previews. The production had to be restarted

at a cost of $300,000 in order to film a high-comedy, action-filled ending in which Kit Carson lassoes the vice-squad cop and Cagney, strictly a laid-back barroom philosopher until this point, beats him up.

"The studio thought Cagney had to use his fists," Saroyan said, and sent a letter to the Cagneys thanking them for having stayed as true as they had to the spirit and letter of the play.

The movie publicity meant new questions about what Saroyan had written lately, and he talked about the cancer-ward play, *The Incurables*, which eventually would be called *Don't Go Away Mad*. "Sometimes I am disgusted with it; sometimes I think it is a great play. People who have read it like it. But it is meaningful and talky. . . . We're all suffering from cancers of one kind or another."

With the date approaching to surrender his house to Mardikian and the summer fog returning, Saroyan's thoughts had turned to Fresno. When Carol had complained that she missed her people, Saroyan had snapped, "Your children are your people now," but it was to the city of his own hundred cousins that he planned to turn. A Fresno realtor showed him forty acres outside of town, a house Saroyan first had seen as a small boy on a picnic. According to the salesman, the barren land was made of "puma tile," an ashy soil Saroyan was assured would be valuable to brickmakers, who would buy it by the ton from him.

ROSHEEN MARCUS: Carol got on the phone and said, "Oh, please, Mother. Bill has found a house in Fresno, and we need ten thousand dollars. They want seventeen thousand down and the rest in payments, and we have to have the money."

So I went to my husband. It was during tax time, and he said, "Christ, I can't suddenly come up with ten thousand dollars like that." Anyway, to make a long story short, he came up with the $10,000 and I took the check, got on a plane to San Francisco and gave it to Bill.

He said, "Oh, like I said, Rosheen, you're a great woman."

Now we get in the car, he said, "Since you brought me the money, I'm going to show you where this house is.

"It's a great house. We'll drive to Fresno. You ever been to Fresno?" I said no.

Now we're on our way to Fresno, and between lights and

things I noticed he was looking at that horse paper, the *Racing Form*.

He said, "I dunno. There's a horse here I've got to bet on."

Well, he had my $10,000 check on him, so I said, "Can I look at the *Racing Form*, Bill?" And I'm looking at the race he's talking about with Blue Boy. So I look at it and I said, "I don't like Blue Boy, Bill. You know something? I think this horse"—and I can't remember the name, let's call it Jupiter—"I think this horse is going to win."

He stopped the car, he said, "What do you mean? What do you know about races? How can you tell about that? You're telling me that, and that upsets me and I've got to know why you picked that horse."

I said, "I don't know, Bill, but I prefer this name to that name. I don't know anything about races. Don't take it so literally. Don't worry about it. I'm sure you know what you're doing."

Well, we get to Fresno, we check in someplace, and he said, "Now, I'm going to show you the house."

I said, "Great." (Now I'm dying to see this house.) And we drive quite a distance, and we drive up a steep hill and there are gullies on each side, and I see a wooden shack. No windows, no doors. It's broken-down. It's something unbelievable. But as you get inside it you can see that the rooms are very large.

"Don't worry about the doors. And we're going to put windows in! And we're growing our own vegetables in our own garden."

And I said, "Well, who's going to take care of all that, Bill?"

And he said, "Well, *Carol*."

I said, "Carol doesn't know anything about growing vegetables or flowers or any of that stuff."

He said, "She'll learn, she'll learn."

I said, "Now, what about these gullies? It's dangerous. It's not a place for children."

He said, "Rosheen, do you realize what's down at the bottom of those gullies? We've got uranium and gold here."

Uranium and gold.

I looked at him and I said, "Uranium and gold? Well, maybe you can do something about that without moving into something as rickety as this. This is terrible, Bill."

"Don't worry. We're going to fix it all up. It's just going to be—the talk of Fresno."

Carol looks at me. "Mother, I guess Bill knows. He knows *Fresno*." She's still a naïve child.

Okay. When we get back to the hotel, he still has the check in his pocket, and he sits down by a telephone at a desk. I walk into their little suite and I hear him say, "All right, Blue Boy in the third race, and in the fourth race, put two thousand on that. The next race, Princess Ann, two thousand on the nose . . ." And he goes down five races, two thousand on the nose, and there's my ten thousand.

If he won anything, I don't know much about it. But I watched him sit there after I raced like a madwoman to give him $10,000, and there he is betting on horses.

A classified advertisement in the San Francisco *Examiner* of June 20, 1948:

NO LIES IN THIS AD

This property could be described another way, but this is the honest way to describe it:

Approximately 30-year-old well-built ranchhouse ready to occupy in dry hill 12 miles north of Fresno. Approximately 30 acres hilltop and river bottom land extending to center of San Joaquin River. Hilltop all hardpan, river bottom all gravel and rocks. 4 bedrooms, 2 bath, long wide hall . . . enormous unfinished upstairs study or play room. . . . No garage, no barn, small pump downhill probably ought to be replaced. 50-gallon water tank in basement probably ought to be cleaned. Underground oil tank for steam heat but heating apparatus out of order. Approximately fifty young olive trees bordering road, but no practical way of watering them. . . . Seclusion and privacy inevitable. Difficult to obtain telephone, 12-party line. Decrepit one-room school 5 miles away, no bus. Apparently no oil, gold or uranium on land or in river. Plenty of squirrels. Owner paid only $32,000 for property one month ago. He is keeping 6 or 7 acres for himself as monument to his real estate sharpness. Will sell balance for $35,000. If interested have head examined or telephone Fresno 2-8574 and ask for owner's Cousin Ross.

Saroyan forgot to notify Ross Bagdasarian about the ad, and so the telephone calls that began that Friday night puzzled him, but there were nibbles. Saroyan said now that he had decided on a place in Fresno itself, a redwood-and-brick house near Fresno State College. He described it as a summer place, but all of the real-estate maneuvers appear connected with the impending loss of the house and the building lot in San Francisco.

Bill and Carol did not move to Fresno. Instead, on the third of July, 1948, they separated. Bill simply declared the upstairs flat on Taraval his official residence.

In his chronicles of this period, Saroyan writes of having hit Carol in play during lovemaking, but the incident is, she says, imaginary. He also records sharp arguments in which he proposes divorce as one of her alternatives, and these recollections are accurate. During one such dispute, in the kitchen, he suddenly slapped her and dissolved immediately into apologies and tender concern. It was not violence, however, but his uncontrolled jealousy that led her to consider divorce.

Gambling at Russian Mike's club, they had met a friendly couple, a plumber and his wife, and during one of their evenings together, the husband had asked Carol to dance. There was nothing untoward about his invitation, nor could Carol comfortably have turned him down. They danced, and Bill brought up the incident to her over and over for a matter of weeks, until she finally telephoned her lawyer. A week after Bill moved upstairs, Carol filed for divorce, charging extreme cruelty and seeking $1,000 a month for her own support and another $250 for both of the children.

When the case was called three days later by Judge Sylvain Lazarus, neither Bill nor Carol was in the courtroom. Her lawyer, Chester Keith, told the judge that Mrs. Saroyan had telephoned him at midnight. The two were reconciled, he said, leaving on a second honeymoon.

But the next move was to New York City, to an apartment on West Fifty-eighth, just around the corner from the Plaza Hotel. As Saroyan explained it, Carol and Rosheen had plotted since the reconciliation to maneuver him to New York, and it was Rosheen who had found the place. The money for it may have come from Harcourt, Brace, who would publish a volume of three unproduced plays in 1949, but the Marcuses recall having loaned Bill money in multiples of $5,000 without expecting repayment, and the New York move is likely to have been one of those occasions.

But this time Bill was having none of Carol's candy stripes and cabbage roses, as at Taraval Street. He hired a woman decorator he had met through Leonard Lyons and instructed her to complete the apartment in an austere modern style.

"He painted all the walls to look black," Carol recalls. "They were black-gray. (I insisted on white woodwork.) And the darkest floors in the world. It was as austere as anything could ever be. And he did it. He did it.

"He had this idea that he wanted black walls—and black oak, rubbed with white. Very modern. Because all of the furniture that we had had gone to George Mardikian for that debt. We didn't have anything. It had a Spartan kind of elegance, but I would never find it attractive in a million years."

But there were other belongings that no creditor could claim, treasures Saroyan had packed into trunks.

ROSHEEN MARCUS: He called me one day from San Francisco and he said, "Rosheen, do you mind? I've got some trunks. I'm not ready to send them to the apartment, but I've got to send them to New York. I'm going to send them to you. Will you hold on to those until we get to New York?"

I said, "Of course, Bill."

Well, these two trunks arrived. It took four men to carry each trunk. They left them in the foyer of my apartment, and one day I wanted to slide them over because they were left right in the middle of the foyer and I couldn't budge them. Nobody could. The maids came in, my husband tried. We all tried. We couldn't budge them.

So my husband said, "What the hell has he got in there? My God! What is it?"

Carol had sent the keys, they came in an envelope, and Daddy said, my husband said, "Let's open that and see."

I paid for it. At that time I think it was $250 or $300 for two trunks, an enormous amount of money then. We opened the trunk, there were chains, snow tires. There was string. There were broken clocks. There were nails—*that* big. Hardware. Broken pieces of things that you couldn't put together. I've never seen anything like it.

Rocks in the other one. No clothes, nothing useful, just all this junk. All this junk.

When I saw what was in the trunks, I said, "What's he doing?" So I asked Carol.

She said, "Mother, he saves things. He likes to save all that."

He said, "Well, they're useful things. There are clocks that I'm going to fix one day."

I said, "What are the rocks for?"

He said, "Those are very valuable rocks."

The trunks were removed and taken to the apartment. Who knows where he sent it or where it went from there. But it was unbelievable. He was an oddball. He really was. A very strange man.

Saroyan was forty now. There were deep lines above his mouth, heavy bags beneath his eyes, the beginnings of a double chin. There was a little money from the sale of the country property near Fresno, $5,000, a net loss of $12,500, and there were modest royalties from a collection of ninety-eight short stories, none of them new.

At Sardi's he had once been introduced to Ferenc Molnár, the Hungarian playwright whose Liliom almost became a Puccini opera, but instead won American fame as the basis for the Rodgers and Hammerstein musical play Carousel. At that first meeting, Saroyan had embarrassed himself by muttering, "But Molnár's dead." It was the Austrian writer Arthur Schnitzler Saroyan had been thinking of, and when he had written Molnár a note to apologize and explain, the Hungarian had responded with a dinner invitation, and the two men had become friends.

Late in 1948 the friendship was renewed. Molnár's customary melancholy had been deepened by the war. There would be no going back to Hungary. He also sympathized with Saroyan's creative crisis, and he told the younger man a story from his own early years, of how the woman he loved had abandoned him for another man and how suicide seemed the only answer. Molnár's father told him to forget his agony by working, and the result was his masterpiece, Liliom.

"Everybody at dinner was amused," Saroyan recalled, "and one of the women said, 'And so again a woman has been the cause of the making of a work of art.' Molnár smiled and the woman's husband said, 'And of course after writing the play the woman meant nothing to you.' Again Molnár smiled, but this time he spoke, too. 'No, I could still commit suicide over that woman. But now I can't sit down and write that way anymore, for any reason.' "

If Saroyan realized now that he was not the same man who had been dragged unwillingly away to war seven years earlier, it became important for him to believe that Carol was not the same woman. The betrayal could not be his alone. For all her loveliness and for all his watchfulness and his only half-disguised jealousy, she had remained entirely faithful, but his dark moods had begun to frighten her. Perhaps her impulse to divorce him had been correct.

CAROL MATTHAU: I was, for the first time, beginning to think, of course, this wouldn't go on. It couldn't.

And I was afraid of him. I was just afraid of him. I never knew how things would strike him, or where they would be coming from.

A fear that he wouldn't love me. Always wondering if he did, and yet, knowing that he really did. I did know that. And I knew that the more he did the more he hated me.

It's very, very hard to explain. He felt that there was some voodoo or something. I don't know whether he would have been happy with anyone. I don't think so, no matter who or where. He just couldn't. It was just too hard for him.

And then there's the other side of it, and that exists—you know, being really passionately in love with someone. And I know that he was, and that made it all the harder. That's what the problem was. Otherwise, I would have left.

You know, when you're very young—I thought that his anger was passion. I thought he was this passionate, angry man because he saw life in such beautiful terms, and life could never measure up. It's the way I guess I feel about people who drink. I think there's some disappointment that I feel I understand.

I gave it all sorts of wonderful ways to think about it, so that I could still love him. You do that when you want to love someone, and I did.

I didn't know that it was just anger about his own gut. He had to belch or something. I didn't know that it was so—when he took to his bed for days at a time.

And yet he was very funny. And there were certain things that I think we shared. But it was doomed. There was no way for that to . . .

I don't know how it survived for so long.

When the break came, in March of 1949, it was immediate and total on Saroyan's part. His motive for walking out on his wife and children was rooted in the very beginning of his relationship with Carol. In his fiction, he explores it most thoroughly in *Rock Wagram*, the first of a series of naturalistic novels precipitated by the breakup.

In that novel Saroyan is the title character, Arak Vagramian, a Fresno bartender catapulted into riches and fame as a movie actor. (He publishes slim volumes of verse on the side.) Carol is Ann Ford, a debutante with a fast reputation. This is the book in which Saroyan rhapsodized with great honesty about the physical attraction he felt for Carol, the one in which he characterizes her appeal as "roses and snow." And in this book Saroyan compares himself to Othello and Carol to Desdemona, confessing his neurosis: "He wants to know the truth all the time." To the jealous-minded husband of a gorgeous woman, the truth means hearing her own confession of infidelity rather than learning about it from a third party, and before they were married Saroyan believed that he had struck an agreement with Carol that if one lied to the other in any significant way the marriage was off.

Carol had been a faithful wife, but by early 1949, Bill found it possible to convict her in his mind of grievous sins of omission, the sins he referred to obliquely when he wrote, "She just happened to be who she was, which she knew and I didn't."

How much or how little did Saroyan know about who his wife was? When he said, long after the marriage was over, that he had fallen in love with her past, did he mean the past available to readers of the society pages, or the truth, which reached the public only forty years later through their son Aram's memoir *Last Rites*?

Charles Marcus actually was Carol's adoptive stepfather. Carol was the illegitimate child of an affair Rosheen had at the age of sixteen, infuriating the grandmother with whom she lived. But Rosheen never yielded custody of her daughter, placing her in a string of foster homes, where Carol often was tormented by other children and generally left to fend for herself, despite her mother's visits.

In an act of misguided meddling, Rosheen's very proper family arranged a marriage with a philosophy professor. Carol was brought home to live with them, but when Rosheen bore a child by her husband—Carol's half-sister Elinor Shepherd—Rosheen's husband proposed putting Carol up for adoption. Rosheen was outraged at the idea and swept out of the professor's life with Carol, leaving behind the daughter he so clearly preferred. But soon both girls were in foster homes. Carol was lucky in hers, that of a warm-hearted Catholic woman in Paterson, New Jersey, named Genevieve Laragay.

In 1933, Rosheen went to Paterson for Carol and brought her back to New York, to a new apartment in the West Seventies, where the little girl was introduced to Charles Marcus. The courtly engineer was enchanted by the child, as he would be for the rest of his life, and soon Rosheen was his wife and Carol his adopted daughter. Later, Elinor joined them, too. Their home was Park Avenue, and Carol's life was one of position and privilege, one celebrated by Cholly Knickerbocker and the other chroniclers of wealth and fashion. The Cinderella debut planned for Carol was far closer to the truth than anyone but her closest friends could have known.

Early in their relationship Bill had seen baby pictures of Carol taken in Paterson. Carol's illegitimacy meant nothing, he insisted, but he was equally insistent that he felt betrayed by not having heard the story earlier than he did. (To his credit, despite his later stance of hatred toward Carol and her mother, Saroyan never used the facts of Carol's birth and childhood in his work.)

But the lie he accused Carol of in 1949 was one he could ill afford to complain aloud about, and it, too, reached back to the days before their marriage.

CAROL MATTHAU: It started so insanely. I had been seeing Bill. He took me to a party, and I don't remember where it was, whose house it was, but there were a lot of Armenians there, and of course the war had started and they were talking about the war.

The Jews. The Jews started the war. The Jews were clever. New York Jews. All the phrases you've ever heard. And I winced.

And he turned around and said, "What's the matter with you, kid? I mean, *you're* not Jewish, are you?"

Suddenly there was a silence and I was looking at all these people who had said all these horrible things, and I was so embarrassed that I didn't know what to do.

I said, "Oh, ah—well, no. No, of course not."

I just didn't have the guts to say, "Well, of course I *am*."

After that he said, "I hate liars more than anything," and I realized that that night at the party I was so embarrassed, I didn't think it really mattered anyway. But because I didn't have that kind of background that it meant anything, I didn't know what it was all about, but I lived to regret that.

I think it came from his—he was brought right up with it. His whole family were like that.

I remember when I invited his mother and sister to New York before he went overseas. They went out one afternoon, and when they came back I said, "Did you have a nice time?"

They said, "Too much juice, too much juice."

I said, "Where did you go?" (I thought they had juice or something.) And then Bill told me what they meant.

But he did once drive me on a very beautiful street in Fresno, and I said, "Oh, this is so pretty," and they had very pretty houses. And he said, "Armenians can't live here." I said, "Really? How horrible!" And he said, "No, the Jews have this all sewed up."

This was festering. I had to tell him, and I did.

ROSHEEN MARCUS: We were not a religious family, you know, and we never discussed religion. Carol didn't have any religious training, and neither did my other daughter. If they felt like attending church, they'd go to church, whatever it was. Nobody ever denied what they were, if they were asked directly, any question. I felt that was an imposition, to be asked, "What is your religion?" I never answered that question.

When Bill married Carol, I assumed he knew she was the daughter of Charles Marcus, and certainly the name indicated, more or less, that they could be Jewish. And I just assumed that he knew everything he wanted to know about her, that we were respectable, decent people and that her father was certainly brilliant, was looked up to as an industrialist in this country.

It only came out when he had gone to a concert one night at Carnegie Hall, and he ran into this cousin of mine. And I don't know how the question came up—I've often asked her. She said, "Well, there was no question about anything. He just assumed that I was Jewish," and he came back to the apartment after the concert and he said to Carol, "I didn't know that you were Jewish. Why didn't you tell me?" That's as much as I know about the story.

In Carol's account of the breakup, reported in their son's biography

William Saroyan, Bill and Carol were lying in bed after making love when she told Saroyan that she was, in fact, Jewish. Saroyan moved immediately to the living-room sofa, but returned to the bedroom in the wee hours, turned on a light, tore off the covers and pointed at her: "Look at you, all white and pink and perfect. Do you mean to tell me that you're Jewish? How can that be possible? Come on, kid. You're not Jewish. How could someone as beautiful as you are be Jewish?"

"My God, what do you think a Jew *is*? What do you think I'm supposed to look like?"

In bitter hindsight Saroyan wrote, "The little bride had confessed it—she had taken six years to do so, and she had chosen the moment that suited her best. She hoped I would continue in the marriage anyway. Really she did, she said. Really."

Exactly *what* his wife had confessed, Saroyan left to the reader's imagination, with only his rage as a clue: "I understood instantly how a father might destroy his entire family and himself. I couldn't look at the woman."

ARTIE SHAW: Carol, I had never thought of her as Jewish, and, as a matter of fact, she has none of the "characteristics," unquote, associated with Jewishness. Not even an ethnic consciousness.

And, when she told me about it, it occurred to me that she must have had reasons, must have heard Bill talking about Jews and thought, "Holy Christ!"

He wasn't in love with her. Not love as I understand love. Let me give you something you can accept or reject. If two people love each other, the welfare of the other person is at least equal to your own. Number two, both people help each other become something that neither could be alone. They are better. That's not true of Bill and Carol.

Bill wanted to *own* Carol. Carol was a thing, a status thing to him. Blonde, beautiful little girl.

He was a black, minority Armenian—a despised minority.

He had a society girl here who knew Oona, who knew Gloria. He didn't *like* that she knew them, but he looked up to her. It was part of his entrée into a world he couldn't become part of. I think he wanted to become part of that world.

She represented a big step up in the world. A little immigrant, second-generation Armenian boy marries this society girl.

You play a game called "masks," because it was true of all the Hollywood women that I knew. I thought I was marrying the most beautiful creatures in the world. People marry each other in Hollywood, and you know, here I am, I got a Lana Turner mask on and you got an Artie Shaw mask. Or you've got a John Barrymore mask on and here's a—what's her name?—Costello mask. Then they get married, and they come together in a room by themselves, and after a few months and the first fine, careless rapture wears off a little, suddenly they take the masks off and they're looking at two people, both frightened, both a little scared.

"What am I doing here?" is what you're saying. "Who the fuck is this?" But you see that makes it very complicated.

So Bill marries this girl, and he's being on his best behavior, obviously, being the celebrity writer. And she's being the little society girl. And they get married, and all of a sudden, there they are—*naked*. Nothing can cover them anymore. What are they doing together?

They had something in common when Bill was a celebrity. She liked celebrities, and Bill was a celebrity. Then she ran into the Armenian culture. She couldn't deal with that.

3. THE FLIGHT

Bill did not seek a divorce right away. He left hastily for Europe instead, so hastily that instead of going by ship, as he always preferred, he flew to Lisbon.

Mixed with his anger and hatred toward Carol was a sense of exhilaration, of new possibilities. It could only be Carol's fault that the marriage was over, but now that it was over . . . what? Not women. There are hints in his fiction of a liaison with an intellectual Portuguese woman, but she is just as likely to have been an invention. His frank admissions of his encounters with prostitutes were accurate. There was a consistency here, the idea that the only women worth troubling oneself over were those who might be the mother of one's children.

A change in his financial fortunes had made it possible, however, for him to turn to gambling. He recently had quarreled with his literary agent, and he was represented now by a firm of literary lawyers whose advice was to write and sell the short fiction he had decided to abandon after the war. There was a market for his stories and a pressing need for them, to satisfy the Internal Revenue Service's demands for unpaid taxes. The money came from rich, slick magazines now, and Saroyan's flight from his marriage appears to have happened at more or less the precise moment it became possible for him to afford it. Like all gambling addicts, he could remember his victories more clearly than his losses, and his luck needed testing. If Carol had been bad luck for him, how would his luck be now?

In Lisbon he instructed the taxi driver to take him to the best hotel, which proved to be the home at that time of the only man with legitimate claim to Saroyan's title as the most famous of Armenians. Calouste Gulbenkian, then in his seventies, had constructed a fortune out of oil and shipping, which conferred upon him, in 1949, the unsought title of richest man in the world.

Saroyan was quick to manage his own introduction, and the old man was delighted to meet with the young author, whose reputation he knew but who, more importantly, spoke an Armenian dialect very similar to his own.

Gulbenkian's eyes twinkled as he explained that the hotel waiters received a good deal of money to eavesdrop on him in all the languages he spoke—except Armenian, which they had never heard. Conducting benign espionage of his own, Gulbenkian mentioned that he knew Saroyan was gambling every night at Estoril. Did he need, perhaps, a small loan? He did, but he did not accept it from Gulbenkian. A brief change of fortune gave him the funds to cover his bill and move on to Biarritz and then Paris.

But the meeting with Gulbenkian stayed in his mind. Saroyan said the old billionaire did not remind him of a father, or even "somebody who was something like a father," but the resonance of their shared Armenian heritage had made the encounter special, and a story began to grow.

In Paris he checked into the Hotel Scribe, the site of the unpleasant scene in the cellar café with Hemingway. He had loved the hotel because its name meant "writer," and now he intended to write something there. He took an outside room on the top floor, where the slanting ceiling reminded him of a poet's garret.

The story he wrote was a thirty-thousand-word novella called *The*

Assyrian, in which Calouste Gulbenkian is embodied in Curti Urumiya, a billionaire, and Saroyan himself inspires the character Paul Scott, a fifty-year-old writer of failing powers who is in Europe after the collapse of his third marriage. Saroyan piles misery upon his fictional shadow: a heart condition, a stroke, but the central equation of the tale is Scott's acceptance of his Near Eastern heritage. Curti Urumiya is a full-blooded Assyrian, just as Paul Scott's own mother had been. Scott has felt this part of himself starting to emerge as he has grown older and his troubles have multiplied. Now his true self will emerge only as his life comes to an end. He boards an airplane for a metaphorical East, his own death.

Saroyan said he needed to write to pay for a divorce and to support his children, whom he expected the court would give to him. It is likelier that he needed to create material that reflected his own life honestly in plainspoken terms, not the tortured allegory of his later plays.

Critics see the hand of Hemingway in *The Assyrian*, specifically a debt to "The Snows of Kilimanjaro," and it is true that his old Paris rival may have haunted Saroyan's room under the eaves of the Scribe. But at about this same time, Hemingway was suffering the creative exhaustion apparent in the overwritten and self-pitying *Across the River and into the Trees*. Saroyan, discounted by many critics even before he had turned to the theatre a decade earlier, was moving with *The Assyrian* into new and rich terrain.

He had written of his Armenian childhood before—directly in *My Name Is Aram* or obliquely in *The Human Comedy*. But the Aram stories sentimentalized what had happened to him in Fresno, prettied it all up, and *The Human Comedy* simply ignored his Armenian background, turning that world into a fantasy as unreal as Metro-Goldwyn-Mayer's back lot. Now he began to reach for the deepest meanings of his personal history, for what it meant to be among the survivors of a victimized race, for the ways in which these survivors treat each other.

Saroyan had used "Assyrian" as a code word for "Armenian" before in his work. He was less interested in conveying feelings proprietary to the Armenian situation than he was in getting across the way the world looked to men who straddled two cultures, one of them so ancient that it survived only in the spirit and attitudes of its people.

Few themes in American literature are so durable as that of the writer who tries, and fails, to return to his authentic beginnings.

Saroyan now began an attempt to return to his ethnic Armenian nature; but instead of failing he appears, to a very great extent, to have succeeded. The novel he would soon begin would be a sustained meditation on race and nationality, on the motives for betraying one's past and the rewards for reclaiming it.

Back in New York, he lunched with editors happy to find Saroyan returning to his old form. At the *Saturday Evening Post* he misunderstood for a moment when an editor, over lunch, offered him "thirty-seven fifty" for a new story, and he recalled the $15 he had received for "The Daring Young Man on the Flying Trapeze." He compared the offer with the $1,000 he had been prepared to demand for the new story. Then he understood. Three thousand seven hundred and fifty dollars. He covered the lapse by demanding $5,000. He got it.

Harcourt, Brace had stood by Saroyan through a period of declining sales and reputation, but after the collection containing *The Assyrian* was ready, he chose to abandon them for a house that was willing to offer more money, $50,000 for three unwritten novels. The contract was with Ken McCormick of Doubleday, who advanced $36,000 immediately.

McCormick himself, in Nevada for his own divorce, was a startled witness to Saroyan's gambling during an evening together at Lake Tahoe.

KEN McCORMICK: We went to have a drink before dinner in the Tap Room, and to get there, you had to go past the gambling table, and as he went by, he picked up the dice and threw them three or four times and won a thousand dollars.

We were a gay party of eight or ten, and in the course of dinner I noticed that Bill was missing, and I thought, "Oh, I hope he isn't sick." So I walked around to the men's room to be sure he wasn't in trouble there, and came back through the gambling room, and there he was, busy at a table. So then we danced and talked at the table, and the show happened, and I went out to see him again, and he wasn't the same person at all. I could see that he was being supplied with a drink, and that all the sharp playing that he had done on the other table was missing, and he was fumbling and things weren't happening.

Along about 3 or 4 A.M., I was absolutely exhausted and feeling horrible because I had gotten the word that he had lost around five thousand dollars. That would seem like, to me, a fortune. I

went over to the bar and there was a rather very handsome
hooker standing there with very few clothes on, and I said, "See
that fellow at that table? Would you get him over here to have a
drink?" I figured if I could get him home with her, in a bed, at
least he wouldn't be losing money at the table. So she went over
and hung over him, to invite him, and later he had no memory of
seeing this girl. She came back, and she said, "You know, this
doesn't happen to me often, but I must admit I got absolutely
nowhere with him."

That afternoon, I received a call to come over to a casino. I was
taken, almost as in a Cagney movie, through a series of doors and
corridors and everything, and then finally ushered into the
presence. And there was a rather pleasant-looking fellow sitting
behind a desk who, I realized, could be very sinister if he wanted
to be.

"You're Mr. McCormick?"

"Yes."

"You're with Doubleday?"

"Yes."

"Are you the editor there?"

"Yes, I am."

"Do you have a contract with William Saroyan?"

"Yes, we do."

"I'm not going to ask you the nature of the contract. That's
between you and the author, but I just want to confirm the fact
that he does have a contract with Doubleday."

"Oh, yes."

"Well, I want to thank you very much for coming in. If you
come to the place tonight, I'd like to give you dinner."

And all he was doing, in effect, was checking a credit reference.
It was practically a sickness with Bill.

Now, October of 1949, Saroyan was in Nevada for the six weeks
required to establish residence for a divorce. He was drinking and
gambling and losing, and in short order half of the Doubleday advance
was gone.

His divorce complaint against Carol charged her with cruelty and
indicated that there were both a property settlement and an agreement
between them giving him custody of the children, but this was wishful

thinking. In almost all cases, it was customary for the divorce to be granted on the wife's cross-complaint, and that is what happened with Bill and Carol. She would keep the children.

When the divorce was granted in the middle of November, 1949, Bill had lost every penny of the $36,000 from Doubleday, and $14,000 more. The new magazine work was bringing in up to $5,000 a story, but now his tax situation was even worse. Perhaps once again relying on George Mardikian's generosity, late that year he was in Mardikian's company, raising money for Armenian refugees in appearances on the East Coast and visiting United Nations headquarters at Lake Success to lobby for greater attention to the Armenians in Palestine.

In his encounters with Carol as he passed through New York on his way to the divorce—the children always would provide a pretext for their meetings—Saroyan believed that she was in a bright mood, and he discounted her suggestion that they try to hold the marriage together. In private, Carol was shattered by Bill's abrupt and angry departure. On more than one occasion she had fainted, and the stress triggered bouts of illness that left her bedridden. She found a psychiatrist.

CAROL MATTHAU: He could only see me at seven in the morning, before his appointments started. For some reason, because I was so young I suppose, I thought, "I'll go there and then I'll know everything."

I got terribly dressed up to go and see him at seven in the morning. And I went in, and when I got there I couldn't think of anything to say.

I said, "I'm just terribly upset. My husband has just left me, and I'm still in love with him, and I'm terribly upset, and I don't really know why I'm here."

He still didn't say anything.

I said, "Well, I'm really embarrassed. I don't know what to say." I told him funny things and tried to be amusing, and I left— never went back.

Now, Bill knew that I had done that, because I had told him so afterwards, so he went to see him. And evidently the doctor said to him, "Now, I understand your wife. I'd like to see *you*." But he never went back.

It's very interesting that he had, as everyone knows of course,

Saroyan and the Nevada lawyer Paul Ralli, just after Carol's cross-motion for divorce had been granted. Saroyan spent six weeks in Las Vegas to qualify for the divorce, losing Doubleday's advance payment for three novels and another $14,000, for a total of $50,000 down the drain. (UPI)

this enormous talent. But he didn't have intellect, and he disdained it. He thought that it was for Jews and stuff, the intellectual and so forth.

Without enormous intellectual power, which he never really did have, nor want, his best shot as an artist would have been to really write out of himself. Like sometimes you see very good performances from people who have no technique, but it's *real*—they know enough to make it real.

One of Carol's later images of Bill would be as a broken-down matinée idol, repeating his starring role by rote. In the novel Saroyan wrote in 1950 this is the alter ego he chose for himself: *Rock Wagram*, the Fresno bartender discovered at Fat Aram's, promoted by Hollywood, betrayed in some unspoken fashion by his high-society wife, Ann Ford. In the novel, the actor returns to Fresno in memory and in fact.

Early in 1950, Bill's mother suffered a stroke. Takoohi lay in a hospital bed for weeks, beyond the help of her doctors. She had remained conscious long enough to receive and recognize her second son, William, and to speak with him in Armenian. When she died at the end of February, she was not really an old woman, only in her mid-sixties.

He seems to have struggled for a time with the growing desire to look back over his shoulder. He spoke of screenplays, of all things, but even these would have been based on the past: "The Parsley Garden," a story about a youthful shoplifting episode, or "Come Back to Carthage," the title of which explains what he had in mind.

Carol would call now to beg him for the money promised under the settlement, but there was none to send, and she was evicted from their old apartment. The landlord's lawsuit made embarrassing headlines.

The Assyrian was published, and the *New York Times* asked for a review from the very editor who had first read and bought "The Daring Young Man on the Flying Trapeze" sixteen years earlier. Whit Burnett wrote that doubt and death had now entered Saroyan's work, not necessarily a bad thing. He compared the novella favorably not only with Hemingway's "The Snows of Kilimanjaro," but with Dreiser's "Free" and Ivan Bunin's "The Gentleman from San Francisco." "To get to such a death it took a lot of living," Burnett wrote.

Death would now become one of Saroyan's principal subjects, eventually his only subject. It was more than Takoohi's passing that inspired this shift in his attention. He came to realize that death had been the very seed and impulse of his work all along, despite his hard-won reputation as life's loud-mouthed celebrant. It dawned on him that this was what the shouting was about, a way of drowning out the final silence.

He moved back to Takoohi's house, where Cosette could be relied upon to bake the bread and guard the door. In July, 1950, he began his novel about an Armenian man reaching out for his lost past.

Early in the book, the Grandmother Lucy figure admonishes her grandson, "For God's sake, grow a moustache and look like a man. Look like your father, the way you were meant to look."

Saroyan did so again, a mustache at odds with the dainty versions worn by Ameche or Gable in those days. It was a vigorous, bristly thing like those he had seen in the pictures his ancestors and uncles had posed for at various points on their routes of flight from ruined Armenia.

Like Saroyan, Rock Wagram treasures something he cannot understand, poetry written in Armenian by his dead father, the alphabet as unfathomable to Wagram as it was to Saroyan when Carol had written to him in that language. In *Rock Wagram*, Arak Vagramian's father has died a suicide, his Armenian spirit smothered by the day-to-day realities of his new homeland. Vagramian succeeds in finding a translator for his father's poetry. Saroyan had not yet searched for one.

In the elder Vagramian's poem, the old man "speaks to God with pity but without love. He says he loves not God but man, and especially the enemy, the Turk. . . . He says he must pity God because God is the Father and His children love Him like fools or hate Him like fools or mock Him like fools." And the final and central message of the dead father's poem is his certainty that, if he is to live, it can only be through the efforts of his son.

Whatever the poetry of the dead Armenak Saroyan might prove to say, this was what his son William imagined that it said at this crucial moment when he struggled to retain his career, his sanity, his sense of self and fatherhood.

"If he is awakened from the sleep of death by this son, he will live and he will love."

Staring across the old oak table at the cold, gray Pacific, half a world

Saroyan and his cousin Archie Minasian in the workroom apartment of Takoohi's Fifteenth Avenue house in San Francisco, 1949. The third mustachioed Armenian (below right) is an imaginary one, painted by their friend Manuel Tolegian. The player piano was salvaged from the set of *Get Away, Old Man*. (Courtesy Aram Saroyan)

away from the shores of Lake Van, where his family's odyssey had begun, Saroyan permitted his life and his work to take a new turning.

Up until now he had borrowed from his past like someone rummaging through an attic for colorful stage properties. The gossip and jokes and cooking smells and bizarre uncles and cousins had crowded his work, and the laughter had been faithfully reproduced. But the terror and poverty had not. There was nothing of the years when, before he could even read, he had struggled again and again to return to the mother who apparently had rejected him. There was nothing of the ambitious and successful relatives who considered their wealth God-given and not to be shared, who laughed out loud at a boy's ambition to walk on a wider stage than they had chosen for themselves. And, certainly, there was nothing of the mother who was sickened by the worthless little daydreamer, a ne'er-do-well so stubborn that not even a broomstick could knock sense into his head: tsoor Willie, poor Willie, daydreamer Willie, good-for-nothing Willie.

"A man is a family thing," Saroyan made Rock Wagram say to himself.

"His meaning is a family meaning."

PART TWO
1908–1939

The four children: Zabel, Henry, William, and Cosette, photographed shortly before Armenak's death. (Courtesy Aram Saroyan)

CHAPTER SIX

TSOOR WILLIE

1. ESCAPE FROM BITLIS

It was Grandmother Lucy, *Noneh* Lucy, who had led the family out of Armenia. Out of Turkey, to be precise, for it had been nearly five hundred years since the Old Kingdom, the last time Armenia had been its own country, with real borders and a true capital. At the beginning of the twentieth century the high tableland once again was becoming a deadly place for the people who had made it their home three thousand years earlier. The flight of the Saroyans repeated an old pattern in the history of their people.

Again and again, thousands of Armenians had fled whenever the danger promised to become overwhelming. Jerusalem, Paris, Warsaw, and cities in Russia all sheltered Armenians who went there not only to keep their families alive, but to maintain the hope of a restored nation. Each of the great sweeps of death was preceded by one of these periods of flight, and on his deathbed Lucy's husband, Minas, reached his conclusions about the new danger and ordered his family to flee.

Their flight actually had begun already, with the departure of their eldest son, Dikran, not long after the renewed massacres of 1893. In that year, the last threads of the old Ottoman Empire were coming unraveled. The Turks, who had been Armenia's rulers for five hundred years, were once more choosing sides in the old struggle atop the Armenian tableland on the border with Persia. This was a clash between a town-building, crop-planting people, the Armenians, and the nomadic Kurds. A victory for agriculture would have left the plateau green, all field and forest. But the climate was just unkind enough to make this goal terribly difficult, and the Kurds and their animals were just numerous enough to keep the Armenians in scattered strongholds that never connected and thrived together.

A handful of Turkish soldiers and administrators were all it took to direct the massacres, once the Kurds were armed. The Turks already had humiliated the Armenians by ordering them to feed and water the Kurds and their animals whenever they passed through. Now the Kurds were being offered the ultimate prize: all of the land the Armenians had managed to wrench from the alpine desert. The murder the Turks ordered and inspired was barbarism itself: Mass bayonetings (to save ammunition). Hundreds of men forced to dig their own graves and a handful spared until the last in order to bury the majority. Women and children marched in great empty circles through the plains without food or water, their bodies left to mummify beside the road.

For most of their common history, the Turks had turned their backs on the plateau and the quarrel between Armenians and Kurds. The conclusive factor in this equation for genocide was the Armenians' religious beliefs. The Armenians are Christians of a most ancient sort, their church so old that the split between Rome and Constantinople is a late and somewhat meaningless quarrel to them. But this made them infidels to the Moslem Turks, and any fate was acceptable for these troublesome Armenians, who might have turned to one of Turkey's many enemies, such as Christian Russia. The idea of guilt over killing hundreds of thousands of women and children was a complete abstraction to the Turks, and it has remained so—officially at any rate—down to our own time. Germany has managed to match Turkey's inhumanity, but no nation has matched Turkey's indifference.

The killings of 1893 and the flight that followed relieved the genocidal pressure on the Armenians for a time, and so did a turn in the political situation. The old Ottoman regime fell into the hands of a group of supposed reformers, the Young Turks, who proposed a fragile peace with the Armenians, a group they viewed as useful as administrators and diplomats. To Minas Saroyan and others who knew their history, the notion of any real alliance was absurd.

Old Armenia was a society built on the strictest of successions from son to son, and Minas Saroyan's eldest already had fled, abdicating his inherited role as family builder. There was another son, little Aram, who turned eight in 1900, but there were also three intervening sisters, Verkine, Parantsie, and Takoohi, and this was a problem. In the granitic patriarchy of Armenia, the most that the father of many daughters could hope for was good marriages. These marriages were brokered and arranged by the parents, romance counting for little or nothing. Minas himself had married Lucy when she was only twelve. A daughter's only utility was as prospective matriarch of an extended family, a sort of small-time queen, and Takoohi's name itself reflected that ambition. Takoohi means "Queen," or, literally, "*Queenie.*" But Takoohi's marriage gained her neither wealth nor power, merely a gentle schoolteacher.

Armenak Saroyan was a poet and philosopher, whose natural home was the Armenian Orthodox Church, a sect in which dogma and scripture counted for less than the binding force of the Armenian language and the church's role in preserving family structure. To Takoohi's kid brother, Aram, who watched Armenak work in his classroom at Bitlis, "His whole ambition was to be able to teach the kids to learn, to obey, and to be a *man.* He was a very religious man, a man with a conscience and compassion towards other people, poor people, unable people, hopeless people."

Saroyan had married Saroyan in the case of Armenak and Takoohi, but the two were in no way related by blood. Armenian custom proscribed marriage even between seventh cousins, although so extended a cousinage ought mathematically to include not only all of Armenia but Turkey, too. Armenak's father, Petrus, had been a foundling, born Hovanessian, who had adopted the surname of his benefactor family, another set of Saroyans altogether. Lucy, Minas, and their children were a far prouder group, secure in their worldly possessions and their heritage as people of Bitlis, a highland city southwest of briny Lake Van. The Bitlisi of Fresno would be a distinct sub-category of Armenians, who viewed themselves as a bit brighter and better-off than their countrymen, even in poverty. The Armenians are one of those cultures who refer to themselves as "The People," or, in their special case, "The Christians," and the Bitlisi envisioned a past reaching directly back to the Old Kingdom. However far they might travel from the plateau, the members of the family would maintain the gigantic genealogical table in their heads. All his life William Saroyan quizzed new Armenian acquaintances on which villages their families hailed from, which branches of their surnames' line they represented, calculating and plotting the clear and implicit relationships, ranks, and stations with the greatest precision he could muster.

As hated Christians in a Moslem country the Armenians were exempt from charity, which they were unlikely to have sought or accepted in any case, but their underdog status made them attractive prospects for the good works of American missionaries. Since the early nineteenth century, with Congregationalists leading the way, Americans had traveled to Turkey to help the Armenians teach their children, fight sickness, and, not incidentally, examine the somewhat more rigorous theology of the missionary denominations. The American travelers appear not to have exploited the Armenians or to have been misguided by colonialist notions. There was a tacit understanding that the role of religion in Armenian life was different from its role in America, and even when an Armenian became a Presbyterian, as did Armenak Saroyan, it was the old doctrines and ways that prevailed, not the new ones. So the relationship was one of collegial Christianity, not of evangelists and converted heathen. When the Turks renewed their slaughter of Armenians in the 1890s, the missionaries became important sponsors for the thousand or so who fled to America each year.

The pattern was for the men to go first to prepare a home and a way for their families to join them, and most of the early Armenian immigrants settled in New England, New York, New Jersey, and eastern Pennsylvania. Their natural work was as craftsmen in business for themselves. They were shoemakers, tailors, carpenters, photographers, and some of them were shopkeepers and merchants to their own community.

The years of escape amounted to a period of unsettling change in the rigid folkways of the Armenians. Sometimes women were promoted to roles as heads of households. This was unheard-of before the troubles. Brides were accustomed to years of quiet subservience before achieving the slightest recognition from their mothers-in-law, and simply to speak to the husband's mother could be an intolerable breach. While many an Armenian wife and mother was undoubted ruler of her own household, even before ascension to the role of matriarch, it was essential that her husband be acknowledged as unquestioned despot in all significant matters. He could be benevolent or not, that was strictly up to him.

With the early departure of her eldest son and the death of her husband, *Noneh* Lucy found herself playing a role with no earlier model in her experience—an independent woman escorting an entire family past the murderous Turks and into a strange new world. But Lucy's status as survivor never was in dispute. The family legend was that she literally had been thrown away at birth, yet another unwanted daughter in a country where only a son had a chance to maintain or improve one's lot. After a night or so of energetic bawling without let-up, Lucy had been retrieved from the village dump, they said, and suckled and reared, more or less as a way of silencing her.

By 1905, when her brood were living in Erzeroum, Turkey, Lucy could be satisfied with the progress they were making in following Minas's deathbed instruction. Lucy's daughter Parantsie remained in Bitlis, to be escorted to America later by her husband. Her son-in-law Armenak had gone ahead to America, under the sponsorship of a Presbyterian minister in Paterson, New Jersey, the Reverend Dr. William Stonehill. That left Lucy in charge of thirteen-year-old Aram, a bright boy whose cleverness at languages and business would soon stand the family in good stead; her unmarried daughter, Verkine; and Takoohi, who had two daughters of her own—Zabel, born in 1899, and Cosette, born in 1902, before the family left Bitlis. A son, Henry, was born in Erzeroum in 1905.

According to Aram, the family never felt itself threatened by the Turks in Erzeroum. Bloodthirsty though they were, the Turks had scruples about killing in their own cities, and the false truce with the Young Turks remained in effect. With no grown man on their journey, the role of *paterfamilias* was played by little Aram, and he played it with gusto. As long as she lived, Lucy really understood no language but Armenian, but when lack of money stranded the travelers in Paris for a matter of months, Aram mastered enough French to handle odd jobs and the big job of feeding the lot of them on next to nothing. Aram excelled at haggling for bread among Parisians and the Armenian expatriate community in Montmartre.

When Lucy, her three teenaged children, and her three grand-children finally reached New York, they were imperiled for a heart-stopping day on Ellis Island because of her inadequate English and the immigration authorities' mistaken belief that her eyesight was too poor to permit her admission to America.

Armenak, by now, was to have been established by his benefactor Dr. Stonehill in a pulpit in Paterson, New Jersey. Lucy would take the others all the way across America, to a place entirely as flat and hot as the Armenian plateau, and as green and fertile as the Armenians' ancient dreams of abundance.

Back in 1898, *Noneh* Lucy's handsome young brother-in-law Garabet had run from Constantinople after troubles involving Greek girls and Turkish sailors. The prospect of arrest there was a terribly dangerous matter for any young Armenian. He had been the first Saroyan to reach Fresno. A relatively new and completely artificial community dropped into the middle of the Central Valley, Fresno was the creation of the Southern Pacific Railroad, whose southernmost stop it became in 1873. It was more than a decade before effective irrigation was financed, turning the desert land into fertile gardens, where every conceivable crop could grow—almonds, figs, vegetables, melons, fruit trees of all kinds, and, the most important crop of all, grapes—grapes for wine and grapes for raisins.

The seed of the Armenian colony at Fresno was planted by a single family, the Saropians, a name now missing in that city whose history they altered. Their packing house dominated the agricultural economy of Fresno in the boom years of the 1890s, but their downfall was sudden. The explanation offered in the Armenian community for years after was that the Saropians had taken in a Jew as partner, and that he had betrayed them to outside backers, securing control for himself. Whatever the truth of that account, its plot contains the archetypes of future conflict between Armenian and Jew in a city that would become home to immigrants from many places. The United Nations–like picnic sequence of *The Human Comedy*, and Saroyan's theatrical fantasy about staging a vaudeville extravaganza of folk song and dance, exaggerated the everyday reality of Fresno at the turn of the century and for a couple of decades afterward. Goodwill and tolerance prevailed with two exceptions: the Jews, who were the butt of guiltless jokes and hatred almost everywhere in America except the largest Eastern Seaboard cities; and the Armenians, far more numerous in Fresno, who were described by many residents of that city as "even worse than the Jews," a double-edged insult.

In the years ahead, the first-generation Armenian immigrants had to choose, in some cases a choice forced on them many times each day, between the old-country way of doing things and the new possibilities that America presented. Some of the Armenians, like young Aram, would thrive in this environment. Others, like Armenak, were destined to suffer—even to die. For Armenak the disillusionment began in Paterson with the little parish William Stonehill had arranged for him.

HENRY SAROYAN: He gave up on the church because he found the parishioners were inclined to be parishioners for the hour that they were in church. Subsequently, they would go on about their un-Christianlike ways, as my father would no doubt consider, and so he gave up preaching because he felt he was wasting his time, he wasn't getting his message across to anybody. So he just figured this is a lost cause, and he left.

Then he came to Fresno, and he had a little church in what was, at the time, an Armenian community called Yettem, and that turned out to be a fruitless effort, so he gave that up and subsequently went into working on a farm. Whichever farm, I don't know—whether it was a relative or someone else, I haven't any recollection of.

In Bill's accounts of his parents' move west, Armenak was satisfied with his Paterson parish. All in the family agree that it was Lucy who contrived Armenak and Takoohi's move to Fresno, where she might keep an eye on her son-in-law, goad him toward whatever opportunities presented themselves, offer him—a poetry-writing mystic and moralist—a chance to redeem himself by turning into a go-getter. Lucy was, after all, a young woman herself, still under forty, and her ambition for her daughter was undisguised and undiminished.

But the only thing that changed once Armenak and Takoohi got to California was the size of their family. Another child, a boy, was born late on the hot last night of August, 1908. It was Lucy who brought the midwife and who helped Takoohi deliver as she stood braced in a doorway. Armenak was half the county away, sleeping where he was working as a fieldhand. Armenak's mother, Hripsime, was not permitted inside the house that night. Armenak decided to name the baby

William in honor of the Reverend Dr. Stonehill, his New Jersey benefactor, who had died earlier that summer.

In the unhappy three years that remained to Armenak, he was one
of those Armenians who were terribly out of place in America. He had
no simple trade that translated easily into a livelihood. The Armenian
children of Fresno did not need to be taught in their parents' language;
they were among the hardest-working and most ambitious students in
the public schools. There were only three thousand or so Armenians in
Fresno at the time Armenak moved there—too few to support more
than the two city church congregations; the little missions, such as his
own, failed in the rural precincts. Some of the more successful early
immigrants had followed the patterns of the old country, offering work
in their businesses or on their ranches to the family newcomers, but
neither of the Saroyan clans had achieved success on a scale which
would permit that—not yet, at any rate.

There was a general understanding among the Armenians of the
time that the prejudice was less intense and the opportunities were
greater 250 miles to the north in the San Francisco area. There the
Armenian community was so small and the cultural mix so diverse that
one's origins were not of such absolute importance. Armenak moved
north alone, and after a few months he succeeded in finding packing-
house work near a San Jose suburb, Campbell, a center of prune production, and rented a farmstead, which would allow him to raise
chickens and vegetables for his family, who soon joined him.

> HENRY SAROYAN: He was working in a packing house, and I do
> recall he came home one day complaining of not feeling well, and
> he laid out on a sofa or something, out in the backyard, and he
> subsequently passed away.
>
> I don't think that there was an awareness that he had
> appendicitis. We didn't have a doctor, and he just came home
> and laid on the sofa out in the backyard. It was a warm day.
>
> I was about six, and I have a very vague recollection of his
> existence. The only major one I have is when he passed away. In
> those days they apparently permitted the coffin to stay in the
> residence, and they had a lot of carnations around, and to this
> day I can't stand the smell of carnations.

Armenak was thirty-six years old when he died, the same age his

Henry, left, and Willie, photographed in Campbell, California, 1911, the year Armenak died. (Courtesy Aram Saroyan)

son William would be in 1945, at the end of the war that so crushed his spirit. Recalling Armenak's death, Saroyan alternately marveled that he had surpassed his father's life span and hypothesized that there was an element of suicide involved, that Armenak had willingly drunk cold water, knowing that this would hasten or ensure his death. Henry Saroyan is baffled by this theory and its origin. In fact, it appears that Armenak died simply because he could not afford a doctor and because pride would have forbidden accepting charity in any event. Now, charity would have to be arranged for his widow and the children.

2. THE ORPHANAGE

Methodist friends saw to it that all four of the children were accepted by the Fred Finch Home, an orphanage in Oakland, sixty miles north of Campbell on the other, eastern shore of San Francisco Bay. The arrangement was supposed to be temporary, just until Takoohi could make ends meet once more. The only work available to her was as a domestic servant, and although no one in her family can, or will, recall for whom she worked—it appears to have been a single wealthy family, or, at least, one family at a time—it is certain that they were not Armenian. This term of service provided something of an unwanted education in American customs and manners for her, and it was a bitter fall for the proud youngest daughter of the ambitious Lucy.

The staff at the orphanage advised Takoohi about how to take her leave of the children. The delicate task would be saying goodbye to Willie, who was not yet four years old. It took place in a small room redolent of institutional furniture polish. Takoohi held Willie and reassured him that she would see him each weekend on her afternoon off. Then, to distract him from his anguish and bewilderment, she gave him a present. It was a wind-up toy, a cheap metal automaton of a black tap dancer that rattled and shuddered atop the little metal drum of a stage, which bore the name of the act: The Coon Jigger. There was no music, simply the random percussion of the little doll's feet. As Willie pondered this device, Takoohi was out the door. A few minutes later, a smiling man in his forties came through the other door and praised Willie for not crying. The boy did not know why he should be crying—not yet.

If there is a "Rosebud" in the life of William Saroyan, an emblematic object like the lost sled of Charles Foster Kane, it is The Coon Jigger, which Willie, grown to manhood and fame, would write of again and again. It accounted for his later fascination with the virtuoso tap-dance artist Bill "Bojangles" Robinson, whose recordings Saroyan would sometimes play while he wrote. Saroyan also viewed the toy as the genesis of the character of Harry the Hoofer, the Gene Kelly role in *The Time of Your Life*, bravely dancing in the face of any and all adversity. Willie cherished the doll because it was the last tangible evidence of his mother, but it was scant consolation for the evident loss of his parents, one right after the other.

Zabel and Cosette were twelve and nine. They had seen enough hardship to prepare them for the orphanage, they were old enough to realize that the situation would not be permanent, and, in terms of old-country custom, they were quite near the age of motherhood. As did the other older girls at the Finch Home, they helped with the younger children, and they also were surrogates for Takoohi, there to remind Henry and Willie that the family would soon be reunited. Henry recalls consoling Willie about Armenak, and he himself has no bitter or sad memories of the orphanage stay. As promised, Takoohi was there each Saturday to see the children and often to take them on excursions, such as a picnic in one of the cool, green parks overlooking the Bay from Oakland's hills.

But at first Willie could not be convinced that Takoohi might not vanish as completely as Armenak had done. And, if his mother could reappear, why not his father? Saroyan would tell his own children about his bitter disappointment at his first orphanage Christmas. A Santa Claus had been arranged for, and when the Santa asked Willie what he wanted, the three-year-old boy said he wanted his father back. In Saroyan's telling he recalled his agony at the wrapped gift he was handed on Christmas morning, too small, whatever was inside, to compensate for his lost father in any way.

At one point, later, after Willie had begun to go to classes with the other children from the home, Takoohi attempted to deal with his insecurity very directly by taking him home with her to San Francisco for a few weeks, even going so far as to enroll him in school there. But the orphanage itself disapproved of this arrangement, and, to Willie's keen disappointment, he was returned to the Finch Home. Takoohi had sent him a pair of cheap, blue coveralls, which he treasured because they were a gift from her, giving them up only reluctantly when he outgrew them. They were passed along to a smaller boy in the orphanage's closed economy, and Willie was distressed and angry at seeing him wearing them, and wetting them. He was angry when the superintendent tried to explain the idea of hand-me-downs. How could the superintendent possibly understand? The coveralls were vital evidence of Willie's usually-absent mother, whom he needed desperately.

As the months stretched into years, Takoohi could see a distance opening between herself and her youngest child. At the picnics the sisters would chatter with her in Armenian, Takoohi's only chance to speak with anyone in the reassuring cadences of the old country. Willie had forgotten what few words of Armenian he had learned, and if the boy appeared puzzled by what his mother and sisters were saying among themselves, Takoohi would offer a few words of attention in English.

Willie was growing up in a melting-pot atmosphere, where orphanhood, not an ethnic family background, was the distinguishing characteristic. On orphanage excursions Willie and the other boys were shepherded in tight groups, their blue short pants and starched white shirts marking them for what they were. Once, when a group of boys taunted them by shouting, "Orphan! Orphan!," Willie observed that one of their tormentors had a peculiarly narrow head and shouted, "Pinhead! Pinhead!" The boy with the oddly-shaped head burst into tears, and Willie ran over to apologize and to comfort him with the gift of a nickel, swiftly accepted.

There was nothing Dickensian or awful about the Fred Finch Home. Willie may have been discomfited by consignment to a Small Boys Dormitory, but the staff were good-hearted professionals supported by a large number of volunteer church people. The superintendent was a Scot named John Wesley Hagen, whose wife, Lillian Pender, retained her maiden name because she was an artist, a portrait painter. Another dominating adult presence was Blanche Fulton, a wealthy spinster who also was a trained social worker. Saroyan would remember her as strict and reserved. And at first there was a fourth important adult, a red-bearded, jolly man in his mid-thirties named John Forderer. He was a favorite of the children, whom he took for drives in his new car, six or seven at a time. But one day, on such a drive, Forderer and an orphan boy were killed in an accident. The child, only five or so, recently had sat for his portrait by Miss Pender, and her painting of him was lithographed into a memorial card, which the orphanage children sold door-to-door in a drive to raise funds for the child's headstone. Willie never had gotten his chance to ride in Mr. Forderer's car, and when it came time for him to sit for his portrait in Miss Pender's studio, he fidgeted too much for her to complete it: one way, perhaps, of escaping premature death and memorialization as a postcard. One day, when a stack of the postcards turned up, Willie and two other boys organized an ad hoc fund drive of their own. The children rarely skimmed more than a dime or so from these efforts, and on this occasion they handed in all that they had raised, but they were punished by being made to miss dinner. The Irish cook, who seemed to live only to gorge her charges, quietly sent for them afterward and fed them even more than usual, in view of the late hour.

Willie was a favorite, then, of the men and women who ran the orphanage. When he disobeyed—for example by whistling, even in chapel—he whistled because he expected to be paid attention to, and then forgiven. It was one way to secure attention.

Another was to run away, and Willie did so again and again, starting when he was only five. He recognized that there was nothing particularly peculiar about a small boy on the streets of Oakland, that he would be mistaken for a neighborhood child and ignored. When he was found and returned the first few times, he was said to have been "lost," not to have run away. While it would be wrong to conclude that the boy was running from a traumatizing experience, it is probably true that he was running toward his mother, symbolically if not in fact.

In the analysis by his son, Aram, in his books *William Saroyan* and *Last Rites*, Saroyan's deeper emotional life froze as a result of the orphanage stay, which would stretch on until 1916, the year that Bill turned eight. Perhaps, in conventional psychological terms, Willie adopted a notion of guilt over his father's death and of anger at his mother's fleeting presence in his life. In the view of some schools of analysis a deficit of early parental love can contribute to development of a narcissistic personality, the sort of character who manipulates people and events to satisfy a gaping hole in his self-esteem. In Jungian psychology, the complex is that of the *puer aeternus*, the eternal youth, whose dazzling displays of brilliance and promise go on for too long, blocking a normal settling-down into a life lived and shared with others and—in the case of an artist—into work marked more by its content than the inventiveness of its surface style.

In the work of his mature years, when content at last had become king, Saroyan looked back and described Willie of the orphanage in clear-eyed terms, albeit devoid of all psychologizing. To the eye of the adult Saroyan, the boy is a performer, a child fully aware of the way he manipulates adults. Whistling where forbidden and running away make him stand out for a few minutes from the crowd of boys wearing identical blue pants and white shirts. When John Wesley Hagen calls him forward at assembly, Willie knows that, if he walks quickly with his head ducked down and his hands in his pockets, loitering and hurrying at once, he will get a laugh. "When I reached him, my cheek felt the impact of his rough hand, a gesture of affection, for he was smiling, but I hated him for it."

What is it that Willie hated? Hagen's expression of regard, his smile? Did he hate himself for seeking it, for the way in which he secured it? Whatever the genesis and motive for behaving this way, the orphanage became Willie's rehearsal hall for his later starring role as the great Saroyan. He liked being "on."

His performance in the schoolroom at Oakland was less disruptive than what lay ahead for him in Fresno, and however much he could read, he had not yet become the omnivorous, voracious sampler and reader of books, flinging one aside to move on to the next in a near-panic: so many books, so little time. But he also was learning lessons that no boy of his kind could get in Fresno. No three-year-old Armenian child left in the hands of well-meaning Methodists could be returned to his family unchanged five years later. Willie's closest two friends at the Finch Home were a Jewish boy and an Irish boy. There were neighbor children he met and knew, and a family who had taken him in, for one night, in a failed experiment at summer hospitality. (It was Willie who insisted on leaving, Cosette who was enraged that he had been sent at all.) There were band concerts and special treats, such as a visit to the Panama-Pacific Exposition in San Francisco, a genuine world of wonders to the seven-year-old boy. In a very particular and at-hand way, Willie tasted the diversity of American life in a five-year overture to his next life, which would be in a ghetto as a member of a despised minority.

But in 1916, when word suddenly came that the Saroyan children were to be put on a train for Fresno, and for good, his heart was filled with joy. They would be back with *Noneh* Lucy, with aunts and uncles and cousins they had merely heard about, but never had seen, and, most important of all, back with Takoohi.

On the last morning at the Fred Finch Home, Cosette exchanged angry words with the Hagens, words about the orphanage's dishonesty in some matter and the children's ingratitude, but nothing could dampen the thrill for Willie of the trip that lay ahead. They left from the station at Fruitvale, and as the train chugged south for Fresno, away from the Bay breezes that cool Oakland in all seasons, the temperature began to soar. The children were merely uncomfortable at first, but then they found the heat almost suffocating. This was summer, and the sun was beating down on the Central Valley without a single intervening cloud. Willie ate a sweet orange. The land along the tracks was totally flat, planted with a hundred strange crops, a bizarre sight to the seven-year-old Willie, accustomed only to the cool, green hillsides of Oakland, the chilly mists, the blue Bay.

There was a new uncle waiting for them at the station, D. H. Bagdasarian, husband of Takoohi's sister Verkine. He welcomed them warmly and drove them to his vineyards outside town. Finally, they were back where they had begun, except that Willie could remember nothing of the place at all—not *Noneh* Lucy or any of the others who crowded in to see the four new cousins who had arrived all at once. The welcomers all spoke the secret language Takoohi had spoken on the picnics with Cosette and Zabel. The food on the table was strange and the names that they called it were even stranger. This is what had made the Saroyan children different from the others at the orphanage—a family. Now they were reunited at last, but for Willie it was not a matter of picking up where he left off. He was very nearly the youngest of this loud, odd gang who crowded around. It would mean beginning all over again.

3. COUSIN

HENRY SAROYAN: We had a hell of a time learning Armenian. I remember one incident, when we lived in Fresno during the early stages of our leaving the orphanage, that Bill and I were out in the backyard and Lucy was trying to tell us to close the gate to the alley. We had a hell of a time trying to understand. We'd look at each other and say, "What the hell is she talking about?" And we kept on talking to each other and laughing like hell because this was a strange language to us.

And either Bill or I—I don't know which one—put their hands

on the fence, and she said, "*Push*," and then we realized that she wanted us to close that gate.

And subsequently we picked up the language, which I've since almost forgotten, because I've had no occasion to use it, because my wife is not Armenian, and neither was Bill's wife.

One evening so early after their return that Willie understood only a few words of Armenian, his Uncle Aram ordered him—sharply, and in the new language—to close a door in the house. Willie replied, in the best broken Armenian he could muster, "I was not the opener of the door." (This is the way such matters were handled at the orphanage.) It meant nothing to Aram. "Then be the *closer* of the door," Willie's young uncle said, and everyone laughed—at Willie's expense, at his pitiful inability to speak the language of The People, and at his audacity.

They defined the boy for themselves in terms of a long-gone relative. "He is Mad Baro all over again," *Noneh* Lucy said, invoking the name of Willie's great-uncle Barunak, *bent* (crazy) Baro, the older brother of Minas, Lucy's dead husband. Baro's ferocity in the face of Turk and Kurd was family legend, but there was something odd and obstinate about the man, and they said they saw it in Willie, in his rebellious nature and his *zavzagging*, his purposeful joking. He was a boy prepared to advance the Saroyans' *khent*, their vendetta against the crazy universe, the secret meaning behind what Bill himself would refer to as "the Saroyan scowl."

They might also see that there was a great deal of Armenak in the boy, but this was Takoohi's family doing the talking. So far as Willie, Henry, Cosette, and Zabel were concerned, the old Armenian ways were turned upside-down. It was a matriarchy that was responsible for their being together and, counting the escape, for their being alive at all. Armenak's brother Mihran was trying to farm outside Fresno at this time, but he and Hripsime, Willie's other grandmother, were dominated and completely supplanted in the children's minds by Takoohi's Saroyans. In Armenia, it would have been Mihran's absolute obligation to care for his dead brother's family. When the time came, however, Uncle Mihran would be there to launch Willie on the most meaningful of his escapes from Fresno, the one that succeeded. If Takoohi's people professed not to understand Willie, Mihran understood him well enough.

Although the Armenian "ranchers," as farmers called themselves around Fresno, were scattered throughout the county, the Armenians who lived in the town itself were concentrated in an area of thirty blocks or so. The very first had rented houses on the wrong, or west, side of the Southern Pacific tracks. By the time Takoohi and her children returned to Fresno, the center of the Armenian settlement had drifted east, to the area just south of the county courthouse. Armenian merchants had their shops on Van Ness Avenue on the west side of the courthouse square, and the backgammon coffeehouses and pool halls reserved strictly for Armenians stretched south along that street.

The house Takoohi rented for $10 a month was on San Benito Avenue in the heart of the Armenian neighborhood. It came with two barns, a producing walnut tree, and a lilac bush, which shaded the window. It was near Emerson Elementary School, whose student body consisted now almost entirely of Armenians.

Despite their poverty, their house was alive with music and good food. There was a piano for the girls, and Henry would learn to play cornet. Surrounded by music makers, Willie came to love music himself, but he had no gift for it at all, hence the player pianos. There was a wind-up phonograph, too, and the stack of thick disks included old World War I songs and, more important, the music of the family's own people—Armenian music and Syrian, even Turkish, music, which Willie found haunting and beautiful.

Now, instead of the meat loaf and hash, the rhubarb and tapioca prepared by the Irish cook at the Finch home, Willie and Henry and their sisters ate kebabs and bulghur, cracked wheat fried in butter, then simmered in broth and served with steamed onions and yogurt. There was a crisp pickled cabbage dish, a Bitlisi specialty called *tut-too*, and another, *pah-chah*, lamb's head stewed with garlic, which Henry would not eat because of the way the head was staring at him. Once more Takoohi could bake the week's bread for her family, frying cakes of the leftover dough as *tazhah-hotz*, new bread, a treat the children dipped in tea. Baths remained a weekly ritual, just as they had been at the Finch home, but now *Noneh* Lucy presided over them, and as Willie and Henry emerged, there was another treat, a glass of *sharbat*, a tall tumbler of cold water with three spoons of sugar dissolved in it. The next morning, Sunday service was not Methodist but nominally Presbyterian, and conducted in a mixture of English and Armenian, which Willie had begun to understand, although he never would learn to read it.

One day Takoohi brought out a rolled-up cloth that contained Armenak's writings and spread them before Willie, telling him, in Armenian, "There was more. He lost some, we lost some, this is all that remains." The notebooks and manuscripts had been made by hand out of brown paper, white butcher paper, anything that was blank and cost nothing. Willie spent an hour touching them and scanning the lines written in the mysterious Armenian alphabet. The boy did not know what the words said, but he recognized that, while Armenak might be dead, he had cheated death by writing down his thoughts. In this way he could speak not only to the son who missed him so terribly, but to the grandsons yet unborn, and to their sons.

None of Willie's uncles could replace the loss of Armenak, but one of them was a huge presence in the boy's life, Takoohi's baby brother, Aram, now in his late twenties and already a grand and self-important self-creation. He must have seen something of himself in this boy who grandstanded so shamelessly for attention. For all her sternness, Aram's sister Takoohi was a woman who delighted in mocking others, giving her impressions of their voices or walks the moment they had left the scene. Whatever they told Willie about deportment, their actions were stronger lessons, and loud Uncle Aram basked not only in the attentions of his mother and sisters, but of Fresno as well. He had moved quickly from work in fruitstands and groceries, through a brief career as barber and into his natural arena, the courtroom, as a criminal defense lawyer. His importance transcended the Armenian community. He was someone that everyone had to pay attention to. Even in his nineties, Willie's uncle was no less certain of his own worth.

UNCLE ARAM SAROYAN: My success was phenomenal. I never stopped. I was a very, very busy fellow—and fearless. I did everything according to my judgment. I never relied on anybody's judgment. I relied on *my* judgment, and worked on it and became a success.

I went to USC, but I didn't stay in school too much. I used to spend my time in courtrooms, listening to criminal lawyers. I never studied. I know the teachers knew that I never studied the texts, and they would say, "Aram, tell us, so we won't get caught up in you asking us questions." I never graduated. I just got out and started practicing law, and made quite a success with it because I was an *actor* rather than a lawyer.

I played in Henrik Ibsen's *Pillars of Society.* I was Rörlund, and they all said that I should go on the stage, but I said, "What the hell? The stage is no good because I can use the courtroom as a stage, defending people, trying to do some good for them."

My hero in life was Clarence Darrow. He came to Fresno, and I met him and loved the man. I had greater admiration for him than any human being or imaginary Jesus Christ. He came to Fresno and tried an arson case, and he made it so tough on the district attorney that the D.A. got up and moved for dismissal.

I became a lawyer when I didn't know the English language, and I defended ten murderers. I got eight of them off scot-free, one or two of them manslaughter and the other as first-degree murder without life.

HENRY SAROYAN: He was a highly respected attorney and shipper and he was a leader in the Armenian community whenever he decided it would be advantageous for him to be present at a meeting, and he'd get up and make a speech and take sides.

I remember one year the company that subsequently turned out to be Sun-Maid Raisin Growers, they were going around to various farms and trying to get people to sign as being a member of this association. In one case, an Armenian refused to talk to them. He told them. "This is my private property, now get the hell off of here." One of them apparently did not feel that this was his right and made some effort to enter his house. And this Armenian farmer, intentionally or otherwise, shot through the door, and he wounded or killed one of the guys.

And my uncle defended him. I remember the trial because I attended a couple of sessions of it. He was a very fiery attorney, and he could move mountains when he got going.

UNCLE ARAM SAROYAN: He just shot in the air. He was trying, with a great big group of people, to scare the life out of the children, who were in bathtubs and so forth.

And during that trial I says, "I'm not defending this man. I'm defending the entire people from the same issues. Today it's grapes. Tomorrow it can be apples. The next day, oranges. There's no end to this thing here," and finally I got him out. Notwithstanding the fact that there was a lot of prejudice created by one factor—I don't like to name names of the people, their racial background—but they accused the Armenians of being boisterous, playing backgammon on their porches, speaking loudly. Eating garlic!

Aram meant the Jews, whom he blamed out loud for a variety of misfortunes, including his personal difficulties in renting a good office for his practice.

"What has the fact that we are a clannish, ill-dressed, noisy, argumentative, uncooperating people to do with the inability of Armenian professional men to rent office space in good Fresno buildings?" he wrote the Armenian newspaper.

In Fresno the financial power of the community is found in the hands of Jews. It is they who have created the feeling of hatred against the Armenian businessmen and professionals, for they well know that in time the Armenians will become their strongest rivals in commerce. It is sad to see how the native Americans have become victims of this Jewish propaganda. United with the Jews are, of course, the American business men, lawyers, doctors, in the effort to keep the Armenians from occupying good offices. By so doing they hope to kill the competition of the Armenians and keep the field free for themselves.

Aram was one of fewer than a dozen professional men among a minority that still accounted for only one out of every twenty Fresno residents. The community was growing and changing because of events in Turkey itself. There, the Armenians had cast their lot with Russia as World War One broke out, and in 1915 the atrocities against the Armenians were renewed by the Ottoman Turks with the tacit approval of their German allies. The Russian forces, even with Armenian support, had proved feeble friends—Russia had its own problems—and there was a hasty retreat northward, into the land that would become Soviet Armenia after the revolution. This time, the massacres were more horrible than ever. No Armenian survived in place. It was flee or be killed. Fifteen thousand died in a single day in Bitlis alone.

Armenian immigration to America stepped up, and Armenian patriotism intensified among the young men of Uncle Aram's generation. Now, as Byzantine Armenia gave way to a Caucasoid Armenia with, at first, an equally puzzling political future, men like Aram became important politicians in this nation without boundaries, using oratory to inspire its people to charity. But Armenia's very self-interest worsened the prejudice. America was involved in the Great War, too, and the citizens of Fresno asked themselves why the Armenian boys were slow to enlist. If Armenians did not enlist, the reason was that the war no longer could affect the country they identified with most strongly. Many of the first-generation Armenian immigrants never took the opportunity open to them to become naturalized citizens of the United States; it would have been a betrayal of their Armenian heritage.

While the Armenian community of Fresno became both larger and more purposeful, formal antagonism against them grew. Newspaper advertisements for new housing tracts boasted of restrictive deed covenants making the new blocks "inaccessible to all races of Asiatic origin. Armenians, Greeks, Chinese, and Japanese, being undesirable elements, will not enjoy the right to own houses on this Kearney Boulevard division for the next twenty-five years." There was talk that Armenians were freeloaders and criminals. Police, court, and charity statistics from that era, however, demonstrate with utter clarity that Armenians stood before judges or entered welfare rolls or charity wards half as often as Fresno's "Anglo" majority. It would be many decades before the antagonism would fade to relative insignificance, and the years of Bill Saroyan's Fresno boyhood were years when his countrymen were forced to prove themselves.

Aram was doing so, not only as a criminal lawyer but as a grape shipper, and so was Dikran Bagdasarian, Verkine's husband, who had met the children at the train. The Bagdasarians' fortunes would flourish, fulfilling every promise of the new country. (Their son, Ross, would begin a spectacularly remunerative show-business career with a small role in *The Time of Your Life*.) But for Takoohi's family there was no choice but for all of them to work. Takoohi herself took jobs in fruit-packing houses. Cosette and Zabel were at first shop assistants and then a legal secretary and saleswoman, respectively. Henry, who quickly had fit into the mold of achievement and obedience expected of a good Armenian son, became a newspaper boy and then a messenger for Postal Telegraph, and these jobs led directly to his adult career.

Willie at first helped with one of the fruit stalls set up each weekend on the courthouse square. His boss was a Syrian named Ahboud, whose skills at haggling matched those of any Armenian shopkeeper.

He shared broken, unsalable melons with his young assistant, and he paid Willie fifty cents each Saturday, a good day's wage for a nine-year-old boy in 1917.

But, as soon as Henry could convince his employers about the matter, Willie always followed his big brother into a job. When Bill began hawking the Fresno *Herald*, he had to pay a dollar for a heavy metal badge that identified him as Newsboy No. 8. As lowest in the pecking order, Bill was pestered for his first day by the seven senior newsboys, who already had staked claims to the best corners, and sometime during that first busy day the badge vanished. Willie searched for it everywhere, without luck, and told his troubles to his Uncle Vahan Minasian, the sad man who had married Takoohi's sister Parantsie and brought her past the Turks to safety in Fresno.

"What is it?" Vahan said. "Tell me."

Willie did.

"Oh, is *that* what it is? A badge that cost a dollar? Paid for and immediately lost? That is nothing. May your soul stay alive."

Vahan's philosophical advice was the first time that any of the adults in his family had talked to him as an equal, which made the words especially comforting. The newspaperboy job took Willie anywhere he wanted to go—into the mysterious coffeehouses, if he wished, although it was understood that he could stay there only long enough to offer papers, and into the White Fawn Saloon on Mariposa Street, with its free lunch and its poker game in the back room. But if the job was an adventure for Willie, it was more of a business for his older brother.

HENRY SAROYAN: I remember on Armistice Day, November 11, 1918, there was a flu epidemic throughout the United States, and I had caught the flu and I'm lying at death's door, in my opinion, and we heard sirens and things like that—there was no radio—so we knew that the armistice had been signed.

So I was lying in bed thinking, "Well, this will be a wonderful opportunity for Bill to sell a lot of newspapers and make a few extra dimes," and when he came home, I said, "How much did you make today, Bill?"

He said, "I didn't sell papers."

I said, "How come?"

He said, "I joined the parade."

He rode his bike up and down with the parade, and I was quite disappointed in his lack of business acumen to realize that here was a golden opportunity, because without radio or TV, the newspapers were the only sources of information, and I just figured in my little tricky head that Bill would sell a lot of newspapers and come home with some extra loot.

I am at death's door, and he comes home and says he hasn't sold *any* newspapers. I was quite disturbed at that.

While the serious Henry always stood up for Willie, advancing his cause in boyhood commerce, Willie soon developed his own circle of friends. His closest boyhood pal was one of Vahan and Parantsie Minasian's three sons, his cousin Archie.

Uncle Vahan was much like Armenak, and soon died of a combination of things—the sickness that can dog the poor and those brokenhearted at being separated from the land they understood. Parantsie and her six children joined Takoohi's family on the roster of poor relations.

Little Archie worshiped Willie, and Takoohi scorned him for this, calling him, in Armenian, a "hind-tit puppy," or "rearward dog," as Saroyan later would translate the insult. To Takoohi, Archie was a mischievous familiar, whose willingness to go any and everywhere with Willie had led her son into more trouble than he could have found alone. The conflicts between this particular aunt and nephew would continue right up until her death thirty years later.

For his part, Archie was mystified that Takoohi and her young brother Uncle Aram, who could do no wrong, were unable to understand Willie, who was slow to anger, quick to forgive, and already creating a special world of his own.

ARCHIE MINASIAN: There's one beautiful thing about Willie. It was what I needed desperately, and what *he* needed. I say "I" because I spent more time with him—I was his mentor, actually. I nourished him. Every time we'd meet, the minute we'd look at each other we'd both start laughing, and it was what was needed: humor.

I remember how many times Willie would be driven out of the house. He was—there's an Armenian word: *tsoor.*

"*Tsoor* Willie."

It's a term for a guy who was a daydreamer, or crooked or crazy, an Armenian term that's loosely used. "*Tsoor* Willie."

That's putting him down on this level, an insect. It's a sad term, but we heard it all through our childhood.

He used to come, when we lived on Raisina Street, I'd hear this little scratching on the door, the window, trying to get my attention. I'm asleep in my little bedroom with rocks all over. Nature man. And in through the window he'd come, and he says, "Archie, can I spend the night here?" And I'd give him my bed and sleep on the floor.

His mother would come in the morning: "Like a *dog*, laying at his feet!" And that stuck. This is the dog, me. "Isn't this strange? Look how he follows him around. Look how he does this, how he does that."

I nurtured myself, but I nurtured Willie, too. Willie, very receptive and warm, used to make us feel like human beings because we were always crushed, always humiliated by rich relatives. We had a few. And let me tell you, instead of nurturing and guiding and giving a kind word, we were treated like bugs.

It's sad: "You're never going to amount to a *damn*." That's all we heard, and when we walked over to El Monte Way, contacted Willie—the warmth, the understanding, because *he* was included in that bug list.

Uncle Aram, I'll never forgive him. Talk about cruel.

"You know, you boys don't deserve to walk on *streets*. Walk through *alleys*." I want to show you how crushing his words were, and cruel: "Walk through *alleys*, where you *belong*, streets are for *people*."

That's right. So we walked through alleys, where we'd find— we never had a toy through our childhood, we made our own. Little peewees. We'd cut a broomstick, tape it at the ends, and we'd find a little wheel once in a while that somebody had abandoned, thrown away, and we'd make a little wheelbarrow with it. This was our entire childhood, finding little things and creating things. Which was beautiful.

But! When you figure out what influenced it all, it was cruel.

My mother was the most intelligent of the whole lot. She was a compassionate woman, she was loved by everyone. All the Armenian women used to come there and weep, and she was a peacemaker. She was one wonderful person. I used to ask her, "Ma, what's wrong with Uncle Aram? Now, I'm going to tell you my reason, and you tell me if I'm wrong. Did he hate my father?" She said, "Yes. Your father was a very proud man—" (You see, they came from Mush. Mush is where kings and warriors—and if you look in the history of Armenia, you'll find that there, all the top echelons of Armenia's history, its greatness, came from.)

She says, "Uncle hated your father for one reason. He didn't want a poor man to feel proud."

What made Uncle Aram the way he was, the sisters. They worshiped him. When he came from the old country, he was just a young kid, and he handled the passage, speaking and taking care of things, and he did a great job. That you can't take away from him. But coming here and all of a sudden finding himself an attorney, a grape shipper with money, it went to his head. In other words, he floated out in space, got away from reason. He became arrogant. But the mother and the three sisters used to spoil him, make him feel like a god.

HENRY SAROYAN: I know one incident that irked the hell out of me at the time. I had found a Plymouth Rock hen under a car one evening when we were going home.

Bill and I, we had one bicycle. He used to sit on the handlebar, and I used to ride him home, and this hen had chicks, and from these chicks a beautiful Rhode Island Red rooster, a beautiful creature.

And Aram was coming over for dinner, and my mother killed the damned thing and served as dinner to him and the rest of us. I wouldn't eat it. It was my pet rooster.

This disturbed me a great deal, that anybody could be so inconsiderate of my efforts to raise these little chickens. She was trying to feed Aram, and maybe that being the largest of the group that I was raising, she felt it would serve the purpose better than one of the smaller ones, but it was very disturbing to me.

In no one's recollection, except perhaps his own, was Aram Saroyan a significant contributor to the welfare of his widowed sisters and their children. Archie Minasian remembers that any sign of charity from him was a signal event. His car pulled up before Parantsie's house one day, and he bellowed for Archie to jump in. "We're going to the ballgame!" Parantsie turned her back to the door and crossed herself. Had some corner been turned? At the ballpark, Aram strode swiftly to the ticket booth, bought one seat, and hurried in, leaving Archie bewildered. "What am I supposed to do now?" the boy called after his uncle. "Sneak in!" Aram shouted at him. The ticket taker shook his head and waved Archie through the gate. Uncle Aram's frugality would rub off on Bill, and Archie was embarrassed in later years when Saroyan would drop a nickel into a newspaper machine and take all the copies:

"Why did you do that, Bill?"

"Ah, I *need* them, Arch."

(Younger women in the family were embarrassed by Grandmother Lucy's reputation for prowling the alleys in search of interesting cast-offs and usable food.)

But Bill did not adopt Aram's hair-trigger temper. The boy might nurse a grudge, but he would not fight, and it took many months for the men in his family to understand this decision on his part.

UNCLE ARAM SAROYAN: He was an amazing person. He would never have an enemy. The worst man, he never would say, "Well, he's no good." Nothing but praise for everybody. He carried the same philosophy as Clarence Darrow. People hate because they have good reason to do so, but those people who don't hold grudges, they are the ones who are helping people, because grudge keeping hurts you, not the other guy. You get no sleep at night.

If Aram believed his nephew shed grudges easily, he was wrong, but the boy was a quiet and peaceful member of a minority with a reputation in Fresno for loud public quarrels and fights. He was no sissy, though, and all the exploits he would celebrate in his stories later were true. Geggenheimer's water tank was Old Man Guggenheim's water tank, and Willie felt guilty about dropping the cat from the top; but he was still writing about it, if not exactly bragging, fifty years later. (The cat lived.)

ARCHIE MINASIAN: Those are the days of the *topal* gang, a group of the older Armenian kids, fourteen or fifteen, who created their own little gang on M Street. *Topal* in Armenian means "cripple." *Topal* gang. Fat Khashkhash was a fat, chubby guy about, I would say, fifteen years old then. There was an empty lot, and there were tunnels under there, and the *topal* gang used to go in there and hang out, like big shots, you know: candles in their little niches. One day, what the hell happened? The police had picked up three or four of the Armenian kids, and Fat Khashkhash was one of them. I wish I remembered exactly the names of the kids—Al Kalakian and several of the kids that lived there—and the cop was having fun, meting out justice on the street.

Fat Khashkhash was just trembling.

The cop had them all lined up. He said, "Six months for this guy. Two months for this guy." Playing games. He comes to Fat Khashkhash, he looks at him, and he says, "*Life,*" and Khashkhash collapsed. It was so beautiful.

School was Bill's particular ordeal. He was ten before he could read and write with any facility. "All of a sudden it was all very simple. I could read, I could write, and I was awfully happy about it."

He wrote what he pleased, however, which meant digressive essays filled with his opinions, not the simple assignments about summer vacations. It got attention.

"So you're William Saroyan?"

"Yes, ma'am. Did I do something wrong?"

"Well, yes, I suppose, but not *really*. It's all right. You may return to your class now."

The Human Comedy's most realistic episodes recreate the spirit, if not the letter, of Bill Saroyan's school days. When the teacher snaps Homer Macauley back to reality and permits him to give his extemporaneous lecture on noses (the subject is the Hittites), Saroyan is recalling himself as class character, although the real-life episodes were considerably less sunny. More realistic was his portrayal of what happens next, when Homer Macauley is made to stay after school, along with his wealthy rival, Hubert Ackley III. Ackley is one of the school's track stars, and Coach Ek (whose name has been celebrated in "Believe It or Not," a marvelous Saroyan touch) insists that he be released by the boys' teacher, Miss Hicks. The coach does not care whether Homer is released to compete in the same meet, which infuriates Miss Hicks. There were real-life Miss Hickses and Coach Eks, teachers who passed over skilled Armenian boys in selecting varsity squads and who considered all such children unruly, lazy, even dirty. ("They refuse to take showers at school," a janitor sniffed.) Half a century later, their insults still rankled with Saroyan. "Miss Clifford, whoever you are these days, wherever you may be, whatever you may think about anything at all, I despised you then and I cannot now say I am sorry I did. I had no choice. You were despicable, dishonest, rude, stupid, hostile, and unfit to teach anybody anything. You marked me as your personal enemy and started every day with sarcasm about my appearance, my clothing, my manners, my intelligence, and my impatience with your inability to get your work organized or to perform it effectively. And you never learned that any sarcasm from you would be answered in kind by me."

But he held warm memories of Miss Brockington, the real-life model for the fictional Miss Hicks, Miss Brockington who "did not hold against me either my nationality or my personality, but on the contrary struggled decently with each, impelling me in return to struggle with them on [her] behalf."

There was a teacher, Miss Carmichael in Saroyan's memoirs, who asked him to stay after on the last day of school.

"This is not punishment," she said across the room to Bill, who was seated in the last row, by the door.

"I know about your family background, I've looked into it, I know there isn't a lot of money, but please don't let *anything* keep you from going to college. Will you remember that, always?"

Bill never would go to college, not for a single day, but learning to read and write told him what he wanted to do with his life. His strange essays, off the subject and full of himself, made the teachers pay attention to him. His handwriting was clear, perhaps the best in the school, and he used the language well. He had pondered painting or singing or composing, but he had no skills in those directions. It was clear to him almost at once that while everyone could write—a letter, a school assignment—not everyone could convey feelings with words the way he could. This must be what his father had done in the brown-paper notebooks rolled up in the piece of cloth. It was something worth spending one's life doing.

Bill's true education happened according to his own lesson plan, in the Fresno Public Library. Henry remembers him with teetering stacks of books on every conceivable subject, and Archie remembers the scorn with which Takoohi greeted her son's habit. Saroyan always said that it was a story of Guy de Maupassant's, "The Bell," about a crippled tramp, that confirmed him in his ambition to write. Maupassant was merely one of the writers whose work the boy inhaled without, at first, much attention to the quality of what he read. But he also read critics and, now that he was to be a writer, their autobiographies. There is little question that he read Sherwood Anderson while Anderson's material was fresh, including *A Story Teller's Story*, which appeared the year Bill turned sixteen, and none whatsoever that he paid attention to Hemingway. He also haunted the periodicals room, and he was enchanted by the world of the stage, which was reported in *Theatre Arts* magazine. Bill read every issue, and he read the plays that were mentioned there, such as Noël Coward's *The Vortex*, a very advanced melodrama about a strange mother and son, an odd bit of reading, indeed, for an Armenian teenager in California's Central Valley.

It was clear that he would have to escape from this place. Writers, he knew, no longer worked with quills and a copperplate hand. They typed, and at the age of eleven or twelve (he came to forget exactly when), he enrolled in Technical High School, where the greatest number of Armenian boys chose to go.

"The woman in charge of transfers was required to ask why I wanted to transfer. I said I wanted to learn typing, which impelled her to ask *why* I wanted to learn typing. I couldn't tell her the truth, so I said, 'I'm going to need it in looking for work.'"

That is what he told his family, too. Aram and Takoohi were furious. Even though practical reasons made most Armenian boys choose a vocational education, the ones who stayed at the academic high school outperformed their non-Armenian classmates, despite, or in part perhaps because of, the antagonism of the teachers.

Henry had become a messenger for the Postal Telegraph Company by this time, and Bill had begun to ease his way into that organization, too, starting by telling the office manager that he would clean the premises for half what the regular janitor was being paid. By the time he began typing classes, he was a messenger working full shifts, and when there was no telegram to deliver, he could practice on the machines in the agency office. The people who worked there were close models for the characters of *The Human Comedy*, especially Old Man Grogan, the Frank Morgan role in the film version. Postal Telegraph connected Fresno to the outside world, a world that was becoming more attractive to Bill all the time.

In 1922, raisin prices collapsed. Although many in Fresno were eager to blame the Armenian holdouts for the inability of the co-ops to control the market, the fact was that the crop was overplanted. Land speculation had turned everyone into a rancher or ranch owner, and when the bubble burst, Fresno sank into a depression, as much of rural and small-town America did, almost a decade before the stock-market crash involved the cities, the banks, and the general public.

Uncle Aram was not ruined by the price collapse, but Armenak's brother, Uncle Mihran, was among those who gave up farming. He would build himself a business that would carry him through the depression and beyond, a small ladies' store, the Mona Lisa Dress Shop. For this gentle bachelor with no family, it was perfect.

ARCHIE MINASIAN: We pulled a fast one on Mihran. I told Willie one day, "You know, this guy worships Leo Tolstoy. That's his idol." I said, "Watch the act that Kirk and I are going to put on."

"Don't give him a bad time."

"Well, watch this."

So we're all sitting at Eugene's house on the east side of Fresno, and it got quiet after supper, and they're sipping coffee, and I turned around and told my brother, Kirk, "You know, I just don't believe this about Tolstoy."

And the minute Mihran heard "Tolstoy," he perked up, sat up in his chair.

Willie was looking, figuring, "What the hell have they got going now?"

And then Kirk said, "It's true, every bit of it."

I said, "I just can't believe that Tolstoy *murdered* those guys. . . ." And then we went on, built it up, built it up, and finally, Mihran blew up.

"What are you boys *saying* about Leo Tolstoy? When did he do these things?"

I said, "Mihran, we're talking about *Gus* Tolstoy."

"Damn your hides, you—" I pulled so many of those things.

*   *   *

Mihran was frank in expressing his complaints about Aram to the boys. "He has no *nobility*," he would say.

ARCHIE MINASIAN: Aram was cruel. I use the word "cruel" because he *was* cruel. When you crush young kids growing up . . .
   We used to walk to the library, city library: "Where the hell do you think you're going? Stay away from there. You're not Shakespeare." In other words, don't read, don't aspire for anything good.
   I filled out a little card—I'd just started Fresno State. I went there three years. I filled out a card for a free folder, and it was Dr. Eliot's five-foot shelf.
   Instead of sending me the folder, would you believe? Dr. Eliot's five-foot shelf, in a crate, arrived at the door. And who drives up—and he drives up all the time, every day he drove up. God, when he saw that.
   We had just opened it, and there was Shelley, there was Keats, there was Shakespeare. That guy went into a rage.
   "Learn to pick up a *broom* and find your right place in life." In other words, don't tackle, don't aspire for good things.
   For Christ's sake. Oh, God, I remember the arguments and the fights. But I'll never forget the most beautiful thing. When we lived on Raisina Street—now this was real comedy—Uncle Aram drove up in a brand-new Apperson.
   So he drove up one day, and this is so beautiful, and came in with his stance, and he struts around, all the Armenians in the neighborhood looking at him. Parked it and left his door open on the San Benito side.
   Willie and Henry had just bought a model-T Ford, and they drove up alongside, and they came out to discuss something. And when they left, Henry had left his door open, and Uncle Aram's Apperson's door is already open onto the road, and when Henry drove off, two doors fell off on the road.
   If you saw Uncle Aram . . . He almost had a heart attack. He couldn't talk. He was in such a rage he couldn't talk.
   Armenians have a lot of comedy anyway. They love to laugh, especially our family. And God, I'm telling you, we laughed.

* * *

But there were serious conflicts with Aram, and with Takoohi. Bill's obstinacy in school now imperiled his graduation.

HENRY SAROYAN: He wasn't sassy, he just *digressed*. For instance, if they were discussing Shakespeare, or an American writer, he'd change the subject and bring up some other writer—or some other subject—and they couldn't stand his digressions. So they kicked him out.

Bill got kicked out of high school on three different occasions, and each time I'd go see the vice-principal and talk him into putting Bill back in school.

But he says, "I can't understand. You're such a good student, and your brother will pay no more attention to classes—as a matter of fact, he's a very disruptive influence."

And he eventually got kicked out, and I couldn't get him reinstated, so he never did graduate from high school.

At that time, at my age, I was not too concerned. I was disturbed that he wasn't making any money, because we depended on the income, to live on.

But Bill was too independent. He did what he wanted to do when he wanted to do it, and if it didn't coincide with what I might have wanted or his mother may have wanted, it did not disturb him one bit. He just went his own way.

In 1925, when he was seventeen, Bill made his first break from the family and Fresno. "I seemed to be fighting everybody," he said. Why could he not finish school? Why did he always have his nose stuck in a book?

He would be eighteen soon, and he had no high school diploma. His jobs were fill-in work with the telegraph agency, office errands for Uncle Aram, and as a fieldhand in the vineyards Aram owned with D. H. Bagdasarian. Henry was working for Aram, too, as a part-time accountant, and there was a serious misunderstanding between uncle and nephews that summer, a matter only hinted at in Saroyan's memoirs, a quarrel so severe the family refuse to talk about it sixty years later.

Bill's first tentative attempt to live away from home was a move to a former tool shed in Fresno that rented for $2 a week, but this proved unsatisfactory. It was time to go—anywhere. He went to Aram and told him so.

"I think that's a good idea. You've been giving my sister a bad time long enough. Get out and stay out. When are you leaving?"

"Right away, but I haven't got any money."

"Bums don't need any money. Go out to the S.P. and grab a freight, the way all the bums do."

"I thought you might pay me."

"For what?"

"For the work I did for you."

"This place has been a college for you. You should pay me."

The quarrel escalated into a shouting match, and Aram switched to Armenian, Turkish, Kurdish.

"You want to be a writer. Get money in a bank and write *checks*. That's the way to be a writer. That's the kind of writer *I* am, not a stupid poem writer. *The moon is sinking in the sea.* The moon is sinking in your empty head, that's where the moon is sinking."

Saroyan could confect comedy from the argument like this, but it was wounding, brutal, final, and even after Aram had become the most memorable of the stock characters in Saroyan's repertory company of relatives, the sharp memory of the humiliating dismissal could paralyze the nephew with rage.

Bill left the Rowell Building that morning and went to the garage of the Californian Hotel, to find out if anyone was leaving town. An elderly gentleman was, and offered Bill a ride. In Bakersfield, they stopped for lunch.

"I haven't got any money."

"I know that. You'll have a dollar in your pocket when we get to Los Angeles, too, and forget it."

"I'll never forget this," Saroyan said as he was let out in the middle of town.

"Forget it."

That very morning, he found work as a stock boy for Bullocks department store. The foreman loaned him a couple of dollars, and he took a room in a cheap hotel behind the Los Angeles Public Library.

There, after a very few days of work, he began to feel ill. He left the store, went to his rented room, and drank water. He fell into a fevered sleep, awoke drenched with sweat, and went out to buy a dime's worth of grapes. There was forty cents left in his pocket, and he was in a city where he knew no one. The single short piece of writing he had been able to sell before setting out on his own had sold to a magazine unable to pay him. In his anger at Aram, he had left Takoohi, Henry, and his sisters behind without telling them where he was going, and the truth was, he did not know that himself.

CHAPTER SEVEN

WRITER

1. THE DARING YOUNG MAN . . .

In a tent in a park in the middle of Los Angeles, Saroyan joined the California National Guard. The recruiter explained that a man had to be eighteen, and Bill said that he was. He was given a uniform and sent to Monterey for basic training. Naturally, he hated it, and since he was free to quit, he did so after only two weeks. Back in Los Angeles, he was standing on a corner waiting for the light to change when he spotted a familiar Buick convertible with the top down. It was Uncle Mihran. Bill shouted after him and jumped in.

Mihran was as warm and kind as Aram could be cold and mean-spirited. Earlier that year, Mihran and Bill had stood together at Armenak's grave in a cemetery beside the railroad tracks in San Jose.

"What are you crying for?" Bill had asked Mihran. "He's not here."

"Where is he, then?"

"Oh, many places . . . Where he was born, where he had his childhood and boyhood. I'm here, so he's here, too."

Now, in Los Angeles, in provident coincidence, his dead father's gentle brother had appeared at exactly the moment he was needed.

They drove to a telegraph office and sent Takoohi a wire saying that her youngest was alive and well. Then Mihran took him to a Greek restaurant, where the food and the smells were very much like home, and his spirits revived. He went back to Fresno to plot his departure a little more carefully. The next job was to be with the U.S. Forestry Service in Sonora, but when Bill got there, he disliked what he saw, left a note saying so, and went on by bus to San Francisco, where he applied for, and got, a job as a clerk-typist with Southern Pacific. He worked for eight days in the office that directed the passenger ferries criss-crossing the Bay and the Sacramento Delta. The boss, Captain Heath, reprimanded him for whistling and humming and for wearing his cap indoors. "Hang your cap up when you come in," he was told. Bill explained that it slowed him down when he had to grab his cap before leaving on an errand. The next day, the argument was repeated. Bill typed his resignation, was paid, and left.

The logical place for him to work, of course, was Postal Telegraph, and Henry's good offices would provide the opening. The feisty little company was just right for Saroyan. It was founded on a grudge.

HENRY SAROYAN: John Mackay had made his money in silver in Nevada, and he wanted to send some telegrams or something to New York, and the Western Union either refused or somehow they did not do what he wanted them to do, so he found a small telegraph company running from Albany to New York, called Postal, and he bought the company and started it. And then he got his Western movement until it became a national competitor to Western Union.

I came up to San Francisco January 1, 1927. I came up here, actually, to go to Cal. When I got here I talked to the general manager of Postal Telegraph, a wonderful old man, L. J. Miller, and he said, "Look, Henry, you're going to come up here by yourself. Your family's in Fresno, and you can't sustain your body and soul at Cal doing nothing, or doing part-time work." He said, "I've got a good job for you," and he said, "By having that job, you can bring your family up here."

So I abandoned the idea of going to Cal and went to work for Postal Telegraph again, over on Clay Street, and it went on from there and I progressed, moved from that little branch that was in the produce district of San Francisco, and I got their main branch in San Francisco, on Market Street. And I was doing pretty good for them and they were doing pretty good for me.

And so, as I progressed, other members of the family would move up here and we eventually rented this place on Sutter Street.

Bill began as a counter clerk at the Market Street office, which adjoined the swanky Palace Hotel. A little over a decade later, he would be sipping whiskey at Artie Shaw's personal ringside table in the Palace's Garden Court. His recreations were more plebeian in 1927: the joints along Third Street, such as Breen's, which was surviving Prohibition by serving 3.2 beer and bitters along with its hearty German cooking.

Saroyan was thoroughly indoctrinated in the notion that Postal Telegraph was in some essential way better than Western Union, and the go-getter attitude of Homer Macauley in *The Human Comedy* is simple fact, not embroidery. He asked for raises and bigger assignments, and he got a promotion without a raise, as manager of the small branch office on Brannan, near the Southern Pacific depot. Saroyan understood the manager to say that, if he could increase business, he would get the raise he wanted, and he became a hard-working salesman, calling on nearby clients with Postal Telegraph call boxes and urging them to test the company's service. By Saroyan's accounting, business doubled, then tripled, and he hired a squad of eight messenger boys from the nearby Filipino ghetto. But no raise.

HENRY SAROYAN: At that time he was the youngest person ever to become a branch manager, and he did it very beautifully, made a lot of friends, made a lot of customers, but every once in a while, the branch supervisor used to call me, and he'd say, "I can't get ahold of your brother."

And I said, "Well, keep trying."

So, eventually, I'd get hold of Bill, and I'd say, "How come the supervisor couldn't reach you today?"

He said, "Hell, I'm a manager, so I did what managers do. I went out and played golf."

I said, "You don't play *golf*."

He said, "Well, the other guys did, so I went along with them."

He was a very independent-thinking person, even in those days. But he was very conscientious—up to a point when he felt that he had fulfilled his obligations. That was it.

He'd get annoyed at it, and he'd quit. He subsequently took over the branch office where I had worked, Market Street, and then subsequently there was a branch office on the corner of Powell and Market, and he worked there, too.

Mainly, he did not want the managerial responsibilities, so he'd just be a clerk or whatever, because he didn't want to be the boss man.

He wanted, as he had for ten years now, to be a writer, and he had made a bargain with himself not to sink to commercial writing, to journalism or advertising, in order to survive.

What did he write? "I wrote working-class Armenian writing in English. It was always bad writing, but I was stubborn."

In the summer of 1928, as he neared twenty, he decided that it was necessary to go to New York, where the books and magazines were published. "I was an immigrant, and all immigrants go to New York," he said, and Armenak *had* gone there, and people remained there who had known him.

Henry thought it was a stupid thing to do, and said so, but Uncle Mihran loaned Bill $200 for the trip. (Cross-country bus fare then was $38, and *Noneh* Lucy sewed most of the rest of the money into a sweater, safe in his suitcase.)

The bus trip crops up several times in Saroyan's early short-story collections. It took ten days, and included two key adventures. In Kansas, the bus plowed into a ditch and tilted over on its side, although no one was badly hurt; and in Cleveland, where Bill had to change buses, he passed the two hours in a burlesque theatre. "The revelation was blinding and gave a boy a baseball bat in his pants."

When he arrived in New York, his suitcase with the money sweater was missing—"lost, stolen or misdirected," as the clerk told him. He was given a claim check and stepped onto Fifth Avenue. It was almost midnight, and he had less than $2 in his pocket. He ran for a couple of blocks, downtown, and shortly was at Twenty-third Street, where a comforting YMCA sign was visible in the distance. He took a room there and bought a sandwich for a dime from the lunch-counter cook, who was just closing up. He had arrived.

The suitcase was found—in Memphis—and returned to him, but he also called on the freemasonry of Postal Telegraph for help, and his evident familiarity with the company and its policies earned him a job opening the tiny branch office on Warren Street in the wholesale produce district, a setting and atmosphere that would find their way into many a story, including the novel *Tracy's Tiger*.

He stood in the little office watching the snow with Peter Beaufrere, one of the messengers, a survivor of a year and a half in a mental ward.

"Pete, there's style for you, there's real style for you, that snow falling is the finest style I've ever seen, and if I could ever learn to write the way that snow is falling my fame and fortune would be made."

"Don't let anybody hear you talking that way or they'll take you to Central Islip," Beaufrere whispered.

Saroyan bought a brand-new portable typewriter, a Corona, for $60. He could have had a used one for half the price, but this was to be an important typewriter: "the machine on which I was to do the writing that would make my name." He wrote an essay called "The Mentality of Apes," based on his conversations with Beaufrere, and sent it to *The Brooklynite*, which never replied.

And, while gazing longingly at the Great Northern Hotel on Fifty-seventh, which he imagined as much grander than it would prove to be, he settled for a room at Forty-third and Seventh in what had to be one of New York's very last gaslit boardinghouses.

The great advantage of the room was its location beside the theatre district. He saw *Congai*, a failure of a play, because it was directed by a man named Rouben Mamoulian, and although Saroyan had not encountered the name in *Theatre Arts*, he recognized him to be a fellow Armenian. He paid fifty cents for standing room at O'Neill's *Strange Interlude*, whose length and seriousness convinced Saroyan that he could do better himself. He saw *Blackbirds of 1928*, with its Sissle and Blake score, and went to his favorite theatre of all, the Palace, as often as he could. The Palace still was dedicated to vaudeville, top balcony went for a quarter, and it was there that he saw James Barton, whom Cagney would hire as the old scout, Kit Carson, in the film version of *The Time of Your Life*.

On nights when he did not see a play, he explored every corner of the city by subway, by elevated train, by trolley, and on foot. Greenwich Village was a particular favorite, and so was the main branch of the New York Public Library, where he consulted the telephone directories and found that the widow of the Reverend Dr. William Stonehill, his namesake, was living in Brooklyn.

When he knocked at her door, she said, "You are Armenak Saroyan's son. Please come in." She told him about his father's work with Dr. Stonehill, and about the Church of All Nations, the Bowery mission where Armenak had both preached and worked as a janitor. Bill immediately went there to walk the same streets, a walk he would repeat during all of his New York years to come.

Finally, in January of 1929, the novelty of the city had worn off. He had spent the holidays three thousand miles from home, and he had suffered a bad bout of flu. Standing on the library steps, he was overcome with a homesickness so strong that it was a physical sensation. He returned to San Francisco immediately, cowed and embarrassed that he had not conquered American literature and the theatre in one fell swoop, but happy to be back.

The family were together again in San Francisco, in a third-floor flat on Sutter Street in the Western Addition. Takoohi hated the climb, so they moved a block away, to a flat on Divisadero, where Bill could watch pretty nurses at Mount Zion Hospital from his workroom window. He had a one-day-a-week job in a market, which paid him $5, but he outraged Takoohi and tried Henry's patience with his insistence that his main job was writing.

"Why aren't you writing?" Henry asked, when he saw Bill looking out the window.

"Henry, man does not live by writing alone."

A decade earlier, Takoohi had been infuriated when he spent $10 on a new wind-up phonograph. Now he spent $10 on a used baby grand piano, which he could not play. As often as not, bulghur and onions was all they had to eat. Henry was moving into accounting and management now with Postal Telegraph, Cosette was a legal secretary, and between them they were their mother's support. (Zabel wed early.) Bill's jobs were increasingly short-lived and trivial: a month in the downtown office of Cypress Lawn Cemetery Company; three days as staff writer for *Macaroni Review*, a tiny trade journal of the pasta industry.

In earlier years, Takoohi had struck Bill with a broomstick when her anger got the best of her. Now she fumed, wishing for him the relative dignity of a steady janitor's job. Willie already had visited Fresno friends who wound up in San Quentin prison for armed robbery, and he ran into another one day while touring the Third Street joints, and was interested to hear that he was a pimp. This was the sort of color that a writer could soak up and use. Bill Saroyan was no hoodlum, but he was, even when dead broke, a hopeless gambler. He even had a street name, the New York Kid, or, simply, New York. (He had lied about his origins one day when joining an ad hoc crap game between boxcars on the Embarcadero tracks.) Cousin Archie, Takoohi's troublesome hind-tit puppy, had moved to San Francisco and was witness to Bill's habit from the beginning, although only rarely placing a bet himself.

ARCHIE MINASIAN: At Breen's Rummy Parlor, we used to walk over there: "Arch, how much have you got?"
"I've got seven cents."
"Let me have it."
Mind you, seven cents. He's got *fifteen* cents.
He'd sit in a penny game. Half hour later, he's in the nickel game.

He won four or five dollars, we'd walk down Third Street from Breen's, and we'd get to Market, by the alley there, there's a bookie standing there, one of these sidewalk bookies. "Ah, who do you like, Arch?"

Listen, this is just the beginning of horse racing. I didn't know anything about it. I wish to hell I could remember the name of the first horse . . . I says, "Put a dollar on him."

"That's a lot of money, Arch. You don't know anything about the horses."

So he did bet the horse that I gave him—I can't think of the name now—and the horse came in. He collected thirty-four bucks. And I'll tell you this, that was the beginning of Archie's getting involved. And then it was Tanforan, it was Bay Meadows, it was Tanforan, it was Bay Meadows, it was Tanforan.

Parimutuel betting was legalized at the two Bay Area tracks in 1933, and Saroyan was there from the beginning, venturing out by train just to watch when he could not afford a one-dollar wager.

Soon after the family moved to a new flat near Golden Gate Park on Carl Street, Bill became a habitual gambler at the Menlo Club at No. 30 Turk Street.

HENRY SAROYAN: It would be two or three o'clock in the morning and my mother would come in and shake me. She said, "How can you sleep when your brother isn't home?"

I said, "Ma, he's a mature person. He can stay out till three o'clock."

"You get up, get dressed, catch a streetcar, go down and find him."

So I used to catch the N-car and go down to Third Street and go into these damned card places, and here would be Bill— *eventually*. I'd have to go to four or five of them before I'd find him. He would be sitting there with his cards in his hand, and I'd eventually tell him, "Bill, you know it's three o'clock in the morning? Your mother sent me to come get you. Come on, let's close this out and go home."

And then we'd go and stand on the corner for the N-car, to get us home. And we'd get home, and that would be it.

I'd, naturally, go to work the next day. But that didn't bother me as much as the fact that he had this strong urge to gamble. Where he got it from I have no idea. He just had a strong urge to gamble, and where he got it from, I don't know because, to the best of my knowledge, my father didn't gamble. He wasn't brought up in an environment where that would be accepted.

It only manifested itself in San Francisco, and, at that time, Bill was not working. He had left Postal and he was attempting to make his way in the writing field.

Whenever he got an urge to get something out of his system, he'd go down and sit at a card table and gamble until my mother would come and awaken me and tell me, "Hey, your brother isn't home. Go get him. How can you sleep?"

By the 1970s, the psychologists who study gambling were discovering that the great majority of heavy gamblers are men, and that the great majority of these men experienced a big win at the beginning of their gambling careers. If William Saroyan ever enjoyed such a win, it went unrecorded in the writings published by the time of his death. For many years, those who studied gambling were struck by the intelligence and capability of compulsive gamblers. In later years they have come to recognize other signs, such as chronic impatience with others,

Behind the door of the Menlo Club, you could name your game, but
generally was low-stakes poker, given the Depression. The San Fra
cisco *News-Call-Bulletin* blanked out the faces of the guilty in this ea
example of investigative reporting (above). Saroyan was a freque
habitué. (San Francisco Archive)

an enforced distance from one or both parents, and, perhaps most important of all, a feeling that they deserve to win—have been *chosen* to win.

Since the day he had stormed out of Uncle Aram's office, Bill had known which of them was the hero and which the villain, and his life had been a true trapeze act of hairbreadth escapes: Uncle Mihran in the Buick, the reappearance of his suitcase, the $34 horse payoff. It was the same when he sat down to his typewriter in his street-front room in the second-story flat on Carl Street. "For a long time I imagined that I would suddenly write something so right it would get me straight to the top, famous and rich."

It was in Uncle Aram's office, in 1932, that the dream began to crystallize. Aram remained a key leader of the Fresno community, something like an Armenian shadow mayor, and he was host to Armen Bardizian, a Boston visitor who wrote for, and helped to edit, the Armenian newspaper *Hairenik*. Bill had seen the paper in the backgammon parlors and had wondered what its columns said. Because of second-generation immigrants like Bill, *Hairenik* had begun to run several columns of material in English in each issue, and Bardizian invited him to contribute.

Saroyan later would speak of the pieces as essays, although they were collected and reviewed and praised as short stories. They are memoirs, sharp and direct and accurate in terms of feelings, if not in the facts, which sometimes had to be changed for the effects he wanted.

His first published work in *Hairenik* was poetry—poems to the Armenian tenor Shah-Mouradian, to Lake Van, and to the River Euphrates, written mostly in a clumping iambic pentameter with very predictable rhymes. These three poems appeared under his own name, but with the story "A Fist Fight for Armenia," which appeared in May, 1933, he was writing as Sirak Goryan, the surname of a fifth-century Armenian writer, and the story is a moving, naturalistic account of two Armenian boys trying to repay a racial slur. They lose the fight but achieve a moral victory.

The story that followed was too long for a single issue of the little paper. It had to be serialized over three issues in June, 1933, and this story, "The Broken Wheel," is written in the accomplished, clear tone of voice that is unmistakably Saroyan's own. It is really the first of the Aram Garoghlanian stories, and the whole family is there in the house on San Benito, described down to the cat and the volunteer peach trees, which grew from pits tossed to the border of the property. Aram and his Apperson appear (although not the incident of the doors), and the broken wheel of the title is the front wheel of the bicycle Henry and Willie had shared, which had buckled under their weight. "Don't you boys realize you've grown? You're much too big for one bicycle now."

In their own accounts, Whit Burnett and Martha Foley would delight in telling about their discovery of William Saroyan through the unsolicited single-spaced manuscript of "The Daring Young Man on the Flying Trapeze." The truth is that Saroyan arranged for his own discovery. He remained as avid a reader as ever of the latest books and authors winning praise, and he scanned Edward J. O'Brien's annual of the *Best Short Stories* for clues to taste-making editors as well as to that powerful editor's own tastes.

Burnett and Foley's *Story* magazine, begun while they were foreign correspondents in Europe, was intended as a showcase for exactly such new talent as Saroyan's. Indeed, their first idea had been to mimeograph batches of stories for limited circulation among editors, serving merely as agents, midwife and middleman, in what they perceived as a shrinking story market. Faulkner, Farrell, Stein, Mann, Conrad Aiken, William Carlos Williams—established authors struck by the taste and intelligence of *Story*—showered their work on Foley and Burnett. The magazine's effect on O'Brien's anthology was powerful and immediate, and their new role as literary kingmakers was solidified when Random House arranged to shelter them upon their return from Europe. Until then, the new publishing company begun by Bennett Cerf and Donald Klopfer had been mainly a reprint house. By supporting *Story*, Random House was supporting a magnet for the best new talent.

Saroyan knew all this. It was the sort of intelligence he gleaned during his long hours in the periodicals room of the San Francisco Public Library, and now he wrote his own applications for permission to live—two letters. One letter, signed by Sirak Goryan, 348 Carl Street, San Francisco, went to O'Brien, enclosing his first three *Hairenik* stories. The other, signed William Saroyan, went to Foley and Burnett at *Story*, enclosing the same three pieces and revealing the pseudonym. The third story, "The Barber's Apprentice," launched Saroyan's playful style, a straightforward delight in making words do whatever he wanted. It is at once a skilled updating of one of *Noneh* Lucy's pointless fables, whose morals explode later, and a parable of his own young life—the drunken young storyteller, apprenticed to a barber, who has no need at all for his services (a sort of benign Uncle Aram), and brought back to his senses by his brother, a mix of Henry and Archie. Yes, the Burnetts said, send something new. What did he have? He had an experimental fiction, which he thought of as a novel, called *Trapeze Over the Universe*. The most important story editors alive had asked him for something new, so he collapsed this novel into "The Daring Young Man on the Flying Trapeze," coming as close as he could to "something so right it would get me straight to the top, famous and rich." Thus the epicenter of his career, the gorgeously polished and complete "Trapeze," was not mailed away to a murky fate, but was written more or less to order for editors whose appetites had been carefully primed. They bought it instantly, and word soon followed that O'Brien had selected "The Broken Wheel" for his next volume.

This was the big win.

Were there more stories? Yes, oh yes, there would be. New stories? Give him a month and there would be thirty of them.

HENRY SAROYAN: I remember when he was writing those thirty stories that he wrote, he converted the front room on Carl Street, next to Poly High School, into his office, and while he was working there, he was so engrossed in what he did, when I came home from work, I'd poke my head in to say "Hi" to him, and on several occasions he'd say, "What the hell are you doing in here? Close the door and get out."

And then we'd sit down for dinner, and he'd say, "Hey, Hank, how long you been home." You know, that incident did not happen.

So he was quite serious about what he was doing, his writing, and quite encouraged when Martha Foley accepted the first one, and he kept on going and going.

He had sent manuscripts all over the world. He sent a manuscript to H. L. Mencken and it came back with a rejection slip, but after Martha Foley had published several of his stories in *Story* magazine, he submitted the same manuscript to Mencken's

Mercury, and they subsequently accepted it, and he was so indignant. "How come you wouldn't accept it originally, and now you do? Because I'm known?" And he says, "How the hell does a new writer ever get recognized in this place?" So he was quite disturbed at the policy of the _Mercury._ And I tried to assuage his feelings by telling him, "This is typical American business. You may think you're a success, but until you're accepted and somebody knows who you are, you're not going to get anyplace."

Now he was going places. He had Random House for his publisher and Saxe Commins for his editor. Ann Watkins was his agent. Ernst Reichl, most inventive of designers, was hired to create a striking package for the collected stories in _The Daring Young Man on the Flying Trapeze,_ each copy of that first book encircled with a band of silver as bright and untarnished as the career that it would launch in October, 1934.

2. NEW YORK, EUROPE, HOLLYWOOD

He had rehearsed what to do in case of fame by announcing himself, even at Breen's, as a writer, and writers were the attraction for him at Izzy Gomez's speakeasy, which was not far from the old Montgomery Block, where Twain and Harte had had offices. From the listings in the O'Brien anthology he had found the name of a small magazine, _Gyroscope,_ published down the Peninsula in Palo Alto. Bill submitted a poem and received a note of regret that _Gyroscope_ had suspended publication, but adding that its editor would like him to visit for tea. The editor was Yvor Winters, the distinguished critic and member of the English faculty at Stanford University. Saroyan's teacup rattled with his nervousness.

As the Sirak Goryan stories were published one by one in 1933, Saroyan made a reconnaissance into the literary world of Los Angeles and met its unlikely ringmaster, Stanley Rose, the hard-drinking bookstore man. Rose's back room was filled with young writers. John Fante, a year or so younger than Saroyan, already had been published in Mencken's _American Mercury,_ and there were other men at the be-

Saroyan was an animated model for the *News-Call-Bulletin* photographer when *The Daring Young Man on the Flying Trapeze* was published in 1934. These photos were taken in the Carl Street flat. He had his eye on the competition (below left): copies of *Look Homeward, Angel* and *Light in August,* both in Modern Library editions he is likely to have cadged from his publishers. (San Francisco Archive)

ginning of their careers, such as Jo Pagano and the author of *They Shoot Horses, Don't They?*, Horace McCoy.

With his slightly murky past, which included a jail term and a reputation for selling pornography, Rose was an unlikely guardian of literature in a city whose writers howled, quite often in Rose's own shop, at the daily desecration of the written word by the movie studios. One of the older writers in Rose's orbit was Jim Tully, a sort of proto-Kerouac in his ceaseless proletarian traveling, but a big complainer about Hemingway (who stole his simple declarative style) and Chaplin (who used his stuff without paying). Saroyan would make fun of Tully's bluster, which in some ways forecast Bill's own attitudes of later years.

Despite the fact that his grammar and speech were crude, Stanley Rose was not a stupid or undiscerning man. "He had a curiously good editorial sense," recalls Raymond Healy, who was Random House's man in Hollywood in the thirties. "He didn't read the new books religiously as they came in, but he read a lot." The ones he liked he put in the window, such as Nathanael West's and Bill Saroyan's, and while West was killed early without achieving during his lifetime the recognition he deserved, Saroyan's fame was immediate.

Saroyan was no stranger to his fellow writers in San Francisco, although they were a quieter and less colorful crowd than the boys in the back room at Stanley Rose's shop. While he was an enthusiastic collaborator in publicizing himself—the story is absolutely true, not a Bennett Cerf invention, that Saroyan peddled copies of his first collection aboard the Bay ferries—Bill also could be shy and tongue-tied, as he was at the literary afternoon arranged for him by a local gallery owner, Josephy Danysh. In their reminiscences of those days, his San Francisco colleagues recall a young man who wondered whether writing was all that he could do well, who pounded the piano according to some inner system of music, and who showed around sketches, "very bad sketches," as one anonymous artist remembered. "I told him that he was not as good a painter as he was a writer. . . . This discouraged him, I think, for writing was apparently no work for him at all, whereas painting and music required a lot of discipline."

To the political-minded critics, such as Granville Hicks, Saroyan was a fresh, new voice of proletarianism. To those who later would be antagonists, such as Clifton Fadiman, the freshness was enough to celebrate. All of them could find Sherwood Anderson in his work.

Curiously, as Saroyan's first biographer, Professor Howard Floan, has remarked, few of them could see the influence of Walt Whitman. But Saroyan's success was the sort that critics could neither create, destroy, nor at first even modulate. *The Daring Young Man on the Flying Trapeze* went through six hardcover printings, five of them before his second collection appeared.

The new stories came easily, and they were in demand. Skeptical critics wrote of a Saroyan cult, and while it was nothing like the later reigns of the fantasist Tolkien or the acidic absurdist Kurt Vonnegut— whose narrative voice owes some debts to Saroyan—the phenomenon of Bill's popularity bore comparison at the time with that of Thomas Wolfe. Saroyan had taken his place on the stage of American celebrity in the well-defined role he would polish and modify in the years ahead.

Now Saroyan could shake hands and talk with the men and women whose names had been familiar to him from the theatre and literary magazines and in the columns of the New York newspapers he had followed at the library back home in San Francisco. One man he longed to meet was the eccentric Joe Gould, reputedly at work on an "Oral History of the World," a massive chronicle of years of overheard conversations.

AL HIRSCHFELD: When he first came to New York, he came up to visit me. And at that time he told me that one man he wanted to meet in this town was a fellow by the name of Joe Gould. And I said, "I can't believe this, Bill, because in about half an hour from now, that front doorbell is going to ring, and it's going to be Joe Gould, because he comes here every Thursday night"—this was a Thursday night—"for his dollar." (He had a list of about thirty people who gave him a dollar a week to live on.)

And, sure enough, the doorbell rang, and it's Joe Gould: the long cigarette holder and the little briefcase, you know. And Bill just fell on the floor and *salaamed* and said, "He's the greatest man that ever lived," highfalutin praise. And he said, "You know, Joe, I must tell you that if it weren't for you, I wouldn't be a writer." He said, "The old *Dial* magazine had an article in it by you. I read it. I was a delivery boy then, and I decided to write." And Joe unpacked his little briefcase that he had. I always thought he had a sandwich in there, and he opened it, and it was a copy of the

Dial, the only published thing that he ever did in his life, and it was called "Polestar and Pyramid."

Bill asked him what he'd been doing, and Joe told him, this oral history. Bill said, "Well, who's going to publish this?"

"It's too good to be published."

Bill said, "Nah, that's ridiculous. I will get it published for you." So we got into a cab, went down to the Broadway Central Hotel, where Joe had a room—that he didn't live in, but for storing his manuscript. It was from the floor to the ceiling, the whole room. You'd just walk in between these papers—not publishable at all. But we picked up a few of the papers to read them, and it was complete nonsense, all kind of: "Oh, yes?" "Uh-huh." "Ooh." "You got a cigarette?" "Hiya, Joe." Handwritten, the whole thing. You could barely read it. *Millions* of pieces of paper.

Bill went to Random House the next day, to Bennett Cerf, told him about Joe Gould. Bennett said, "Listen, if it's everything you say it is, we will certainly give him a contract to publish it."

We go down to the Village the next night, and there's Joe holding forth at the end of a bar in Minetta Lane, and we said, "Joe, we got a publisher for you. Random House is going to publish your book." There were drinks on the house, great celebration. And as the evening wore on, I got Bill aside and I said, "You know, you may not be doing this fellow a favor, because now he's an undiscovered genius, and you're going to make him another unsuccessful writer." I said, "I'd just let it alone, see what he does."

The following Thursday, he didn't show up for his dollar. He never showed up again. About six months went by, and I went down to the Village again, and there's Joe. And I said, "Joe, what happened to you?" He said, "I told you. Those bastards with all their big ideas. They don't want to publish literature."

Aside from the title "Polestar and Pyramid," which, briefly, would be the working title of *The Beautiful People*, Gould's main contribution to Saroyan's work became the phrase "No foundation, all the way down the line," which the Arab mutters throughout *The Time of Your Life* as a dour commentary on the barroom, and the world in general. In 1935, however, the theatre remained in Saroyan's future.

His royalties made it possible for him to travel, and he set out for Europe, Russia, Armenia. In New York he stayed, as he had dreamed of doing, at the Great Northern Hotel, recognizing its increasing shabbiness immediately, but sticking by his decision. He found his room a comfortable place to write his first play, after reading in the *Times* the mistaken report that he was at work on a drama. And it was during this trip that he made a lifelong enemy for himself, gossip columnist Walter Winchell, who talked and, somehow, wrote out of the side of his mouth about Broadway and all its inhabitants. "So you're Walter Winchell?" Saroyan mistakenly cracked, unimpressed as they were introduced at the Stork Club. He could read the anger in Winchell's eyes, and he would be able to read it later in reviews and columns in the years to come.

He went to Europe aboard the *Berengaria*, albeit in a four-man room, where his companions in third class included a Serbian peasant returning to his dying mother. In London, a bed-and-breakfast room was arranged not far from the offices of Faber and Faber, where his publisher, Geoffrey Faber, asked him to tea. It was an important meeting for Saroyan's publishing future, his first encounter with Frank Morley, who, later in the thirties, would become his American editor at Harcourt, Brace. Saroyan knew that he was brash and loud in this encounter. He thought, "They like me, it must be that I am really a good writer and they don't mind that I am making so much noise."

This trip was a rehearsal for his later life in Europe. He looked longingly at the Savoy Hotel, where he would not begin to stay until 1939, and where *The Adventures of Wesley Jackson* would be written. In Paris, he literally ran from sight to sight, including the Hotel Scribe, and was unsurprised when a girl materialized beside him. She would not do, but could she direct him to a really good bordello? She did, a house in the Opéra district, and Saroyan would remember it as the best he ever visited, although he never could find it again. In Helsingfors he mentioned to a clerk in a music shop his affection for Sibelius, for *Finlandia*, one of the records he played as he wrote. She telephoned the composer, who insisted that he visit. It was a forty-kilometer cab ride away, and the composer's nephew, home from Stanford, was interpreter for the uncomfortable encounter, which included whiskey, cigars (Bill did not light his), and strained silences. "We hear 'Valse Triste' a lot on the radio in America," Saroyan informed him. Sibelius groaned. "Drink whiskey," he told Saroyan.

Bill wrote the incident up that night while the embarrassment was fresh, and "Finlandia" was published in his next collection, along with other undisguised—or only slightly disguised—travel reports.

But one report that was missing was written in Moscow and left in his room, never to reappear, and Saroyan came to believe that his frank comments about the Russian people in that story were the reason he was forbidden to meet, as he had wished, with Maxim Gorky. (He admitted that he wished to visit Gorky as a living monument, not to interrogate him, as he had foolishly hoped to do with Sibelius.) But he met a fellow Armenian, the poet Yeghishe Charentz, who would be imprisoned and die in Yerevan a few years later.

As Saroyan continued to Tiflis, Georgia, and into Caucasoid Armenia, his people's adopted and official homeland, he was stricken by a severe digestive upset. It was not the usual traveler's *malaise*, but Saroyan did not know that. Soon after he returned to San Francisco, he traveled to Mexico City by train, the symptoms in abeyance, but later that fall they returned in force. Saroyan had rented a small office in which to write, but on this morning early in October, 1935, he went by taxicab to St. Francis Hospital, where Dr. Harold Fraser diagnosed the same condition that had killed Bill's father, Armenak: appendicitis. There was no delay about surgery. It happened immediately, and when Saroyan awoke from anesthesia at eleven that morning, he felt that he had been to the land of death and back.

In the little office, just as he had done during his travels, Saroyan continued to write story after story, almost effortlessly, and just as easily got them published, at least in the magazines. But he quarreled now with Random House, where Saxe Commins disagreed with Saroyan's plans for his second anthology, *Inhale and Exhale*. Saroyan wanted it to be a compendium of literally everything he had written since *The Daring Young Man on the Flying Trapeze*, and he was angry to learn that he could not have his way. *Inhale and Exhale*, as large and thorough as it was at five hundred pages, disappointed him in its incompleteness and disappointed Commins, Cerf, and Klopfer in its sales. The first printing went quickly, but the second sat in the stores.

Saroyan also was having problems with his representatives, Pat Duggan and Harold Matson, whom he followed when they left Ann Watkins's agency to set up their own shop in 1936. They had sold to *Esquire* the key Aram story, "The Summer of the Beautiful White Horse," for $200. Saroyan told Matson that *Esquire* was too rich for such a low fee; $500 would do—no less. Matson responded that the story was in type, that $200 was Arnold Gingrich's top price at his then-young magazine, and that to press Gingrich further would imperil other Matson-Duggan clients with a valuable market. Saroyan yielded, but gave instructions that nothing of his was to be shown to *Esquire* again.

Bill already was wary of the magazine for printing an attack on him by Ernest Hemingway in a piece called "Notes on Life and Letters." Hemingway, whose sense of literary humor was so slight as makes no difference, had been prickled by a little passage in "Seventy Thousand Assyrians" in *The Daring Young Man on the Flying Trapeze*. "I have a faint idea what it is like to be alive," Saroyan had written. "This is the only thing that interests me greatly. This and tennis. I hope some day to write a great philosophical work on tennis, something on the order of *Death in the Afternoon*." Saroyan's tennis, in fact, was much like his piano playing, a matter of slamming according to some inner light, and not even his brief romance with the international tennis champion Helen Wills had done much for his game. Saroyan was far less serious about tennis than Hemingway was about bullfighting, and Hemingway was unimpressed by the disclaimer Saroyan inserted into the story: "It may seem to some sophisticated people that I am trying to make fun of Hemingway. I am not. *Death in the Afternoon* is a pretty sound piece of prose. . . . Even when Hemingway is a fool, he is at least an accurate fool. He tells you what actually takes place and he doesn't allow the speed of an occurrence to make his exposition of it hasty. This is a lot."

Hemingway was not assuaged by praise tossed in among Saroyan's jokes. His attack on Saroyan was a tirade:

Anybody can write like somebody else. But it takes a long time to get to write like yourself and then what they pay off on is having something to say. Listen, Mr. Saroyan, maybe I'm a little drunk but this is all right. See? We were all hungry, see? We all hocked our typewriters, see? Only we had something else to write about at the time besides ourselves. . . . You're bright. So don't get sore. But you're not that bright. You don't know what you're up against. You've only got one new trick and that is that you're an Armenian. . . . And we've seen them come and go. Good ones too. Better ones than you, Mr. Saroyan. We've seen them go a long way and we've seen them not come back and nobody even asked where they was gone. They forget quick, Mr. Saroyan. . . . Also your ear isn't so good. And a good ear in a writer is like a good left hand in a fighter. Do I make myself clear? Or would you like me to push your puss in.

Sensing a marketable feud, Gingrich had offered Saroyan a chance to respond to Hemingway's attack in print, and Bill had turned him down, choosing to reply to Hemingway by letter. "Get in there and knock the critics for a loop," Hemingway had answered, and there matters stood until hostilities were renewed in London and Paris during the war. In the sixties, when Saroyan's public career was near its lowest ebb, Gingrich's magazine would publish an article with a more devastating effect on Saroyan, a memoir by Budd Schulberg, whose friendship with Saroyan had begun just as Bill's first collection had been published.

BUDD SCHULBERG: It started when I first saw his stories in *Story* magazine. That was when I began to read him and sort of wait for those stories, and I was enchanted with them. I went to San Francisco with my wife, quite a character. We went and looked up Bill, and he was, of course, totally glad to meet us. I believe I remember having his address, knocking on his door and his calling out a window. We stayed a couple of days, hit the bars and talked a lot, and he read stories out loud. We went to bars where he seemed to be well-known, played little tiny bets on the horses.

When we left, we offered to loan him a little money, and he was too proud and wouldn't take it. But my wife actually put a dollar in his pocket, one dollar, because he had some horse he wanted to bet. (In those days you didn't have to bet a whole dollar, you could bet fifty cents, and he didn't have two dimes to put together.) He kind of talked about it after a while.

By 1936, Saroyan was in much better financial shape, but his quarrel with Random House brought him together with his young friend and admirer Schulberg in a failed publishing experiment. Saroyan's left-over stories would be the initial offering of the Stanley Rose Press, but Schulberg and Rose found themselves overwhelmed, as Random House had been, not only by the sheer number of Bill's uncollected pieces, but by the high percentage that were difficult to accept—or to publish—as fiction. Some were political. When Schulberg pointed out to Saroyan that he might profitably read Veblen, Bill replied, "No, I'd rather not read Veblen, or Engels, or Nietzsche or anybody else like that." Why? Schulberg wanted to know. "Because how do I know that I won't have those same ideas myself, and if I read it somewhere else first it might keep me from writing it on my own."

Schulberg and his wife were ardent progressives in the thirties, and Schulberg recalls Saroyan accompanying them to a rally where André Malraux spoke for the Loyalist cause in the Spanish Civil War. (Saroyan also surprised the Schulbergs by signing the petition to qualify the Communist candidates for the ballot in 1936. Saroyan had been amused by the American Communists he met in Moscow the year before and never was passionately political, much less a Communist. Schulberg analyzed his willingness to sign as a way of helping an underdog while thumbing his nose at the election laws.)

Saroyan's resubmission of stories already rejected by Random House led to his final break with that first publisher, and while Schulberg's publishing experiment with Stanley Rose did not pan out, there was a short interim collection, *Three Times Three*, published by a group of University of Southern California students, whom Saroyan was willing to help with a gift of his manuscripts. But with royalties dwindling from *The Daring Young Man on the Flying Trapeze* and the occasional gambling binges cutting into his magazine income, Bill needed money. Not for the last time (he would do the same, later, for Scott Fitzgerald), Schulberg got his older writing friend a job in the family business, the movies.

BUDD SCHULBERG: My father had his own little studio and company, and then I got the idea that my father should—talked to my father about it, sort of approached him and suggested that he hire Bill at $250 a week.

My father was very literary, had been a writer himself, and was open to that. He had read Bill's stories, liked them a lot, and thought the dialogue in those stories was fresh, so he thought that Bill could really make a contribution. It wasn't a hard sell. "Great, it sounds great. Bring him down." Down he came.

He wrote very good stuff in those scripts. My father did a picture called *A Doctor's Diary*, and he wrote this amazing little monologue for the doctor, to the newborn baby, which was later published as a short story, "Okay, Baby, This Is the World."

That's the kind of thing he would do, write very effectively, write his best work—I mean, as well as he could write—into the scripts. He was better jacking them up that way, giving them some extra quality, than actually writing the whole thing.

Bill had some ideas of his own about doing pictures. He did write some from scratch, but I don't think they were produced. There was one football story I remember that had a very good idea in it, but I don't think there was any one, intact work of Bill's produced.

We all hung out at Lucy's Restaurant on Melrose, which was right near the studio, sort of a hangout for the Paramount people. And my father had a big table there where he sat with all his friends. So Bill did come up against other Hollywood writers at Lucy's, at my father's house, and I remember him quite distinctly at B. P.'s big house in Benedict Canyon. There were weekend gatherings, without being set up. They were just there, people showed up: poker games, lots of card playing.

Two hundred and fifty dollars a week in those days, it was like getting twelve-fifty, fifteen-hundred a week today. He started to branch out, started to gamble more, and there were quite a few attractive girls: a lot of actresses, a woman who worked in a bookstore, a very nice girl—and I can't think of her name—whom it seemed . . . *seemed* . . . that he was serious about.

He was biding his time, planning, he said, to save money. He was going to wait for the right horse, bet the whole bundle and then go off. It was the most harebrained financial scheme I'd ever heard of, but then he said he'd probably go off somewhere, like New Orleans, and write something.

Budd Schulberg accompanied Saroyan to the track the day that $1,000 had been accumulated and all the signs were right. Bill had studied the charts and decided on a horse that Schulberg, in his retellings of that day, calls Shasta Rose. As they waited in line to bet, an old handicapper heard them discussing Shasta Rose and shook his head no, "a silent, almost imperceptible negation." The old man pointed at Missouri Boy, and Saroyan followed his lead, betting everything on the stranger's horse. Missouri Boy was ahead by six lengths when he stumbled and broke his leg. Shasta Rose won, paying in the neighborhood of seventy-five hundred. Bill thanked the old man. "Only God could have known he was going to break his leg."

Saroyan had disliked assignments like *A Doctor's Diary*, and the elder Schulberg was unimpressed with his original screenplays, such as *Man Alive* and *Daily News*. But the seeds of Saroyan's dramatic career were growing. Schulberg halfway recalls that Saroyan wanted the money for the New Orleans trip in order to write a play there, and *Three Times Three* contained "The Man with His Heart in the Highlands," a short story written a year earlier, in the fall of 1935, which would become his first produced play. It also contained a vignette in which the Saroyan figure, as telegraph messenger, delivers a death message and stays to spend an hour with the bereaved mother, going over her scrapbooks. It became a key scene in both novel and screenplay versions of *The Human Comedy*. And the very night before he had flown to Hollywood, Saroyan had gone to a bordello in San Francisco. The girl he chose was simple, pretty, lonely, and he lingered with her and smoked, drank, and made love all night. She spoke in a husky voice and described her upbringing in a Polish-Lithuanian family in the Midwest: Kitty Duval of *The Time of Your Life*. They explained themselves to each other. He was off to Hollywood the next day and—the whiskey talking—he offered her a chance to go with him. "I'll never see you again," she said to him, and, knowing it was true, he had to fight back tears. The girl joined the others in Saroyan's gallery of as-yet-unwritten characters.

It was easy to make fun of what Hollywood did to writers. That was the table talk every lunch and dinner at Musso and Frank's grill down the street from Stanley Rose's shop. The agents occupied the bottom rungs of the writers' world view, and Saroyan remembered one who asked Stanley for a tip on new novelists.

"There's this Boston man, Nat Hawthorne," Rose said, handing him *The Scarlet Letter*. "I think there's a good movie in it, and I know just the right boy to do the adaptation."

"Why not get Nat himself?"

"He won't leave Boston."

Agent Jim Geller of the William Morris office, a one-time writer himself, got Saroyan a new writing contract as he parted ways with Schulberg. It was for even more money, $300 a week at Harry Cohn's Columbia, where he was paired with Dalton Trumbo on the task of converting three stories by *Saturday Evening Post* writer Clarence Buddington Kelland into a comedy. Neither Saroyan nor Trumbo wished to collaborate, so they reached a sporting proposition, flipped a coin, and Trumbo did the work while Saroyan collected three months' salary. He returned to San Francisco $40 ahead.

3. THE TIME OF YOUR LIFE

"No more *tsoor* Willie," Archie Minasian noticed. The money and the publicity had taken care of that, and it was likely as not Archie himself who had *tsoor* hung around his neck by Takoohi, especially when he arrived at the Carl Street flat to accompany Bill on a day at the races. Archie and his mother lived only a few doors away now, and when Takoohi mistakenly attacked her young nephew on his home ground, in Parantsie's kitchen, Archie shouted at her to leave, shouted so loud and long that she did leave. He thought it would be a final break with the Saroyan cousins, but Bill himself arrived soon afterward to marvel at his daring.

Bill had a new publisher now, the distinguished firm of Harcourt, Brace, and while his old colleagues at Random House gloated that his first two collections for the new editors were far from bestsellers, they sold well enough. The agents Matson and Duggan were handling requests for commissioned articles, radio scripts, even screenplay work, although Saroyan rejected the latter.

In San Francisco, Saroyan was easy in any society. There was a mistress of sorts, a vivacious and intelligent professional woman with a good view of the Golden Gate from her smart apartment. (Saroyan was one of those considered important enough to have taken the elevator to the top of one of the towers of the sweeping new bridge that spanned that strait.) When famous writers came to town, as did Carl Sandburg, it was essential that Saroyan meet them. He was a tourist attraction himself.

On a visit to Fresno, Bill went downtown to see his Uncle Aram and was distressed that the elevator operator in the Mattei Building was an old classmate, an exact contemporary who had been known as the biggest comic at Emerson School. What had made one of the school comedians an elevator operator, the other a world-famous writer? Saroyan left the meeting by the stairway, not the elevator.

Soon, work would begin on a new house for his mother and sister, a place that would cling to Red Rock Hill in the Sunset District. In the old flat on Carl Street, next to the noisy schoolyard of Polytechnic High, Saroyan worked with the windows of his upstairs front room wide open, no matter the weather, which usually was cold. He tossed his Chesterfield butts right onto the street. Above his oak work table, still painted bright blue with pink trim, a big chart tracked the forty or so stories circulating among Saroyan, his agents, and the magazines and anthologists.

"I had plenty of money, it just kept coming in, but if it began to let up I just sat down at the typewriter and worked a few days or a few weeks, and again the money began to come in." Where was the Saroyan novel? This was the plaint of the critics who had begun, one by one, to drift away from his side. There was none, but the plays were beginning. Saroyan had converted "The Man with His Heart in the Highlands" into a one-act play at the suggestion of the editor of *The One-Act Play Magazine*, and when the play was finished and anthologized, Saroyan expanded it into a piece that would run about an hour. Through his agents it reached the Group Theatre.

IRWIN SHAW: They asked me to write a curtain raiser for it. I went up to the country, and in two days I wrote a curtain raiser, a one-act play, but it was so different in style from Bill's play that they said they'd just put on Bill's play by itself, which they did. And my play was done by other people and is still being done, a little play called *The Shy and the Lonely*. So Bill and I became friends.

It was a group of *actors*. They were left, you know—very liberal, very liberal—and they would look for things like *Awake and Sing!* or *Waiting for Lefty*, but they were not interested in propaganda per se. They were interested in the art of acting, so much so that they scorned playwrights. That's one of the reasons why they didn't hold together. Sidney Kingsley, who gave them *Men in White*, which they did brilliantly, wouldn't give them another play because he felt that they scorned him.

I was there the opening night of *My Heart's in the Highlands*. Lovely. Lovely production. It was at the Guild Theatre. Bobby Lewis did it, very stylized and lovely, the perfect production, wonderful cast. Sidney Lumet was in it, playing the boy, and he was a very good child actor.

Saroyan's nearly formless tale of the old Scot with the bugle took form in the hands of Bobby Lewis, a Group actor who would become an important director with a special talent for making fantasy work (*Brigadoon, The Teahouse of the August Moon*). John Mason Brown wrote that it was "not a play that says a precise thing in a clear-cut manner. Yet its whole point and glory is that it *does* something to you—some-

thing poignant and exquisite and indefinable." The five-night showcase run was extended, and while it closed before summer, a financial
failure, it announced a new voice in American theatre.

To Saroyan, 1939 would be remembered as "one of the enormous
years of my life," so enormous that he once considered writing a full-
length memoir dealing with the world's unwilling movement into war
and his own struggle in the theatre. More than twenty years later,
Saroyan would tell his son that writing and acting were different versions of the same thing, and in the spring of 1939 Saroyan was a writer
who acted, soaking up the attention and striking poses. As *My Heart's
in the Highlands* folded, he pouted that he would leave the theatre after
his debut effort.

LILLIAN GISH: George Nathan wanted to bring him up to have
dinner with me. At that time, I lived on East Fifty-seventh. I had
the penthouse, and Mother was downstairs.

And they came up, and I was fascinated by his mind and ideas,
and during dinner I asked him how long he took to write a play,
and he said, "Ohhh, about thirty-six hours."

And I thought: "Hah! Isn't that astonishing?" (It shut *me* up.)
And I listened to them talk and thought about it. And I heard
Saroyan say that his last play had such bad notices that he was
never going to do another one.

And I thought, "This talent, this man—not another play, when
we need him so badly?"

So when dinner was over and they were ready to leave, I said,
"Mr. Saroyan, I'm sorry to tell you, but I'm not going to let you
leave this apartment tonight. You see, I'm in a penthouse and I
have the key to the elevator. My mother lives downstairs and I
can stay down there—and I *will* send your food up. But if it only
takes you thirty-six hours to write a play, I am not going to let
you out until you write that play."

Well, they laughed, but they found out I was serious. We
talked about it awhile, and I said, "If God gave you a talent like
that, and you don't use it, He'll punish you. You just can't do
that, and we need plays too badly."

He said, "Well, all right, then. I'll take your word for it. I'll
write another play."

And I said, "All right, then, I'll let both of you go home."

JULIE HAYDON: He expected to take Broadway by storm, and he should have. The play was worthy of it, but only two critics really endorsed the play, and George was one of them and John Mason Brown the other. The day after the closing of the play it was announced in the *New York Times* that "William Saroyan is brushing the dust of Broadway from his boots forever, never to return!"

And I always spoke to Nathan at noon every day. That day, George said, "You read the *Times* this morning." He said, "William Saroyan must be convinced that he stay in New York and write another play at once. The theatre needs him!" And he'd already telephoned Saroyan and made arrangements to meet him at George's corner table at "21." (You'd enter the bar, turn to the left, see the great red banquette, spacious and inviting, and the table where Nathan always sat with his friends. And on the wall above it, the plaque saying "George Jean Nathan, his corner." Except it was on the other side of the room at that time—on the other side of the bar, in the corner.)

Anyway, *The Time of Your Life* was written because George invited Saroyan to his corner table that afternoon when he was going to brush the dust of Broadway from his boots forever, and Saroyan admitted that he had another play brewing under his hat, but that he needed a definite production commitment or he just couldn't transcribe it to paper. So Nathan immediately thought of Eddie Dowling, and he decided he'd bring the two men together under the most favorable circumstances possible, and that would be at the Critics Circle award dinner. But that would be a bit of a problem because, to be invited, you had to have an award.

He was president of the Critics Circle and sure of his own powers of persuasion, and during the voting—although he knew that Saroyan's play *My Heart's in the Highlands* hadn't even been mentioned in the critics' earlier discussions—he decided to give that play a one-third vote. And that aroused a discussion among the critics of a play they had otherwise ignored. And finally he convinced the other fellows that Saroyan should be given a citation as the most promising young playwright of the season, and then he would be invited to the dinner. And now all he had to do was to see that Dowling sat opposite Saroyan at the table, which he did.

EDDIE DOWLING: He sat across from me at the Algonquin at the Critics Circle dinner. I read it. Nathan gave me a copy of it, and I had read the little play and I liked it very much. I said to him, "Mr. Saroyan, I'm glad that you got some recognition here tonight. I think you write beautifully. And if you ever write another play I'll buy it sight unseen."
  He said, "Do you mean that?"
  I said, "I certainly do."
  He said, "I need money. I'll be in to see you in a week."

The setting was very much like Izzy Gomez's joint, and Kitty Duval was the little farmgirl hooker of the proverbial night before Hollywood. The benign meddler, Joe, whose source of income never is explained, was a little like Saroyan, still bemused at his own ability to spin words into money, money that could vanish in huge quantities in a single phone call to a bookie, or money that was, as he wrote the play, building his mother a new house. When Joe sends his major domo out to buy little toys to play with at his habitual table in the barroom, he will not explain his motive. But The Coon Jigger, while written without reference to race and played by a white actor, is there as big as life. The Arab's repeated statement, "No foundation, all the way down the line," was lifted directly from one of the few published fragments by Joe Gould.

Another meeting, at "21," was arranged between Saroyan, Dowling, and Nathan, who also saw to it that Julie Haydon was there. Saroyan always said that he wrote Kitty Duval with Lillian Gish in mind, but he was always willing to listen to Nathan.

JULIE HAYDON: They were sitting and they were talking along, and they didn't notice me. I just sat and I listened. They were saying farewell, and Saroyan had delivered his manuscript to Eddie Dowling and the Theatre Guild, who were co-producing. Just as we were about to leave, Nathan casually glanced at me and said to Bill, "Here's your Kitty Duval."
  And Bill said, "Yes!"
  I couldn't believe that I didn't dream it.

So then we all sauntered out into the glorious sunset. I'll never forget it. It had turned everything to gold. The whole street was shining—we were all made of gold. And Bill turned, said to me, "Could you lower your voice about two octaves to play the part of Kitty?" And I piped, "Oh, yes, I'd be so delighted. I'd do anything to play Kitty."

The Theatre Guild—specifically the Guild's Theresa Helburn—thought Haydon was exactly wrong, especially after recent, saintly roles. "*Ju-lie*, you know you cahn't play that part," Haydon recalls Helburn's saying. To acquire the voice that Saroyan had demanded, the young actress went to the Lower East Side and sought out an old Polish woman to coach her.

Shortly after the Critics Circle award, the cast and crew of *My Heart's in the Highlands* had staged a ceremony of their own, in an Armenian restaurant, honoring the work as "the best Saroyan play of the year," and praising its director, Bobby Lewis, who was now hired to direct the new Saroyan play.

Saroyan was content, at first, to step back from his brainchild. He went to Ireland that summer, returning at his agents' behest, not because of *The Time of Your Life*, but, rather, to discuss an abortive musical revue project with Vincente Minnelli. His new house was ready in San Francisco, and, having arranged that his cousin Ross Bagdasarian would be discovered by Lewis, Dowling, and company, he watched the play's progress from afar, until warnings from Ross brought him east by airplane. He arrived at a New Haven tryout almost unparalleled in the annals of theatrical disaster.

EDDIE DOWLING: We open in New Haven for a weekend—Friday and Saturday, I think it was, just two days. We dress-rehearsed on Thursday, and we opened on a Friday night, and it was a frightful, frightful experience. We opened to frightful notices. It was the weekend of the Harvard-Yale football game, and they were all half-plastered. The scenery fell in on us. Oh, it was a terrible thing.

You can always tell the kind of trouble you're in when nobody comes back. My family were there—my wife, my daughter, some other members of my family, my boy. There were a lot of them there, but nobody came back, not a soul.

Julie Haydon and Eddie Dowling would team again (Saroyan's own *Hello, Out There*, Tennessee Williams's *The Glass Menagerie*), but the dream Joe asks about in *The Time of Your Life* was right on stage for the audience. (Vandamm)

Saroyan poses warily with the two key members of the Theatre Guild, Theresa Helburn and Lawrence Langner, and the distrust that erupted into open warfare seems plainly written on the faces of the playwright and his producer Langner. (Vandamm)

Gene Kelly was discovered beside the Langners' suburban swimming pool and soon created the role of Harry the Hoofer in *The Time of Your Life*. But, in this scene from the 1940 revival, it is his brother, Fred, in the part. Veteran character actor Henry Jones is at right. (Vandamm)

I was sitting in this little dressing room all by myself, feeling sorry for myself, just off the stage two steps down, a little tiny bit of a thing, just room enough for one chair and a mirror on a makeup shelf and some lights around the mirror—nothing else. Everything was quiet. The audience had gone. By the time the curtain had come down there wasn't hardly anybody there except I guess Mr. Shubert and the Guild and my family and the ushers and a few others—that's all. And I knew it was a dreadful failure.

And across the bare stage—of course, there's nothing as eerie as a dark theatre, late, not a sound . . . and you hear a pair of squeaking shoes come across. Mr. Shubert was a dapper little man, and he had an odd-shaped head and he never could get a hat that would fit him properly, and he always wore derbies, hard hats you know, and he had a slight lisp. He was a very reticent little man, very quiet, dapper as could be. It was him with the squeaking shoes coming across the stage, but I never looked up. I kept looking right in the mirror in front of me, fearing the worst, you know, and then I heard these two steps come down and then quiet. And I looked in the mirror and he looked in the mirror, and he said very quietly, "Eddie, I don't want to put no more money in this."

So I said, "Mr. Lee, it wasn't that bad."

He said, "I'll see you in New York," and he was gone.

Thornton Wilder was next to visit Dowling. "This thing has great beauty. It needs direction, Eddie, and it needs a new production, and it needs several new members of the cast," he said, but he urged that the play be saved. The Guild, Dowling's wife, the great majority of cool heads who had been out front voted for a mercy killing, but it was, again, Nathan who prevailed in the all-night meeting at the Taft Hotel. The play was due Monday night at the Plymouth in Boston. Bobby Lewis was out, Dowling would direct—along with Saroyan himself.

AL HIRSCHFELD: Bobby Lewis had—a cocktail bar. And Bill said, "That's not right, I want a bar, a regular bar," and Boris Aronson, who designed it very carefully, said, "It's not that easy. . . ."

Bill said, "The hell with that. I'm going out and get a *bar*!" And he went out and bought a bar. And put it onto the stage. And

Boris, being Bobby's friend, left—although he greatly admired Bill. And Bill put a bar on stage, a real bar. What he wanted, how he had visualized the thing.

And it worked. It *worked*.

In his memoirs, Bobby Lewis cites a letter Saroyan had written from San Francisco, blessing the director's plan to stylize the production in the same way he had treated *My Heart's in the Highlands*. "Be a poet," Saroyan had told him. Julie Haydon recalls that Lewis had directed the play with Dowling's character, Joe, as the quiet hub of a wheel with the other characters spinning around him, faster and at a distance. Despite Lewis's removal, this and other key ideas stayed in the minds of surviving cast members, although there were wholesale changes— Gene Kelly replacing Martin Ritt as Harry the Hoofer, Bill Bendix in for Karl Malden. Lawrence Langner of the Theatre Guild, an inventor in private life, was recruited to design the pinball machine whose patriotic payoff climaxes the play, the single fantastic element in a setting (by Watson Barratt) that now was far closer to Izzy Gomez's dismaying dilapidation than the Italian restaurant with trelliswork and twinkling lights that Aronson had confected. On one dreadful Boston night as the changes were being installed, the lighting men dropped in new amber gels without burning them in, and everyone on stage looked like a jaundice patient.

Saroyan joined Dowling at the side of the stage, eating the pears that everyone connected with the production remembers. (He had wanted grapes or apples and found the available pears "mushy and punk," but, as he tossed the cores into the footlight trough, to the crew, they became nearly as famous as Cézanne's pears.) With Nathan back at work in New York, viewing other people's plays, it was the producers, especially the Guild's Langner, with whom Bill now clashed.

"What the hell is the matter with the actors?" Saroyan shouted at Langner one night.

"Do you really want to know?"

"Yes. What is it?"

"You are what is the matter with the actors. If you'll keep out of the theatre the next three days, we will be able to bring this play into good condition. Otherwise, we won't."

Celeste Holm, one of the replacements, had been cast as Mary L., the closest thing to a love interest provided for Eddie Dowling's Joe.

She enters in the last moments of Act One and for the first ten minutes or so of the second act plays a tender conversation, which was in no way a conventional love scene. It was one of the acting challenges that makes the play's duets and solo turns staple items of scene work in all drama schools. Joe's attempts to guess the woman's name from the "M.L." on her handbag almost imperceptibly becomes something deeper—and then Mary L. must leave. It was Celeste Holm's first Broadway role, and she won it in an open call held by the Guild in New York on Columbus Day, 1939.

CELESTE HOLM: They were all very good, and I kept listening, wondering what it was they weren't doing, so I tried something quite different, and I got it.

You see, he had written it like an interview: "Is it—Madge Laubowitz?" whatever it was, from the initials on the bag. So, in something like twelve minutes, fifteen minutes, the last line is "Would it surprise you very much if I told you that I loved you?" And she says, "No." And I had to get there. And the point is the kids were playing it moment to moment, and it was realistic, but it didn't add up. So I realized that when two people are discussing something that they both love very much it's as though they're loving each other, and so I played it that way. They talked about Paris, about having been in love. I created it as though it *had* been them.

I went to Boston that night and I went in about three days later. And I never had any direction at all. I read the scene, Dowling said, "Learn it that way," and that was it. I don't think I had more than one conversation with Saroyan in my life. I always thought he was afraid of me. (He talked to some of the *guys*.) He had a morose quality that I think hid a very tender nature.

Miss Holm recalls the cast's confusion when Barratt's realistic set was dropped into place with little notice, and the Boston audiences seemed to like the play even less as the changes were made. Only Elliot Norton of the *Boston Post* was encouraging, and from New York, Nathan wrote a *Newsweek* article condemning the way the Guild had wrecked Saroyan's beautiful script.

EDDIE DOWLING: As an example of how bad it was, the old priest who baptized and confirmed me was a cousin of my mother's. He was retired now. And he was living quite well. He was a great theatre buff. He came out and all he said to me was, "Eddie Dowling, I'm ashamed. I'm ashamed of you and I'm ashamed of this play. I never thought I'd live to see a relative of mine sit on a stage and hear a frightful man say to a little girl, 'You're like all two-dollar whores in the morning.' Now," he said, "please don't ever tell anybody that I christened and baptized you. I'll never come to see you again." And away he went.

In New York, the feuding between Saroyan and the Guild intensified. The playwright was dissatisfied with the sightlines at the theatre, and Langner later would tell people that Saroyan had proposed pushing out the walls of the house. Nathan was on hand to make suggestions, and he became convinced that the short scene set in Kitty Duval's bedroom should take place, instead, on a small stagelike area of the saloon setting. The idea was to avoid slowing down the play. Joe's speech on the evils of money already was out at the insistence of the Guild and with Dowling's agreement—supposedly in the interest of an earlier final curtain. Langner and the Guild now refused to make the change in the bedroom scene, arguing that the set had been designed and built, not once but twice, and that they were determined to use it.

EDDIE DOWLING: Opening night in New York. The fellow I used to write musical comedies with—Jimmy Hanley, a very wonderful composer—well, Jimmy was a drinker. And we hadn't written together in some time now, but he was out there for the opening. And again in New York, strange to say, that Wednesday night in New York, nobody came back.

My God, I thought, the same thing had happened in New York that had happened in New Haven and in Boston. I had a great big Lincoln car, and we were living in Bayside at the time. Jimmy Hanley was, too. So we all piled into the car about midnight to go home. But before I had left the theatre he had come in and, oh, he had a good snootful. He leaned against the door jamb like Mr. Shubert did in New Haven and he said, "Kid, you got it . . . I just come from Sardi's. You got it, you got it, you got it."

So my wife and all the rest of my friends, including Jimmy's wife, we start across the Queensboro Bridge to go home, and there's a man who used to broadcast the reviews to the shows on WOR. He said, "I'm awfully sorry, folks, tonight because one of my dearest friends, Eddie Dowling, opened in the mad Armenian's *Time of Your Life*, and I'm afraid the man on the flying trapeze will have to go back to the trapeze, because it looked like this was a bust tonight. I know Eddie will understand that I would like to say nicer things, but I don't think it has a chance."

So anyway, now we ride home. I'm pretty exhausted now, and I think I'm finished. I asked my family please not to awaken me. I said, "Good news will wait and bad news can wait, too. We'll get the bad news too soon and the good news can wait." So they promised. I went to sleep about three o'clock in the morning . . . and it didn't seem like I'd closed my eyes before they were pulling the bedclothes off me and shaking me, and I awakened and said, "Oh, please, what is it?"

And they were all standing. One had the *Times*. One had the *Tribune*. One had the *World*, which was still being published then. One had the *Mirror*. One had the *News*. They had all the morning papers. And in turn, like the Christmas carol singers, they sang the notices to me, each one a different one. And of course they were sensational notices, the best any new playwright had gotten since O'Neill, really.

So we were home again.

Lee Shubert didn't come back that night. The first I saw of him was Wednesday. He came to the Wednesday matinée, and he leaned against the thing again, with the same little derby and cigar, and the same little lisp, and he says, "Eddie, gee. How could I make thutch a mithtake?"

Saroyan was famous again, terribly famous, and his opinion was solicited on every subject, including the war that had begun in Europe. Hitler? A victim. Stalin? Another victim. "I understand him easy." Women? "I want one who is beautiful, young, and who doesn't interrupt. I hate women who try to think; they're all so shallow. It's all right for them to feel." When the war had begun in September, 1939, Saroyan had been impelled to make it part of his work (*The Well-Known Soldier*), but by accident and Nathan's design his work as director had intervened. It had been a tiring fight, but to Saroyan it was clear who had saved *The Time of Your Life* from the warehouse: Saroyan.

In the glow generated by ecstatic notices, the Theatre Guild might forget its differences with him and prepare to work the next season on *Love's Old Sweet Song*. But at a deep level Saroyan himself was less forgiving. Dowling, he would say (but say only after Dowling's death), was not quite right for the role of Joe. And whatever Lawrence Langner and the Guild might have felt and done about Kitty's bedroom scene, the authorized scripts of the play would place it firmly on the barroom stage. It would play that way, Saroyan's way, in all of the thousands of stock and amateur productions that have followed, and Joe would say his speech about money, and young actors everywhere would read and memorize the spoken overture to the play, which had been cut in tryout:

> In the time of your life, live—so that in that good time there shall be no ugliness or death for yourself or for any life your life touches. Seek goodness everywhere, and when it is found, bring it out of its hiding-place and let it be free and unashamed. Place in matter and in flesh the least of the values, for these are the things that hold death and must pass away. . . . In the time of your life, live—so that in that wondrous time you shall not add to the misery and sorrow of the world, but shall smile to the infinite delight and mystery of it.

PART THREE
1950–1981

CHAPTER EIGHT

EXILE

1. THE SECOND MARRIAGE

It was as if Saroyan believed that the divorce decree would merely alter his relationship with Carol, not end it. The thirty days that the laws of Nevada had required him to spend in that state had been the worst binge of his life. He would remember it as a month without food. He drank heavily only when he gambled heavily, and he never gambled more heavily in his life than in the autumn of 1949, when he lost $50,000 while waiting for the court to declare his marriage dead.

But almost immediately he began to want Carol back, and his desire intensified when he saw her in New York at Christmastime that year.

CAROL MATTHAU: He said, "How are ya, kid?"
"Oh, fine, Bill, I'm fine."
He said, "It's good to see you."
And I said, "It's nice to see you."
And he says, "Ahhhh, you look beautiful. I'd love to take you to dinner or something."
I said, "That's very sweet, but I can't."

He said, "Why not?"

I said, "I—I have plans. I can't."

And he says, "Well, how about tomorrow night?"

And I said, "Bill, I really can't and I'd rather not."

"Well, who are all these plans with?"

I said, "Well, I have a beau."

He said, "Oh. Yeah, but it's nothing—*serious*, is it?"

I said, "Well, I like him a lot."

"Yeah, but—you didn't, you wouldn't have an affair with him, or anything like that?"

I said, "Well, of course I would, and I do, and I am."

Ah, well. He went crazy. He had me followed. He was under my window in the snow. Hired detectives. I used to give them notes to tell them where I was going. I had told him the truth.

He went from threats: "I'm going to take the children. . . ." And I said, "I don't want to talk about it. . . ." It upset him very much who the man was. He was very, very upset by then. Went from threatening me with taking away the children—because it was a married man—to wanting me back, and I wouldn't go back. And I think the thing that ended that siege was that his mother was sick.

In the Saroyan family, memories of Takoohi's death remain intimately associated with Bill's campaign to retrieve Carol for his own. In Armenian tradition, faithlessness was the only excuse for divorce. Although she had been faithful as a wife, now, in Takoohi's eyes, she was making a cuckold of Bill, and Takoohi was furious at her son's foolishness. First he had gambled away the $50,000 advance for the books, now he was trying to get back the wife Takoohi considered him well rid of.

Saroyan's financial and literary affairs were in new hands, the law firm of Ernst, Cane and Berner, where the problem of unpaid taxes in the mid-$30,000 range could be answered by the solution of large royalties the firm negotiated for its powerful literary and show-business clients. Just as Saroyan had left behind Random House, Schulberg, M-G-M, and—most recently—Harcourt, Brace, he now abandoned Matson and Duggan as his agents, incensed at their continuing share in the rights to *The Time of Your Life*. (Saroyan proposed a buyout and was furious when Matson told him he expected to earn a million dollars in agents' fees from *The Time of Your Life* alone.) Early in 1950, after Takoohi's death, the new lawyers were overseeing Saroyan's discussions with 20th Century–Fox. *Come Back to Carthage*, the screenplay he was discussing, was in all likelihood the seed for *Rock Wagram*, the novel in which he began to retrieve the reality of his Armenian boyhood. In addition to straightening out his literary and financial affairs, Saroyan now called on his new lawyers for help with his marital situation, and a very junior member of the firm was assigned to help.

PAUL GITLIN: I remember Bill being very upset about Carol. She was living near the Hampshire House then. She was dating. He was suspicious because, after all, she was the mother of his children.

We had her followed. The whole purpose of that was to show she was an unfit mother. That was his idea, to get the kids back. He was capable of these temper tantrums that would last for years. He wasn't doing anything much except blowing his own legal situation.

She came in to see Berner, and Pinchas had me sit in, see what we could do to get Bill to stop these tactics. (I think the real reason he stopped is, he just ran out of money. Private detectives are terribly expensive.)

Cloak and dagger. My first experience in this stuff. I'd just joined the office and the idea was, he was sure it was ———— ————, and somehow or other he'd found out that this particular night, that she'd be going out with him. There was a bar on Fifty-eighth Street, on the back side of the Hampshire House. He was convinced that she would sneak out, come back with the fellow, and then go back in with the fellow, and the idea was to watch that exit all night long. I never got home until five o'clock because she never came out. She didn't have a date that night.

I was in the bar with the detective, and the idea was I could identify her. Everyone knew what ———— ———— looked like, but no one knew what she looked like. Pictures. But they wanted someone there who knew. But I didn't get home until four, five in the morning.

It was one of these erratic moments in his life.

She lied to him, the fact that she's Jewish. I said, "I'm Jewish, too."

"That's beside the point, she lied to me."

I even, out of sheer curiosity, said, "Why are you so mad about this?" And he started giving this whole story. But I resented the fact—I told him I personally resented the fact that it smelled of anti-Semitism.

"Oh, no: she just *lied*."

I said, "Would you have married her anyway?"

He said, "Sure."

He was madly in love with her. (She must have been a very beautiful girl.) But this was a kind of paranoia that was going on—you don't believe what you're supposed to believe. You believe what you want to believe, and you live that paranoia.

Bill did not keep the facts of the situation to himself. Budd Schulberg ran into him that winter at the Copacabana and mentioned, in all innocence, a recent professional encounter with Carol's suitor. "It was a different Bill. It was sad because it was a bitter, angry, hurt, different Bill from this person who, really, in his life earlier had been like his stories: everybody should love everybody else and things will work out, shouldn't have any wars. I remember feeling that "I've lost that Bill Saroyan that I really liked a lot, that he'd never be—he wasn't—the same."

ARTIE SHAW: Carol and I got talking, and I said something about Bill—they'd been divorced, and I said, "Whatever happened?"

She said, "Oh, Christ, Artie, it's such a story, it's hair-raising." We had dinner or whatever and went up to her apartment, kept talking. So she told me the story that I then wrote. I asked her if she minded if I wrote it, and she said, "No, I hope he reads it." She was very bitter. I understood the overtones in the story, but I didn't spell them out until the very end, which was, why did she lie to him—or not lie, but omit to tell it? Which came at the end of the story. I showed it to Carol. She read it. She said, "That's it, that's it. You've got it."

I was living on my farm in Dutchess County, but I'd come into New York occasionally, and I was living in the Windsor Hotel, a suite, and I got a call one evening, and it was from Lenny Lyons. Lenny said, "A friend of yours wants to say hello."

"Who's that?"

"Well, I'll put him on."

It was Bill. I had just written this story, and I was filled with a peculiar set of mixed feelings about him. I still liked him, and I even think I understood a little bit why he felt that way, but it was a horrific story. Anyway, he said, "Gee, come on over. . . ."

I said, "Bill, I'd love to, but I've got something very important I want you to see before I do." I thought, "Well, let's have this out between us." I mean, if I'm going to be a friend to somebody, I've got to—as I say, "Here I am. This is where I am. You tell me where you are."

"Is it important?" he said.

I said, "Yeah, it's important enough for you to bust up what you're doing and come over here." So he came over, and I handed him the twenty-five pages, just as I've described, and he started reading it faster and faster. Obviously he knew what it was. Clearly. And it was pretty vituperative, some of the things he said.

I wanted it out of the way. I wanted him to know that I knew. If he could tell me something that would add to my understanding, I was perfectly willing to accept it, but having been victimized by that same kind of idiotic hatred and virulence, it was a disease I didn't want to be exposed to.

When he finished, he made the comment, "Well, you know there's truth and there's *truth*, and there's a lot of layers to truth."

And I said, "Bill, I understand that. It's all true."

He said, "Well, anyway, the fact is, she *did* lie."

And I think I asked him, "If she did, why would she have? What would have made her think she should lie?"

And he looked at me, and I looked at him, and nobody said anything. That was the end of that. We got past, somehow, that funny little embarrassing moment, where we both knew that we knew what the other knew.

Artie Shaw's story, "Old Friend," would be published fifteen years later as the central novella in a collection called *I Love You, I Hate You, Drop Dead!* His original idea had been to include it in the chapter on anti-Semitism in his autobiography, *The Trouble with Cinderella*, but distance and disguising were needed in order to publish it. (Saroyan becomes "Steve Larsen," a best-selling Chicago novelist.) Despite the strain on their friendship caused by the story, Bill still turned to Artie at a key point in the next phase of his campaign to get Carol back. The idea now was to woo her, and he determined to court her as he had not had time to do in 1942.

CAROL MATTHAU: I was free and I was beginning to come back to life. I was very happy.

And Bill kept pulling on me, and pulling.

And there *were* pulls left, there were. And there were very ambivalent feelings. I would think to myself, "Well, I would never marry anybody else, and I would certainly never marry *him* again."

I said to him, "I can't marry you again, because I don't love you anymore."

And he said, "That's because you have no reason to. But you *will*."

ARTIE SHAW: Bill said, "I've got to get back together with her. She's lost her head with this guy. It's stupid. She's just making a God-damned fool of herself. She's the mother of my children, and I'm the father." And he went on and on, in this mystic way he talked about the mother, the father, the important biblical dah-dee-dah-dah, mother, father, and children. "You gotta do me . . ."

I said, "What?"

"You gotta go talk to her and . . ." You know the guy, John Alden, "The Courtship of Miles Standish." "You've got to go over and see her and talk to her about getting back together with me."

I said, "Jesus Christ, Bill. After that story? Really?"

"Ah, she misunderstood the whole God-damned thing! Christ's sake, it wasn't against her."

I said, "But it *was* against her."

"I'm not denying it. I was a God-damned fool, but you've got to talk to her." Booming away. So I said, "All right, but it's against my better judgment. I don't know if I'm going to be able to do it with a great deal of enthusiasm, but I'm going to try."

So I called Carol the next day, and I said, "You know, Bill's in town."

She said, "Yes, he called."

So I said, "Look, I gotta talk to you. I had a long talk with him last night. I have to talk to you."

Slimmer, mustachioed, Saroyan in 1950 as he undertook his successful campaign to win back Carol's hand in marriage. (Courtesy Aram Saroyan)

She said, "What about?"

I said, "I'd rather not do this on the phone." So I went over there. With mixed feelings. Got there about—she had a dinner date, got home about ten-thirty, eleven. We met at her apartment, and we talked and talked and talked and talked, until about three in the morning, but in between there, she had gotten into bed, and I was sitting in her bedroom, talking to her and saying, "Look, the guy absolutely feels," and "I can't recommend him, but I feel responsible. For Christ's sake, I got you two guys together to begin with," and "I can't say I'm recommending him, but, God, give it some serious thought. He seems to be honestly in need of whatever it is that being together with you could bring him."

She says, "I don't believe I could do it."

Well, about one-thirty in the morning, the phone rang and I could hear the booming voice: "GRRRR, GRRRR, GRRRR!" And he was screaming and hollering.

(I used to say to him, "For Christ's sake, why don't you talk to her quietly?" And he said, "God damn it, I'm sore at her! I told her I *love* her, I *love* her." I said, "Jesus, that sounds like 'I *hate* you, I *hate* you.'" And I said, "That's what she's hearing.")

Well, she finally said, "All right, I'll talk to him. . . . I'm talking to him. *NO!* God damn it, I'm *talking* to him!" And she put the phone down.

"Do you know what that son-of-a-bitch asked me just now? He said, 'Is he in bed with you?'"

The crazy son-of-a-bitch! I'm over there only for one reason, for God's sake. I wouldn't have been near there if it hadn't been for him. I was really pissed. I said, "Christ, Carol, forget it. I'm sorry I came over here."

ROSHEEN MARCUS: The warmest episode I had with Bill Saroyan was when he wanted to remarry Carol. Carol had absolutely said no soap and he came to me and he said, "Rosheen, you're the only one . . . you're the only one that understands, you're the only one. You're a great, wonderful woman," he kept telling me.

He, on his bended knees, he had a talk with my husband and me, and I cannot remember the conversations, but all of it—*all* of it—pertained to Carol. All of it. Every moment of that conversation. But for hours. We couldn't get rid of him.

And my husband kept saying, "Well, you know, ah—you've proven yourself. What is this? We won't have her unhappy like that." I don't remember. You know how fathers talk.

I sat on the sidelines and I listened to most of this, too, and then, finally, he got me. I went to my bedroom, and he got on his knees, and he stayed on his knees until six o'clock in the morning. I sat in a chair and he was on his knees.

He said, "Please, Rosheen. You're the only one that can make her come back to me." (Because she kept saying—she was adamant about it: "Nope. No soap. I will not go back to that life.")

He said, "I know Mr. Marcus doesn't want it, I know she doesn't want it, but you can do it," and he sat on his knees, his bended knees, and I couldn't get away from it. Until six in the morning.

Finally, I said, "Well, I'll do what I can, Bill, but you know, she's been married. She's now a woman, and she's going to have to make up her own mind. I'll do what I can."

And I did. I did it.

Carol came to believe that, now that Bill knew everything about her background, marrying her once more was his way of telling her that it did not really matter to him. And there were the children to think of. By Thanksgiving, 1950, Aram was seven and Lucy was four, and on that day, after a telephone call from Bill, Aram wept for the broken family, and his tears touched Carol.

CAROL MATTHAU: I put it together when I saw Aram crying like that, and the three of us just living together, and knowing it wasn't a whole life, really, in a sense. But, I'm very selfish, and I don't think I would have just done it—*just* done it for that, if I didn't think it had a chance.

It was very difficult to tell the other man that I was leaving him to go back, and he offered me and my children everything in the world, and without ever having to see him again, which was not what I wanted. I'd never do that.

But I decided that I would go back to Bill, and I was very— heavy about it. I think it was just like committing suicide.

The remarriage was in March, 1951, in Los Angeles, where they

At the second wedding, left to right, Ross and Armen Bagdasarian, Bill, Archbishop Calfayan, Carol, Araks and Manuel Tolegian. (Courtesy Aram Saroyan)

would start again in a rented house on Rodeo Drive. They honey-mooned with a cruise to Catalina on the Chaplins' yacht, but the honeymoon ended swiftly.

CAROL MATTHAU: The minute we got married, I just heard about the other man for breakfast, lunch, and dinner. That's all I heard about: what a whore I was, I'd had an affair.
I invited Oona and Charlie over for dinner. I was going to cook an Armenian dinner. And, at the same time, Jane and John Gunther were going through to Japan, and they called, and I said, "Oh, come over for dinner. I'm cooking an Armenian dinner tonight." So they said, "We'd love to. Can we bring a friend?" I said, "Of course." And at the same time, Sid Perelman called. I said, "I'm glad you called, Sid. I'm cooking tonight, come over." And so I cooked this dinner, and they came, and Oona and Charlie, and the Gunthers brought Garbo, and it was a very pleasant evening, and that was the end of the evening. This story was in one of his books as a great testimony to my social climbing. Oona being my oldest friend (and Gloria), the Gunthers coming through—it was not a party that I gave. But it wasn't a scene that he could star in, he wasn't the star.

Frank Loesser and his wife invited us to a party. We had a *terrible* fight, just a terrible, terrible fight. And finally, I'm all dressed for the party, and don't really want to go, and he's yelling and screaming and calling me every name in the world. (I have no memory what the fight was about. I wish I could remember what the fight was.) But he was yelling in the car—they lived a few streets away—calling me *the* vilest names in the world, and we keep moving toward their front door, and I'm saying, "Please, I don't want to go . . ." and for some reason, although it was a party, Frank opened the door. And in that split second, Bill said, "My beautiful bride and I are so happy to see you." But I'm left there with my head and heart pounding, and I was like that for the rest of the night. And he was so charming, so divine. They must have thought that I was crazy. I could hardly say hello.

I think that one of the things that I really hated about him was, if he got mad, he stayed mad for months, and he always got mad. He just couldn't let go.

Money was less of a problem, despite the loss of the Doubleday advance. *Rock Wagram* had been published to reviews praising its seriousness and craftsmanship; it showed Saroyan, as one critic put it, "on back to life again." Saroyan worked a bit with movie producer and agent Charles K. Feldman, who was trying to put together a deal on John Steinbeck's *The Wayward Bus*. But the real money came from a surprising and unexpected direction. In 1939, driving across the country (specifically, driving across New Mexico), Bill and his young cousin Ross Bagdasarian had invented new words for an old Armenian folk song, a sinuous singing commercial for love: "Come On-a My House." Now an actor and a musician, Ross sent a copy of the song to Mitch Miller, then a powerful artist-and-repertory executive with Columbia Records.

ROSEMARY CLOONEY: Mitch had a demonstration record of it, and he heard it one day and wanted to record it the next, and he was absolutely sure that it was going to be a huge success for me.

Now, the fact that it was an Armenian folk song, he wanted an accent. I don't know how to do an Armenian accent, so I used what I laughingly called an Italian accent because that was the band I sang with, an Italian band, Tony Pastor.

It is a strange piece of material, but it took off like a house afire. It was one whole summer. That was the one that Mitch Miller called the sales department and said, "Ship three hundred thousand on consignment," and if he does that, everybody listens. And they did it.

I went to Florida for a week and came back, and at that time on Broadway there were four big record stores, and they had loudspeakers on the outside and they'd be playing the top records they were selling. And I came back from Florida and drove down from La Guardia, down Broadway, with my head stuck out of the cab, and listened to myself for the first time on Broadway, just out of these record stores.

The record sold 900,000 copies almost instantaneously, and it was the inescapable soundtrack to the summer of 1951.

"Ross and I have made about fifteen thousand dollars apiece out of the song so far," Saroyan said that summer. He and Ross had a small office in Beverly Hills where they dealt with the business aspects of their sudden success and tried to extend it by converting other Armenian material in the same vein. "What we do with these songs is, we just grab them. If they ain't in the public domain, why, we sort of ease them over into the public domain," and all of the material was based on Near Eastern themes. "Oh! Beauty!" had been "Akh, Yavroos" in the original Armenian, and, like the others and despite its merit, failed to replicate the success of "Come On-a My House," with its recitation of delights, including that most Armenian of produce items, the pomegranate. (Ross, however, would go on to very considerable success as a commercial jingle writer; a character actor—he is the piano-playing neighbor in Hitchcock's *Rear Window*; composer of the novelty hit "The Witchdoctor"; and creator of the Singing Chipmunks, whose exasperated human boss, "David Seville," has a distinct Armenian cast in his animated incarnation.)

LUCY SAROYAN: I remember the day they went off to get remarried. Aram and I were standing there, and we said to each other, "They think we don't know about divorce, and what divorce is and marriage is. They think we're too young to understand what they're doing, but we know. They're going to get married again." And we did understand. Kids understand everything.

I remember once, they were having a very big fight. Aram and I were peeking around the corner, and Aram was behind me going, "What's happening? What's happening?"

My mother picked up a pomegranate, and she threw it at him, and it hit him on the head and cracked on his head, and some juice came running down. He wiped the juice off his head and looked at it and said, "God damn it, Carol, look! Now you've killed me."

And Aram said, "What happened, Lucy, what happened?"

I said, "She killed him, she killed him"—because we didn't know what "killed" meant yet. I remember that. It was the same day I took a hairpin and stuck it in an electric socket, so it was a big day for me that day. My mother killed my father and I almost electrocuted myself.

And they were laughing five minutes later.

But in *William Saroyan* Aram recalls a fight in which Carol was pushed down a flight of stairs and Bill tried to strangle her, stopping only when the children appeared in the living room. Bill had been right, the second marriage was different. It was worse.

"Suicide was suicide, divorce was divorce. I flipped a coin and it came up divorce," he wrote long after, but it was Carol who left with the children, for an inexpensive apartment, and who brought the separate-maintenance suit in October, 1951.

CAROL MATTHAU: My lawyer said, "You know, I'm very fond of you, but I don't think you're being a good mother." And I said, "Why?" And he said, "Because you put how you feel about money ahead of your children's well-being. You have this very airy-fairy idea of 'No, I won't take this' and 'I won't take that,' but you have no way of taking care of them.

I filed the second time, and he was going to countersue for custody. *Horrible* papers and depositions and things. He served me with the papers that said things like—that I was an atheist and that the woman taking care of the children was a religious fanatic. That I was illegitimate. That I had had an affair with a married man. That I was insane, and that I shouldn't have custody of the children, because I was insane. And that my mother and father were not married, which indeed they were. Oh: and that I had had an abortion in Oyster Bay. I had never. In Oyster Bay I don't think I spent two minutes without him. I did have a miscarriage, and he was right there when it started, and he was mad as hell. And he decided that it was an abortion, and he had this in his deposition.

So I went down the list. I said, "Bill, this isn't true, and you know that isn't true. And you also know that I'm not insane." I went down point by point.

And he said, "Yeah, but you want your freedom. That's the price." He said, "Yeah, you'll go to court, and you'll prove this isn't true and that isn't true, but people will just read the accusations. And everybody thinks you're such an adorable, darling thing, and this will be in their minds now. You want your freedom, that's the price."

I said, "But, Bill, it is not—I mean I'm sure there are some

At the second divorce, Saroyan, writer John Fante, Carol, and Martha Stevenson Goetz. (Wide World)

really rotten things that you could say about me that are true. Why do you—"

"You want your freedom, that's the price."

That was the answer to everything. I went down the whole thing.

I said, "You know, Aram and Lucy go to school now. Don't do this. Why do you want to do this? We can't live together. That's why I want my freedom. We can't live together, and you know it. And why do this?"

"You want your freedom, kid, that's the price."

So I said, "I'm literally on my hands and knees, begging you not to do this." Finally, I said, "Okay, I will be examined by court psychiatrists," which the thing said. I said, "I probably won't do very well because this great, Pulitzer Prize–winning author has described me as crazy. Because of peculiarities of my manner and so forth, it will be very easy for them to assist you. I realize that. But I'll have to take my chances—because I am going to fight you."

And I said, "But I'll tell you what, though. We're going to go in even. You and I are going to go in even. You were in a Section Eight ward, and I'm going to get your Army papers from Washington, and they will go into the information that the great Pulitzer Prize–winning author also spent a lot of time in a Section Eight ward, and then that'll even us out. Then you can talk to them and I can talk to them, and I'll go only on the condition that you go, too."

Well, he went insane. He dropped the lawsuit immediately.

Bill bought a house in Pacific Palisades for Carol and the children and, for himself, a little house on pilings at Malibu. A card table, a redwood picnic table, a player piano, these were the furnishings. His writing turned even more toward his past, his real feelings:

"Morning is best when it begins with the last hours of night. . . . Enough of culture's hours. I am a peasant. Enough of feasting. I want hunger. Enough of fat. I want muscle. Enough of pity. I want humor. Enough of vanity. I want pride."

He shed many pounds, consulted (and used) a plastic surgeon, regrew the mustache. The marriage was over, again.

2. THE SEPARATE LIVES

"I was forty-three years old. I was very tired. I was very broke. I was very mad, but in that house on the beach I had the feeling that I was home, I was back in the world of the spirit, the world of truth, and I began to get back my soul."

This was an isolated occupation for him, however, and the money problems recurred. None of his Doubleday books earned enough to go significantly beyond the advance money that he had lost gambling, and in 1952 a new $10,000 lien was filed against him by the Internal Revenue Service. The child support agreement with Carol gave her $400 a month to cover her mortgage and feed the children, but as often as not the check was late or short.

Official though the split now was, certified by not one divorce, but two, a shadow of the marriage remained. Carol had no job skills, no way to escape the responsibilities of small children (Aram eight in 1952, Lucy six). She began work on a book of her own, a short novel called *The Secret in the Daisy*. Bill loaned her a typewriter (although she threw it at him during a quarrel), and he dropped in to check on the children and Carol, too, frequently arriving late at night and trying to coax his way back into her bedroom. Some evenings he succeeded.

Friends occasionally would try to fix him up with someone, and in one passage of autobiography he confesses—offhandedly boasts, actually—of a one-night stand with Marilyn Monroe. But he also was becoming isolated by his worsening deafness. Henry Saroyan blames Bill's hearing loss, and his own, on their days with Postal Telegraph, when long-distance phone lines went into use and careless operators sent ringing current down the line while a message was being taken. Bill told his children that his hearing loss began when, as a child, he blew his nose too hard. He remained an enthusiastic, trumpeting nose blower all his life.

For many years, Saroyan's loud laughter and talk had disturbed theatre audiences. In 1952, as Bill commented loudly on *The Red Badge of Courage* at a movie house in Hollywood, a fellow patron, the actor James Mason, slapped Saroyan for refusing to shut up. Loud public talk, dominating conversations, ignoring what others were saying— Saroyan exhibited the classical symptoms of hearing loss. He evidently never sought medical help, and he did not wear a hearing aid. It seemed to suit the loner role he was adopting.

Saroyan wrote later of being accosted by an agent who said, "Tell me something, will you? What's *happened* to you?" This postmarital period of the early fifties was the time of eclipse, when the question first became poignant and important. Aside from the short fantasy novel *Tracy's Tiger*, in which a man's id strides alongside him in the form of a tiger, Saroyan's work now was quite serious. *The Laughing Matter*, his novel of a marriage destroyed by a faithless wife, was turgid melodrama, severely damaged by Saroyan's very earnestness in painting the Carol figure as the villainess and himself as the hero. (Saroyan himself spoke of it as "sick.") But the work that counted was autobiographical, and in the 1952 volume *The Bicycle Rider in Beverly Hills*, Saroyan reveals for the first time to his readers the true story of his childhood, of the orphanage years and how his father's death shocked him into a very early recognition of mortality, which had shaped his choice of career.

The career now was mostly in the hands of Paul Gitlin and the other lawyers, who negotiated ceaselessly and successfully with the Internal Revenue Service, avoiding a tax lien against their law office, clearinghouse now for all of his royalties. They arranged deals, which he would turn down (a "Wonderful World of William Saroyan" television series never reached pilot stage), and negotiated top dollar for him with the leading magazines, such as the *Saturday Evening Post, Holiday, Cosmopolitan*. They also got him out of gambling jams. Lawyers from Miami presented them with $50,000 in promissory notes Bill had signed to cover gambling losses, but the New York lawyers prevailed, threatening to approach Florida authorities if the debt was pressed; Saroyan claimed that the game had been fixed.

Even though the productions had ended with *Get Away, Old Man* in 1943, the plays continued to pour forth, and one of Saroyan's most marketable properties was *The Girls*, a play with only two characters, named Carol and Gloria, sitting in a hotel suite and discussing their love affairs and those of their friends. More than one producer was interested, and the lawyers' technique always was to describe to Saroyan a project's potential revenues (and effect on the tax debt) before revealing what was for sale or the use of the material intended. Saroyan refused to let *The Girls* reach the stage.

He did, however, appear in 1954 on the Ford Foundation's television magazine *Omnibus*, hosted by Alistair Cooke, and introduced his own short comedy *Vive*, performed by Bert Lahr and Bobby Clark. Saroyan

Lean and nautical, Saroyan in a Malibu pose for *The Bicycle Rider in Beverly Hills,* the first of the memoirs in which he began to express his undisguised feelings to his readers.

was receiving a retainer from CBS for contributions such as this, and invented the running feature on *Omnibus* in which older people described incidents from their past directly into the camera, a role Saroyan himself declined to perform. He did, however, dramatize some of his boyhood recollections, and Sal Mineo played young Willie in the sketches. Royalties could be attached by the IRS; salaried work such as for CBS could not.

In 1955 the New York City Center proposed a revival of *The Time of Your Life*, and Saroyan exercised his authorial rights by seeking a degree of control over casting. He secured the role of Elsie Mandelspiegel for Gloria Vanderbilt, a witty bit of casting against type, and saw that Carol was hired to play Mary L., the role Celeste Holm had originated on Broadway.

Carol had completed her novel, *The Secret in the Daisy*, which Random House now bought and published as the work of "Carol Grace." The pseudonym, however, was explained away by Carol's biography on the dust jacket, in which she mentioned how "I began marrying and divorcing William Saroyan, twice each." The book's short chapters are a little like Saroyan, a bit like John O'Hara, but at heart a sincere recounting of Carol's childhood up to, and including, the beginnings of her affair with Saroyan. Their lovemaking and her pregnancy are relegated to a fantasy in which she wonders to herself whether confessing that pregnancy to her mother would be one way of finding out about her real father, a man who is a mystery to the girl in the book. At the end of the flap copy, Carol wrote, "I have just written a play and the best part in it is for me." While the play vanished without being staged, her declaration was true on another level. The publication of her novel and the return to New York for *The Time of Your Life* reminded her that she had friends and a family there, that there was no real reason to remain a housewife in Pacific Palisades, and so she moved back to the East Coast. The good part she would write for herself next would be in a happy new marriage.

Carol was hired as understudy to Jayne Mansfield in George Axelrod's play *Will Success Spoil Rock Hunter?*, a satire on Madison Avenue and the pneumatic school of acting represented by Miss Mansfield herself, and it was in this cast that she met a struggling young character actor named Walter Matthau.

Saroyan now told his children that he would write a book for each of them. The one written for Lucy, nine years old as Bill began it, is

Saroyan at fifty, Pacific Palisades, 1959. (Courtesy Aram Saroyan)

Mama, I Love You, an exercise in wishful thinking, which reviewers unanimously found cloying, but which makes more sense if viewed as a forty-seven-year-old author playing the role of a child Lucy's age. Carol is Mama Girl, a divorcee with custody of her daughter, and Bill is Papa Boy, with custody of their son. Mama Girl and Twink, or Lucy, head from Los Angeles to New York, where the mother's ultra-rich girlfriend, Gladys DuBarry (a victim of "polio of the soulio" in Saroyan's telling), bankrolls the play that lifts the *daughter* to fame as an actress, coattailing Mama Girl along. The play itself, a fantasy-comedy about death, sounds like purest Saroyan, and Papa Boy and brother Peter arrive from Paris for opening night, reunion, a remarriage. (*Papa, You're Crazy,* the book for Aram, is a plotless set of aphoristic monologues, father to son, which resembles Bill's lectures to the boy—a very minor work in Saroyan's later style.) But for all the sugar, *Mama, I Love You* was a commercial hit, beginning with a big serial sale to the *Saturday Evening Post* and ending with a $100,000 offer for the movie rights.

As usual, the lawyers began by describing the amount of money to Saroyan, then revealing the property they were discussing, and, finally, the potential buyer and use. When told it was M-G-M that was interested, Saroyan snapped to attention. Of course they could have it for $100,000, provided they yielded his long-sought rights to *The Human Comedy.* No deal, of course, and Saroyan was unswayed by reminders that Louis Mayer had been forced out of M-G-M six years earlier and had absolutely nothing to do with the studio that still bore his name.

For Aram, a better gift than the book was the chance to sit next to his father at the 1956 World Series. They witnessed the Yankees' Don Larsen pitch his perfect game against the Dodgers. Robert Creamer, then an editor of *Sports Illustrated,* the magazine that had assigned Bill as a celebrity reporter, recalls Bill's delight in going to one of the late-season games at Ebbets Field in 1957, the last year the Dodgers played there. Saroyan was charmed when the Dodgers' press agent pulled out of his billfold a wrinkled keepsake clipping, a funny letter Bill had written to *Life* magazine, and even happier when introduced to Clem Labine, the brainy Dodger relief pitcher, who shook hands and said, "I was reading one of your books last night." In the stands at that game at Ebbets Field, Saroyan struck up a conversation with a boy about his son's age, eleven or so, which eventually led to an argument, then a bet. The wager was a quarter, and when the boy lost, Creamer was delighted to see Saroyan stick out his hand and collect.

Just as the New York production of *The Time of Your Life* had revived Carol's theatrical ambitions, it returned Bill to the theatre in a roundabout way. While working on it, he stayed in the Great Northern, then on its last legs, but near City Center, cheap and resonant with memories of writing *The Time of Your Life* in May, 1939. On this stay, Saroyan wrote *The Cave Dwellers*, and it took eight days, not six.

Bill fretted over the contracts the lawyers drew up for the production, quarreled with Carmen Capalbo and Stanley Chase, the young men who produced it, and sat out opening night. Nonetheless, the reviews were generally favorable, and the praise was neither stingy nor directed merely at the production and the players. Many felt the shadow of Samuel Beckett, specifically his *Waiting for Godot*, hovering over Saroyan's allegory set in an abandoned theatre on the Lower East Side. *The Cave Dwellers* ran for a hundred performances in a theatre with eight hundred seats, and despite its relative success, it did nothing to save Saroyan from the tax man. The bill the Internal Revenue agents pressed on Saroyan's lawyers was now in the $50,000 range. The tax troubles alone were not enough to send Saroyan into exile, but Carol's remarriage jolted him.

She was appearing in an S. N. Behrman play called *The Cold Wind and the Warm*, and Bill had sent a telegram to her theatre that said, "You're the greatest actress in the whole world, the trouble is, you don't live in it."

One night during the run, she realized that Bill was going to discover the seriousness of her affair with Walter Matthau. It was, in fact, the very day Matthau had returned with the divorce he needed to marry Carol.

CAROL MATTHAU: Aram called me one night before he came home for dinner and said, "Can I bring Pop up?" And you can't say, "No, you can't bring your father up to where you live," so I said, "Okay," and I was fixing dinner for Aram and Lucy, and then I was going to the theatre. (I was working in a play.) But Aram had had a date to go to the fights with Walter that evening. Aram had asked Walter to take him to the fights, so Walter had made this date with him.

Now, Walter was coming up to the apartment to pick Aram up,

Aram and Bill in the stands at the 1956 World Series, historic on more than one account: the last ever played in Brooklyn, and Don Larsen's perfect game. (Photo by Art Daley, *Sports Illustrated*)

to take him to the fights, and Bill was coming up with Aram, and as luck would have it, they both came up at the same time, and all I could hear in the hallway was Walter saying, "Oh, I—gee, I thought you were much taller. I didn't know you were short."

I knew that I was doomed—*doomed.*

So I opened the door and they came in, and Bill said, "Well, what's he doing here?" and Aram said something about the fights. And Bill looked at him and said, "You don't have to go, my boy. You don't *have* to go," as though this had been something that had been perpetrated on Aram. But Aram (I forget what he said) wanted to go. "You know you don't have to go," and Aram said, "I know," and anyway, I had to leave for the theatre and Bill said, "I'm going downtown. I'll drop you off at the theatre."

So he gets in the taxi, and he said, "So it's *Matthau.* That's who it is, Matthau. You're having an affair with Matthau. A married man."

And I said, "He isn't a married man."

"Why are you such a liar? You're having an affair with Matthau, and everyone knows Matthau is a married man."

I said, "He isn't a married man. He isn't. He's divorced."

He said, "You are a liar." (This is the same Lon Chaney, Jr., deal again, and this goes on and on.)

I was absolutely dying. This is years and years after we were divorced—in fact, it was just before I married Walter, and I said, "No, he's not married—he's *not.*"

He said, "You're a liar, you're still a *liar*, you will always be a *liar.* . . ." On and on and on.

And so now, we're nearly at the theatre. And he said, "He *is* a married man. When did he get divorced?"

I said, "I have to go," and I jumped out of the taxi. Walter had just come from the airport, that morning, from Mexico, with his divorce, and I just didn't have the guts to say, "Today." I just didn't have the guts. But that's my whole relationship with him. There would have been nothing wrong if I said "Today," but I knew that would corroborate to him that it would still be a lie, although it was the truth.

Saroyan fled from the truth of Carol's new romance and marriage.

The lawyers had sold *The Time of Your Life* for a television production with Jackie Gleason, and had cleverly sheltered the $10,000 check from IRS seizure by acting as packagers. They gave the money to Bill in the form of a cashier's check, which he promptly converted into traveler's checks at Thomas Cook & Son. This transaction set off bells at the IRS, rude questions that the lawyers would have to be paid to answer. But by then Saroyan was gone with the money. He sailed to Venice and took a train to Belgrade, where he was going to discuss producing a movie for the state-run film organization.

He said he might be staying away from America for the rest of his life, because of the taxes. "I haven't been a playboy. I haven't squandered my money. I've done some gambling, but that goes back more than ten years."

But there was nothing, really, to the Yugoslavian movie plan. In Belgrade he spent $1,400 for a nearly new red Karmann-Ghia and drove west, and when he reached the casinos on the Riviera he gambled and lost every penny he had in the world.

3. EXILE

Saroyan was fifty. He had spent most of this landmark year traveling for commissioned articles and working on a book he wanted to call *Fifty-Fifty*, an autobiography written in daily installments. He would boast that it came to amount to a million words. Paris, he decided, was a good place to stop and be broke in.

Bill now put himself once more at the mercy of Hollywood, specifically, the plans and charity of Darryl F. Zanuck, mogul of 20th Century–Fox. Zanuck was well known for placing his girlfriends in the movies in a charmingly old-fashioned way. Some, such as Bella Darvi, sank like rocks from public view, but Juliette Greco, his current flame, had genuine appeal, and Zanuck, who lived in Paris, wanted material for her.

Bill signed on to write a play for Greco and to work on other properties Zanuck held for the movies. The resulting play, *The Dogs, or The Paris Comedy*, took Saroyan an uncharacteristically long thirteen days to write; it opened to good reviews the following year. Less came of the film scripts Saroyan tinkered with, but his fee was large, $80,000. However, as with the television money, he gambled much of it away. He

Returned from exile, Saroyan appeared on NBC's *Omnibus* series once more, 1961, and began alternating between America and Paris, as he would for the remaining twenty years of his life. (NBC)

became a regular at a fashionable club on the Champs-Élysées, populated by a ritzy *demimonde* of hookers, hustlers, pimps, and gamblers. A gambling companion noted Bill's loud theatricality at the baccarat table, a far cry from the studious demeanor of the pros, who were winning more often. Whenever Saroyan won, he distributed 100,000-franc chips like cocktail peanuts. His friend noted, however, that nobody offered Saroyan any chips when he was losing.

In 1960, Saroyan matched his Paris comedy with *The London Comedy, or Sam the Highest Jumper of Them All*. The idea, he explained, was for a whole string of comedies about expatriate Americans, "a series, like *Granddaughter of Lassie*." He already had finished a *Moscow Comedy, or No One in His Right Mind*, and another set in Australia. The play for Juliette Greco had been a brittle affair about a family of courtesans, utterly conventional. *Sam*, on the other hand, took place on a tilted stage, and its plot was difficult for the audiences and critics to make out. The *Times* of London was unimpressed: "The characters who tell the audience what is happening, the 'ambassador' from the audience intervening and questioning, even those moments when an actor comes forward and says something like 'We all hope you know what the hell this play's about, because we certainly don't'—all are the hoariest conventions, radiating a delicate period charm impaired only by the patent conviction of all concerned that they are daring, new and up to the minute." As if to atone, Saroyan turned next to collaboration with the popular British novelist and jurist Henry Cecil on a comedy entitled *Settled Out of Court*, about a case retried in the home of a judge. It was no great success, but it demonstrated Saroyan's ability to work with every possible theatrical form. Although Saroyan was capable of playing the old fogey about the youth culture of the sixties, for example, because of his own iconoclastic beginnings, he was an interested and tolerant observer of theatrical experimentation for all of his life. His very last works were unproduceable "plays" that dispensed with conventions such as plot in order to remove the barriers between the dialogue and the audience. In 1961, Saroyan collaborated on an *Omnibus* hour that examined avant-garde theatre and, as his own contribution, included two readings of the Mary L. scene from *The Time of Your Life*—as originally played and as an exercise in existential distance, à la *Godot*.

Once Saroyan had cut ties with a colleague, the break usually was permanent, but in the early sixties he saw money as a way to buy himself back into America, even though it was highly unlikely that the Internal Revenue Service would attempt to extradite him. When Harold Matson, his former agent, approached him with talk of an autobiography, Saroyan was willing to listen. The advance would be $25,000, quite a large amount at that time, and Saroyan was to be paid in shares of stock in the publisher, Trident Press. The arrangement backfired for Saroyan because the stock took a dive after he was paid off. And his personal stock was low, if critical commentary on the book is an accurate gauge. *Here Comes There Goes You Know Who* is written in fifty-two short, rapid-fire sections—if not a sharply-edited version of the long-projected autobiography *Fifty-Fifty*, then inspired by it. Saroyan never had written more frankly or movingly about the orphanage years, his family's scorn for his ambitions, and his sometimes strained relationships with his children. He was caught in a trap: if he was sentimental in his writing, he was living in the past; if he was frank and outspoken, as in *Here Comes There Goes . . .* , he had soured into a cynic. "With a lover like this, humanity needs no enemy," sniffed *Time*'s anonymous reviewer.

Late in 1961, Saroyan consented to a term as playwright-in-residence at Purdue University, inspired by his experiment with the Theatre Royal and *The London Comedy*. The play he put together on this occasion, *High Time Along the Wabash*, concerned racism and nuclear arms. (A British atomic scientist teaching at Purdue is administered ad hoc justice for putting the make on a teenaged coed.) During this sojourn, Saroyan would visit his sister Cosette in the Fifteenth Avenue house and relatives in Fresno, but Paris continued to exert a greater pull.

In 1961, after months of having moved among hotels and apartments during his Paris stays, his earnings from the autobiography made it possible for Saroyan to buy a permanent Parisian *pied-à-terre*. He used an agent who assembled a list of ten or so apartments for the first day of the search, and the first of these was in the 9th *arrondissement*, on the sixth floor at 74 rue Taitbout, a street that climbs north toward Pigalle from the Grands Boulevards. It is in the Opéra district, the neighborhood where Saroyan would search again and again for the bordello he had been unable to find since that first visit in 1935; also, the Armenian community of Paris were sprinkled among its streets.

Saroyan glanced at the flat and said, "Okay, I'll take it." The agent was dumbstruck, begging him to go down the list (no one ever took the first!), but Saroyan was adamant. The building had no elevator, no central heating. The windows would not close tightly and the floor-boards were rotting. Bill complained about it unceasingly for the next twenty years. But he also called it "this old building which I have come to believe in and to love, although it is falling to pieces." One entered beside the kitchen. To the rear were a dining room, where no dinners were held, and a storeroom, which would become crowded over the two decades with junk books, "trash books" as he called them, books picked up at stalls along the quais for a few centimes because their jackets or illustrations or the names of the authors reminded him of something or someone.

"I buy trash books, I make a drawing, and I put the date and everything, and twenty years later I look at it and study my mind of that time. Why did I draw like that? And it's interesting. I don't want any day to go by without *something*."

The front two rooms, each with a fireplace, were for work and music. The furniture was shabby and utilitarian, and the first important purchase was the pianola. He took along his new Paris lawyer, the Philadelphia-born Armenian-American Aram Kevorkian, to negotiate for him. In all his Paris years, Saroyan never learned to speak French well enough to negotiate really complex transactions; it may be that his deteriorating hearing added to his difficulty in understanding the language sufficiently.

Paris he called "a city of enlightenment, culture, awareness, intelligence, wit and beauty. . . . And yet one almost never believes any of the people who are in the streets, or anybody one happens to meet anywhere else, is especially enlightened, cultured, aware, intelligent, amusing or beautiful." The city was not, he insisted, "one big roaring lark," and if the occasional woman climbed the six flights with him it was "for its own sake, no strings attached, no questions asked, no demands made."

The main point of Paris was to write. The daily schedule went uninterrupted. If he tired of the writing, he might paint or draw or go to the pianola. When he was alone in the flat, he confessed to Jack Kevorkian, he would dispense with the piano rolls and play the improvisatory secret music he had played since the first piano on San Benito Way in Fresno.

By the mid-1960s, the efforts of Paul Gitlin and his legal colleagues had begun to erode Saroyan's tax debt, although Bill was fond of tossing around for the press large estimates of what was still owing, always ranging from thirty to fifty-five thousand or so. His books still did not sell well, nor would they ever again, and while he returned for a time to his old firm, Harcourt, Brace, he would argue again with them, like all the others, and move on to a new house. In some cases, it was obvious that he was being published simply for the value of his name. The tiny firm that brought out *The Dogs* misspelled Saroyan's dedication to Lillian Gish—"Gist," as it was printed. Nevertheless, the royalties from the plays never stopped. Every time a school or amateur company performed *The Time of Your Life* and sold tickets, a small royalty found its way to William Saroyan; and not a day went by that *The Time of Your Life* was not on the boards somewhere.

There was enough money to allow him to split his time between America and Paris, and his first notion was to move to New York, where his children were still in private school. In much the same way he bought the flat on rue Taitbout, he rented a Third Avenue penthouse on a three-year lease at $600 a month. It was a spur-of-the-moment decision, made before the building was complete, and it soon ended in litigation. Once he had moved in, in 1963, Bill was disturbed by the sound of ventilation machinery on the roof immediately above his head. He walked out on the lease, was sued, and successfully fought back, although Gitlin and the law firm had to rely on complex technical measurements and testimony to prove Saroyan's point.

The logical American home was Fresno, and later in 1963, on one of his visits to his sister in San Francisco, Saroyan drove his Karmann-Ghia to Fresno, parking away from the middle of town and simply walking around, remembering. It was a hot summer day, and a mug of draft root beer recalled Fresno of the twenties in Proustian fashion for him. Driving north along Highway 99, where generations of Armenians had worked vineyards and orchards, he saw that tract houses now proliferated, and, out of curiosity, he stopped to look at some of the new construction. He wound up buying a house impulsively, just as he had purchased the Paris apartment. He bought two houses, in fact, one to live in and one in which to store his manuscripts and stones and jars of coins, the things that reminded him who he was and had been. There was a vineyard across the street, but it too soon gave way to tract houses. Now Saroyan had homes in two cities, and the pattern for the rest of his life would be half a year in each place. He usually came to Fresno at the end of summer, harvest time.

The decreasing popularity of his work—his plays would now be restricted to revivals or tiny workshop productions, and no more fiction would be published in his lifetime—allowed him introspection, but this did not mean that he was pleased with the relative obscurity.

ARAM KEVORKIAN: He was terribly pained by his eclipse after the war, by the attitude of the New York critics. He was greatly bothered.

We would often talk about that because he was a natural—with strangers he had a sort of natural braggadocio and seemingly impervious thick skin, but obviously he was very, very sensitive and he was living in a different world underneath that, and I think I was one of the few people who was privy to his internal suffering.

For example, when he'd come out with a new book, he would go through what I'd call an optimistic stage where this was going to do well and it was a great book, a good publisher, and everything. And then I would often hesitate to ask him, but at some point, it came out that the book didn't sell well. You'd find out that most of his books at the period I knew him sold at most a few thousand copies. And after a while it was the sort of thing that we could talk about, because it became an accepted understanding between us that he wasn't fooling me. (I used to do his taxes.)

And he'd say, "Now, why do I keep on writing?" And he would say he just has to keep doing it, that's all, and it was a sort of a—the image was a sort of heroic plugging away, a guy fulfilling himself, doing his thing because he had the talent and he had his voice and whatever he had to say.

It's a form that gave him an opportunity to do his thing. It's like Bach saying, "Well, today I'm going to write another fugue." The fugue is the form, not the content, and I think that's what Bill was trying to prove, "I can take any subject and be a writer."

I remember when I first did his tax return and it says "profession" and I had put in, like a lot of people, "author." And he said, "'Author' is an awful word. I'm a writer." He was proud of the word "writer" and the fact that he earned a living at it.

One hot August day in Paris, having let his mustache go untrimmed for a year, he cut it back to the dapper brush he had affected when he first grew it, trimmed his hair, looked in the mirror, and saw himself when young, as well as the face of his people, staring back. Saroyan walked twice that day through the Paris heat, and among the regular stops on his walks were the shops of Armenian compatriots, such as the old tailor Krikor Atamian. They worshiped him in some cases. He was, after all, *Saroyan*, and large pictures of him still hang in some of the Armenian shops of that city, beside the portraits of Christ. Atamian's devotion was an important element of Bill's Paris existence, a boost to his suffering ego. Another friend was a shoemaker, a year or so younger than Saroyan, a powerful little man who had been a wrestler and who kept a tame owl, which would touch its beak to its master's upper lip when he asked, in Armenian, for a kiss.

Saroyan was a welcome and frequent visitor in the offices of the Armenian newspaper in Paris, *Haratch*, and while he had a realistic, sometimes self-mocking view of his adulation by fellow Armenians, in a gathering place like this he could, at least, expect to be understood. He used the *Haratch* office as a rest stop in the course of his hours-long perambulations around the city.

One of his Armenian friends in Paris was Garig Basmadjian, a poet almost forty years his junior. They had first met on one of Saroyan's visits to Jerusalem, in that city's large, old, and important Armenian community. Basmadjian was only a boy, but already a poet, and he presented Saroyan with copies of his work. Later, as they walked along the shore, talking, Basmadjian was appalled to watch Saroyan use the sheets of manuscript poetry to wipe and wrap the wet rocks and bits of wood he was collecting as souvenirs of the day. When the acquaintance was renewed in Paris, Basmadjian found himself being interrogated at length by Saroyan, who was curious about the pedigrees and reputations of a variety of Armenian writers in France, Israel, Yerevan—anywhere. There were many Garig Basmadjians, younger Armenian writers who apprenticed themselves to the master and who came away from the experience with a glimpse into Saroyan's innermost thoughts, surpassing anything that he shared with his family or in the work published in his lifetime.

He might be petulant and jealous about Basmadjian's command of the written Armenian language, or the frequency with which the younger man found it possible to visit Armenia itself, but these feelings were signals of the seriousness with which Saroyan viewed his heritage.

"I am unable to conceive my identity apart from being Armenian," he told Basmadjian. "It is as central as the spark of life from the beginning. It is part of me. I could never live not being Armenian, because of the fact that's what I am. If somebody came today to me and said, 'Mr. Saroyan, there has been a terrible mistake, your father and your mother both were Turks, and you also are a Turk,' I would repudiate that. It could not enter my being, because if it had been, let's say, genetically possible, the life that supplemented that genetic falsehood would turn out to be a falsehood. I owe everything, everything to the unaccountable, which is in each of us, arriving in the center of himself and a part of a family and a part of a region and a part of a culture.

"I am not a very good student. I do not know cultures historically and in terms of scholarship. I know them by living them only. My debt to Armenia and therefore all Armenians is incalculable. It is enormous, that's what it is."

Alone in the house in Fresno set aside for work or the house set aside for memories, or sitting by himself in the Paris flat, that city deserted in August, staring into the mirror at the face with the one-year mustache (now gone white) or the dapper stub of a mustache, he had come to the center of himself and found—an Armenian. It wasn't an object such as a mustache that one could trim, or a nose one might reshape with a little plastic surgery. It was no adopted attitude, but something absolute and essential, and it was the heart of his last quarrel with the world, the sad and endless argument with his own two children.

CHAPTER NINE

FATHER

1. LUCY

LUCY SAROYAN: Papa always was a force for me. I worshiped this man, always. It was easy for me to please Papa. I could make him laugh. I could settle his arguments with Aram. I had a great time with him. I loved him. He *thrilled* me.

He had a house in Malibu, and I remember this because it was a very specific moment. My brother and my father were listening to the pianola and singing along. I was sitting in the bathtub, with the door slightly open so I could see them. Papa had this aluminum bowl that he would pour water over his head with in the tub. He had it by the side of the tub. I had the bowl, and I remember putting the bowl in the water and pouring the water over my head and thinking, "I've never been as happy as I am right this minute. This is the happiest I've ever felt in my whole life. I will always remember how happy I am at this moment," and I do to this day.

> So long, my dear old mother,
> Don't you cry,

> Just kiss your grownup baby
> Boy goodbye.
> Dry the tears in your eyes,
> Don't you cry,
> Don't you sigh,
> So long, Mother,
> Kiss your boy goodbye.

That one always used to get to me, because I always used to think, say *goodbye* to these people?

Never, never, never.

Papa used to come over to the house on Maroney Lane in Pacific Palisades and tell us stories all the time. They were the Fat Khashkhash stories—he had a character called Fat Khashkhash—and I loved these stories. "Oh, Papa, tell us a story." Fat Khashkhash was a fat boy, a little fat boy.

The type of thing was that kids would all put their money in and buy a box of Good 'n' Plenty, but Fat Khashkhash wouldn't have a penny to put in, so they would hand out the Good 'n' Plenty's around among the little group of kids, and they would pass up Fat Khashkhash. So at the end of it, when everybody had a handful of Good 'n' Plenty's, Fat Khashkhash would say, "Gimme the box." I always remember that phrase, "Gimme the box," and we'd roar with laughter.

It was not until Carol moved back to New York with the children in 1955 that Lucy realized her father was a famous man. It happened in school, where the teacher asked if she was related to the writer, and at first she was fearful that her father was simply notorious, rather than a man of achievement. ("I thought Papa was a gambler who wrote books.") The *name*, whose specific gravity was a work of art in itself, had now settled upon a new generation, and for Aram the essential thing came to be readjusting the question: not "Are you William Saroyan's son?" but, rather, "Is William Saroyan your father?"

In a moment of great frankness with Basmadjian, Saroyan told the younger man, already a parent himself, that he liked to believe his children were being raised badly as a result of the divorce and his isolation from them, but that he was prepared to admit that they were better off because of the split-up. As in any broken marriage, the children could carry messages, direct or implicit, between the now-distant

Aram and Bill at Malibu, 1957, in a publicity photo for *Papa, You're Crazy*. The book written for Lucy, *Mama, I Love You*, had been deft fantasy. "Aram's book" was a far more ponderous affair. (Richard Tolbert)

partners. They could—through simple gestures or the curve of a chin—remind Bill and Carol of each other. They could, and did, become tokens and counters in legal games about their welfare and the way in which the court's orders were being carried out on their behalf. It seemed to more than one member of the family that even the unpleasantness of a deposition or a court appearance was tolerable to Bill because it was a connection, however left-handed or strained, with Carol. It was common knowledge that, for Bill's part, the torch never had gone out.

Bill's gambling and on-again, off-again income through the fifties and sixties had left him far in arrears on the support owed Carol for the children, and in 1963 she sued him for it. Saroyan's tax situation also had resulted in minute accounting by Gitlin and his colleagues, and the amount spent on the children exceeded what Carol was due. The point was Bill had spent it on them as he chose, not as the custody agreement required, and the court documents, as did his autobiographical books, listed the trips they had made together. They had ventured to New York from the Coast and, on more than one occasion, to Tijuana. In 1957, he had taken them by ocean liner to Venice, and then on to Trieste, Yugoslavia, Greece. Perhaps Bill assumed Carol could rely upon the wealth of her family, that the $400 a month he owed was unnecessary. The children's trips with Bill aboard luxury ships were small comfort to Carol, who actually relied upon the generosity of the neighborhood grocer she had known since childhood. Her account at his store surpassed $2,000 at one point, according to Aram.

Sometimes the trips became occasions for tirades against Carol. "My devotion to my mother was so strong that I just didn't believe any of it. It didn't bother me," Lucy recalls, but she also believes that Aram could become trapped from time to time in the game, defending Carol to Bill while they were together and then, on his return, behaving toward his mother as though Bill's stories about her were true. Aram recalls that Lucy was exempted from Bill's rages against Carol: "It was like, meet your mother, son. It's the death-goddess Kali." To Aram, Bill's motive in attacking Carol seemed to be an attempt to bring about a fundamental change in the way the boy viewed not only his mother but women in general. It also could be a way of explaining the unusual absence of any new woman from the father's life. For all of his thirteenth summer, Aram listened. Four summers later, he returned to America abruptly, rather than endure Bill's venom. (A psychiatrist helped Aram judge what Bill was trying to do.) When Carol described the episodes to an older adviser, he told her sadly, "Don't fight it. The tragedy is, later the boy will hate him."

Bill occasionally attacked the children directly. Once, driving through vineyards in his Cadillac with the children and their Aunt Cosette, Bill stopped to let Aram pick grapes. They proved to be sour and Aram took none, but Bill railed at him for the unnecessary stop. "My past was kicking me around, and with it I was kicking my son around, and every now and then my daughter a little, too." The harangue went on for hours, and Aram asked Bill to stop again. The boy vomited, "trying to hide behind a tree whose trunk was too narrow for hiding."

"He isn't like you," Cosette said to her brother, in Armenian. "He's like himself." As Bill confessed the incident in print he wrote, "That's the thing that bothered me in 1958 and will go on bothering me the rest of my life. I only hope it isn't the last thing I remember."

Although Aram always would find Bill's heartiness and *joie de vivre* a performance, not an effortless part of his personality, Saroyan was a matchless tour guide, according to Lucy. And with his own children, as with those of his friends (and even strangers, such as the eleven-year-old boy at Ebbets Field), part of the Saroyan magic was that he treated them like adults. This included an early and thoroughgoing introduction to the world of gambling, and Bill believed that Aram had inherited his own betting spirit, admitting that he could not bear looking like a loser to his own son.

> LUCY SAROYAN: At the Casino in Monte Carlo you can't go in if you're a minor, so we used to sit on the steps, and Papa used to say that I was his lucky piece. I had to sit on the steps and wait until he came out. I got to be such a familiar figure there that, as these different people would come to the Casino when Papa was in town, they'd go, "Oh, hi, Lucy! Bill must be here."
>
> We were in Greece and the owner of the race track came and said hello to Papa, and he said to me, "Do you want to see the horses?"
>
> I said, "Oh, I love horses so much."
>
> He said, "Well, come with me. I'll show you the horses." I would go down to where the horses were getting ready before the race, and I would say, "Oh, I think number three is the

prettiest horse, don't you?" And the man would say to me, "No
. . . I like number *seven*. I think number *seven* is the nicest horse."
We were all betting, Pop and Aram and I, so I would bet on
number seven because he thought it was the best horse, the man
who was taking me back there. My horse came in and Pop's
horse lost and Aram's horse lost. And the man would come back
and he would say, "Do you want to see the horses again?"
I said, "Yes, I do." And I'd go and I'd say, "Oh, I like number
two."
And he'd say, "I don't like number two, but I think number *five*
is the prettiest horse in this race."
And I'd say, "You do? Gosh. I guess you're right." I'd go back
and I'd bet on number five. And Pop lost and Aram lost, and I
won again.
Papa says, "What's—ah, what's going on?"
I said, "Oh, you know, when I say to this man what I think is
the prettiest horse and he always thinks it's another horse, well, I
always went with his horses."
And he says, "You didn't *tell* me that he told . . ." Because
these were fixed races in Greece, and the guy was trying to help
Papa out, assuming I would go back and say, "You know, the
prettiest horse in this race is number *seven*."
He wanted to kill me. He went into one of those insane rages
there, but then I knew I had really done something bad. Because I
didn't quite understand. I was saying, "But that's *cheating*, Papa.
That's cheating."
And he said, "You bet your ass that's cheating!"

In the summer of 1959, the summer of *The Paris Comedy* and Darryl
Zanuck's largess, Bill took an apartment on the Avenue Victor Hugo
and invited his son and daughter to join him there. Lucy was thirteen
and Aram would turn sixteen in September. As Bill told his friends,
the children would be adults soon, and the summers together would
become difficult or impossible.

ARAM SAROYAN: It was boring. He was writing. We couldn't
speak French. *He* couldn't speak French. There was nothing to do
except, finally, we discovered the rue de Beaux Arts, where they
had all these exhibits. But I wanted to get out of there almost the
minute I arrived.

The book he was writing was *Not Dying, An Autobiographical Interlude*, and it was both precise and revealing about his self-imposed tax exile, his money problems, and his quotidian adventures with the children. Bill and Lucy marketed together, faking their way among the French shopkeepers, and they cooked together. "He could cook shish kebab," Lucy says "and steaks and stuff like that. But he also made stuffed vegetables, stuffed grape leaves, yogurt, lots of Armenian food. He had a feel for food. He could make a chicken like nobody else could, and he never had to look at a cookbook. He had contempt for people who dealt with cookbooks." Bill also delegated the household chores and insisted that Lucy and Aram rise early, as he did, and invent business to go about, if they had none.

LUCY SAROYAN: I remember the day that a telegram came. Papa woke me up, it was about six in the morning, and he said, "Telegram for you and Aram." I woke up real fast. I didn't know what time it was, but I thought maybe I'd overslept again and was going to get in trouble.

I opened the telegram and it said, "Darling Aram and Lucy, Walter and I have just gotten married. We miss you, we love you, we can't wait to see you—Mama."

There was nothing I didn't want in my hand more badly than this telegram. I wanted it to evaporate in my hands, because there was Papa standing over me.

So I handed him the telegram, and I actually saw Papa go ashen. He said, "It'll never work, it'll never work, and anyway, they'll never have children. You better wake up your brother. Go tell your brother."

I couldn't get out of the room fast enough, because I saw my father just dissolve in front of me. He didn't start to cry or anything, but he lost all the color in his face, and I knew that his dream of remarrying her was over.

That was a tough day. I woke Aram up: "Aram, Aram! Mama got married, Mama got married."

Aram said, "How's Pop?"

I said, "You'd better come with me."

We both frantically ran back to him. And he said, "Yeah, yeah. Well, all right. She married him. He's a nice guy, he's a good actor, he's a nice man. It'll never work, it'll never work. They'll never have any children."

With Carol's remarriage Bill's sporadic child support checks stopped altogether. Walter Matthau, like Carol, had two children by his previous marriage, but they wanted a child together, and the birth of Charlie Matthau provided another, more final, crisis for Bill.

CAROL MATTHAU: I had Charlie, and then when I came home from the hospital, Lucy came home in the afternoon, looking very angry at me, and I said, "What's the matter, Lucy?"
She said, "Well, I've just seen Pop and I told him that you'd had Charlie, and he was terribly, terribly upset."
And I said, "How could he be upset? He knew I was pregnant."
And she said, "Well, he didn't believe me. He's upset because you have everything and he has nothing."
I said, "Lucy, I'm here by the skin of my teeth, and don't spoil it with what he thinks. I don't care what he thinks. He knows I'm married."
"But he didn't think you'd have a baby with anybody else."
And that's how insane it was. He didn't think I'd have a baby with anybody else.

During one of the European summers, Bill caught Lucy in the throes of a Harold Robbins novel. She knew that *The Adventurers* was far from great literature, but she was unable to tear herself away, even when her father lectured her that cheap bestsellers were the bad writing that drove out serious work such as his own. But, when Lucy perceived that Bill was under attack, she sprang to his defense. She already had encountered friends who were surprised to hear her mention him as still alive, and when Budd Schulberg wrote about Bill in an *Esquire* piece called "Ease and Unease on the Flying Trapeze," she was furious. Schulberg wrote, "Bill Saroyan is still a middle-aged man on a trapeze that doesn't swing so close to the top of the tent." While there was nothing gloating or cruel about the facts he had laid out or his tone of voice, the basic idea of the piece was to analyze an old friend it was now convenient to label a has-been.

LUCY SAROYAN: I went berserk. I read it and I felt like this man should be killed. I wanted him sent to jail immediately, and I started telling Papa that he had to do something about it, that he couldn't let this man get away with this, and Papa then even started investigating proceedings of libel—was this piece libelous? What happened was that my pride was hurt that anybody would attack my father or put him down, and then I got *him* feeling very defensive about it. I'm sure he felt bad enough about it as it was, but to have his daughter saying, "I can't live with this man having said these terrible things about you."

I really do believe that Papa was a genius—a *personal* genius. I don't even mean a genius as a writer. He had a genius for living.

He used to do amazing things, like he'd be walking down the street and pick up twigs off the street that were just, like—sticks. They looked like little sticks, and I'd say, "Pop, stop picking things up off the street, would you please? You're embarrassing me."

And he'd say, "You watch. You'll *see* these twigs," and he'd take the twigs home and put them in a jar of water, and, sure enough, little leaves would pop out on the twigs. He would make little plants.

He also had big "found" jars—jars full of things—not just the rocks, but he would find things, buttons, on the street. Money. Little bracelets on the street. An earring here, an earring there. And he kept *jars* of all this stuff that he would collect.

He made life exciting. If we went into a lousy little restaurant for dinner, it was an event, it was an occasion, it was a celebration. We just had a sense of humor to ourselves.

I remember my childhood sweetheart's family gave a dinner party of eleven people once, and Papa came to the dinner. It was for Papa, but he didn't know there were going to be other people. He was late and they were all seated at the table when he arrived. We sat down and Papa and I laughed through the whole dinner, laughed real hard. They didn't know what we were laughing about. My friend laughed a little bit because he knew Papa, and he was laughing because we were laughing.

But everybody else was looking at us like "These are lunatics. These are Armenian *lunatics*."

We were celebrating this occasion where I was trying to show him off, and he knew that. And it wasn't working, and we were laughing about this, and this was a great joy to us.

When Lucy performed at the Dalton School, Bill arranged to be in the audience, and when she enrolled at Northwestern University, Bill accompanied her. He never was happier than when she showed him short stories she had written, and he was a silent guardian angel to her acting career when it began, asking the William Morris Agency to advise him of her roles and to send clippings about them along to him. But he also spoke to the children frankly about the burden of the name, the reputation, the inevitable and automatic comparisons and expectations.

LUCY SAROYAN: He always used to say to me, "The only way I've ever handicapped you is by making you second-generation. You don't have the drive that I had. I've tried to give you everything in the world. But I can't give you that. I can't give you that drive."

His expectations for Lucy and Aram sometimes were more implicit than explicit, perhaps because they came from the ancient source he was beginning to tap deeply as his children reached adulthood, his Armenian nature. "A man is a family thing," Rock Wagram had said, and for Saroyan's people there were strict rules about families.

2. ARAM

ARAM KEVORKIAN: I think Bill loved his children as only an Armenian or Oriental father can, and he was like a Jewish father or an Armenian father: he worried about them all the time.

Part of the problem as they grew older was that it was a conflict of generations, and this can happen with any family. I've seen it in my own.

He was an old-fashioned Fresno Armenian who thought a child should get married and not fool around and have boyfriends and be free and easy, and the man—if he had a manchild—the man should get a job, or work, or do something.

What pissed him off was that in the beginning Aram was doing these one-word poems, and Bill thought that wasn't *sérieux*, as the French would say.

But, if Aram had written thousand-word poems, he would have been proud of them. If Alexandre Dumas's son wrote one-word poems instead of novels like the father, he probably would have said, "I don't understand it."

LUCY SAROYAN: Aram was writing poetry at Trinity, in high school. He later edited and published a magazine called *Lines*, which was a poetry magazine. What happened was, he enraged my father when he became a concrete poet.

Those poems!

I remember a terrible scene. We were all in London in this apartment that Papa and I had taken together, and then Aram came over and joined us, and Aram was smoking a lot of grass and writing concrete poetry. He sat down at the typewriter, and Papa was railing on about how Aram and this concrete poetry were terrible, and all of a sudden Aram said, "I've just written the greatest poem ever written," and Papa said to me, "Did you hear the typewriter? Did you hear the typewriter at all?"

I said, "I didn't, Papa. We were talking. I didn't hear anything, but let's take a look at it."

Aram pulls the sheet of paper out, Papa looks at it, and on the sheet of paper, in lower case, is the word "gum." And Aram said, "This is the greatest poem ever written, this is—"

Pop went berserk in the room that night. That was the night that Aram told him that the written word was obsolete. He said, "You're telling me that I'm obsolete, you're telling me that my whole life is obsolete."

I think Papa wanted Aram not to be a concrete poet, to be a writer, or a *something*—something successful. Success was very important to Papa, and if I was going to be an actress, I'd better be a movie star.

ARAM SAROYAN: He was enough of an ego to have preferred the kind of doting and slightly crippled children who would have testified to his being a giant. And at the same time, he was enough of a real guy with a real heart not to want that, to want me and Lucy to go ahead into our own lives and have better lives than he himself had managed.

When I was writing one-word poems, like "lighght," and

showing them to him, he couldn't wait to see the next one. He'd be lying on his bed, and he'd say, "Let me see it." A book of mine was reviewed in the London *Times* that summer, a book of concrete poems. It was 1966 when that movement was happening, and it was bigger then in England than in America. At any rate, he couldn't wait to see the next one. And, at the same time, he would have times when he would rather violently denigrate what I was doing. "Wait a minute. You're off in a dream world. You're on the marijuana and you don't know what's happening." And on a certain level he was correct about that.

I was a young man who was, let's say, *too* sophisticated aesthetically and really green in terms of my own life, and that's really what's reflected in those poems, which are innocent and rather charming if you look at them today.

I saw a tremendous amount of tension involved in being *Saroyan*, and as a survival instinct, I began to look to other role models.

I was afraid of his example. I saw how the marriage with my mother went, and I didn't want to repeat that kind of catastrophe in my own life. And so I turned away from him as a literary example and at the same time as an emotional and life model. And later on, of course, you discover that all your own chosen models have just as many problems as your own parents, albeit different ones.

The Chaplins, Gloria Vanderbilt, Richard Avedon—these were the familiar friends of Aram's mother, and it was impossible for her to live in that *milieu* without special opportunities arising for her children. Aram, for example, worked for a time as an apprentice to Avedon. In later years, Matthau and his close friend and colleague Jack Lemmon found parts for Lucy in their films, and she worked briefly as Matthau's dresser. As for Matthau, he was more of a warm and generous new husband to Carol than a stepfather to Aram and Lucy, whom he did not seek to adopt. But at the beginning of the marriage, well before Matthau's ascent to stardom, money was sometimes short, and he was responsible not only for his own two children by his previous marriage, but for Carol's as well. "He never intruded on my father's place in my life," Aram wrote of Matthau in his autobiographical novel, *The*

Street, confessing that a "fatherly come-on" had inspired Aram to take a punch at Walter during a quarrel at an Upper West Side dairy restaurant. "The fist fight was in a way the most generous of his acts toward me—simply in accepting me as an equal in his anger. He later apologized and indicated his own hedging in not completely wiping me out—instead, boxing with me as a coach would; whereupon I hit him, and the fight was quickly halted by the crowd that had formed."

Matters never came to such a particular head between Aram and his father. In the old country, or in Fresno, it would have been the most natural thing in the world for a son to follow his father's trade, but despite Bill's interest in Aram's poetry and his professed delight in Lucy's stories, there may have been an element of competition that discomfited Bill. There was no way Aram could duplicate Saroyan's spectacular entrance upon the literary scene in 1934. But Bill soon was faced with the fact that his son's books of poetry were printed by Random House, the important publisher he had walked out on thirty years earlier, while his own work reached the public in ever-smaller printings under a string of less prestigious imprints. Aram's editor at Random House, Christopher Cerf, was disturbed to receive a letter from Saroyan attacking Aram's work. Bill gave Aram a portable typewriter and, when it was appropriate for the boy to be on his own, a small apartment on East Forty-fifth Street. While their meetings and conversations could be entirely comfortable, the distance and hostility and fear of each other could shake both men badly, as in the small but cataclysmic street encounter which both would write about later and at length.

Saroyan was walking up Fifth Avenue from Forty-fourth Street one day. Aram, who did not know his father was in town, was walking down Fifth Avenue. Each saw the other, refused to acknowledge the other. They passed.

"I didn't smile and he didn't smile. I didn't nod and he didn't nod. And I didn't care and I didn't care that he didn't care," Bill wrote.

It was Aram who broke and ran back:

"'Pop!' He turned, bewildered, and inspected me, snatching his glasses from his face, squinting," Aram wrote in *The Street*. "'Hello, my boy. I called. I left a message with that service you've got there. That's nice to have. A good idea.' I began to walk with him."

The son said he must have been dreaming. The father said he assumed the son was going someplace important. That night, Aram called on him at his hotel and they walked and talked.

The great complaint, the one which Saroyan spoke of unceasingly to his friends and acquaintances, was the matter of the letters. In writing of the incident on the street, Bill said that Aram had not known that he was in town because Bill had stopped writing to him. Bill claimed that his letters had gone unanswered by his son, but this is untrue. Aram's replies are catalogued as part of his father's estate.

ARAM SAROYAN: When I was going to a psychiatrist in my early twenties after Gailyn and I had gotten together, one of the things I did was to take every letter I'd ever gotten from my father and put them in chronological order into one of those clasp binders that has a spring in it so I could read them straight through as a book. In other words, I was trying to come to terms with my father, at a certain level, because a lot of the information that I'd gotten from him was in these letters. But, if I remember correctly, I was never able actually to finish reading that book I put together, mainly because it was terribly repetitive and dull. His letters, as a general rule—at least to his family—are not terribly telling. I think he wrote with one eye on posterity, on his literary archives.

Anyway, I had this volume, and Gailyn and I had gotten together, and we were pressed for money. We were traveling around a lot, too, and the stuff had to be shipped here and there each time we moved. And since I was selling my literary archives each year to UCLA, I thought, "Well, I should put this in with it. I could get some extra dough, and they'll be safe." So I sold them to UCLA that year, along with my archives. Now, I'd been getting $500 a year for my archives—this was back in the late sixties—and that year I got $2,500 because I included my father's letters.

It was reported to him that these letters had been sold, and at one point he expressed interest in buying them back from UCLA, and UCLA was ready to sell them back to him. But he never did it. So that's what that was all about. Later on, he seems to have made a big issue of it in explaining our estrangement. In fact, it had nothing to do with it. We were friendly for years *after* I sold the letters.

Lucy often found New Year's Eve an occasion for taking stock, spending an hour or so before her party going over the letters her father had written to her on stationery saved from a variety of hotels where he had stayed in the past, some of them with the children. She knew that he did not like the telephone, now that it had become so difficult for him to hear clearly, so she would spend part of the last night of the year writing a long letter that filled him in on what was happening in her life.

LUCY SAROYAN: He never answered those letters. I finally got to the point where I stopped expressing what I was doing with my life because I knew there was nothing that would please him. I didn't have a job. I was not married. I wasn't doing any of the things that were going to satisfy him, so I wrote to him about him, about Aram's children. I sent photographs—he loved pictures—so I would send pictures of me, pictures of Aram's kids, pictures of Aram. Anything that I thought would please him. I would just write conversational letters, but without putting details of my life. I always suggested that I would love to hear from him, but that I did not expect to hear from him.

And I didn't.

"What happens to kids?" Bill wrote. "Yes, my little daughter was a delight to know, just as my little son was a fascination. Until each became a full member of the human race, by choice, by practice, by experience, by pose, by purpose, by fate, by law."

He did not write to Lucy for eight years. The break with Aram came later. Aram and Gailyn had children whose names—Strawberry, then Cream—tickled Saroyan's sense of word-play. (He did not know of Carol's role in inventing those names.) Gailyn is a painter whose work is filled with light and flowers and is reminiscent of an up-to-date Bonnard. For many years, their home was a small, simple place on the mesa of artists and poets above Bolinas, a village on a tiny peninsula north of San Francisco. Bill visited often, delighting in the children and in the fact that his youngest grandson was named Armenak. When Aram asked Bill for help in buying the cottage, his father's reaction was, once again, kindness on his own particular terms. Carol had won, on appeal, her lawsuit against Bill for the unpaid child support and had held the judgment over him, renewing it on behalf of the children whenever it was about to expire. Now Bill was made to understand that she would forget the matter if he helped their son and his family. Saroyan bought the house for himself, conferring a life estate upon Aram and his family, but writing into his will instructions that the property would not go to them upon his death, but would be held by the foundation he had devised to perpetuate his property and his name. As he approached death, which became, increasingly, the central subject of all that he wrote, Saroyan had cut his family away altogether.

CHAPTER TEN

SAROYAN

Now he was *Saroyan*—to himself and to everyone else as well. The lawyers, a few of the fellow writers, his sister or brother or Cousin Archie—any of these might address him as Bill, but his meetings and conversations with them became fewer and further between. Years of letters from old friends like Hirschfeld went unanswered.

Saroyan had maintained routes and routines in all of the cities of his past, but now he began to edit out cities as well as people. The vibrating penthouse was the last New York apartment. (Even the Fifty-seventh Street Automat was gone now.) A hotel—usually the Royalton—would do as staging area for his visits there: a call on an editor from the distant past, a reconciliation with the lawyer he had not spoken to for five years. Paris could provide relief from Fresno, Fresno from Paris, and Yerevan, in Armenia, the ultimate refuge from anywhere and everywhere else. His new life was one of peripatetic isolation, the journeying of a well-seasoned hermit.

"From a swift young man," Saroyan wrote of himself in *Days of Life and Death and Escape to the Moon*, "delighting in new clothes, moving everywhere with noise and laughter, I became a sloppy old man in old clothes with a careless posture and a lazy walk, going nowhere. What did I expect? Well, the fact is everything of an external kind that I expected I got, such as fame and money, but it always turned out to be only for myself, and that had never really been the idea."

Saroyan arranged for other, more manageable sons, younger men with whom the relationship would be in his control, and in and out of whose lives he could pop at his own whim. "He made a thing of appearing and disappearing," one of them recalls. "You never could count on an appointment." And, while he might walk away from an elaborate dinner party in his honor after the first five minutes, he might just as easily appear unannounced and stay for many hours, delighting in the company and in himself.

One of the surrogate sons was Michael J. Arlen, the writer for *The New Yorker*, whose own father was born as Dikran Kouymjian into a family of well-to-do Manchester, England, merchants. Dikran Kouymjian metamorphosed into the best-selling author of *The Green Hat*, the Michael Arlen whom Saroyan had heard praised at Anthony Eden's table during the war. After the war, just at the time Saroyan had grown the patriarchal mustache, he had embarked on a little project to bring the elder Arlen back into the Armenian fold, writing to the editors of the Hairenik Association in Boston that he would persuade Arlen to contribute to their journals. Saroyan failed in this task, but he rejoiced in the younger Arlen's rediscovery of his own Armenian nature, as chronicled in the memoirs *Exiles* and *A Passage to Ararat*. In the latter the young Arlen records his journey to Soviet Armenia, a country his father never saw, and confronts the enormity of the Turkish genocide in personal terms. It is this book that led to one of the last meaningful conversations between Saroyan and his daughter.

LUCY SAROYAN: I was reading the book, and I got to the place where Michael takes a flower—his interpreter gives him a flower to put into the eternal flame for the Armenians that were killed, and he can't put the flower in, he can't bring himself to burn it for these Armenians. I was so stunned by this shame that he was feeling that I called Papa in the middle of reading the book and said, "Papa, Papa, what is the matter with this man? Why is he so ashamed to be an Armenian? All my life I've been so proud of it and bragged to everybody that I was an Armenian, and I don't understand."

Papa said, "It's wonderful that you're reading the book. This is very good for you. It's time for you to know now. I wanted always to protect you from that. I wanted you to feel that it was a great and joyous experience, that it was full of laughter and love and fun." And he said, 'Those are some of the dimensions of being an Armenian, but not all of them." He said, "The sorrows and the grief and the moaning and weeping over the losses—I always sheltered you, both of you, from that, because I didn't feel that it was necessary for you to get into that dimension of the Armenian experience."

MICHAEL J. ARLEN: I used to feel, in an uncomfortable way, that I was the good son. Bill used to say, "Your father would be proud of you," and "I'm proud of you."

I felt him very hard trying to be a father to me—I was then, really, in my late thirties—as though he could sort of act the part to me that he couldn't in real life. He would be thoughtful and considerate. He would come in and be very dear.

But Bill was somebody, I always felt, with a sort of surface, character-acting kind of thing. But underneath he was—not a lot colder than many writers are (writers tend to be cold underneath)—but cold and selfish and self-protective and all those things that many writers, very good and very bad, are, although they don't also have this kind of Akim Tamiroff persona to go with it.

My guess is that Bill started as many Armenian boys do, as my father did. My father, I suspect, grew up in such a *strictly* Armenian household, and as the adored youngest son—these were *haut bourgeois* Armenians in England. To guess about these things, my guess is that my father was so *Armenianed* as a child that he was free to become his own strange construction of a quasi-Englishman, and to be very offhand, truly offhand, about his Armenianness, enough to mystify me later on. My guess is that Bill, for all the whooping and hollering, also grew up in a thick Armenian household, but must have felt such lacks—maybe simply parenting, or whatever it is—that when Bill began his young man's journey and got out into the world, the American-Anglo-whatever-it-is, and was soon enough a big success, and found, as so often happens, the Fitzgerald thing about there being no second acts in American lives. (All that really means is that some people really have a sound emotional infrastructure in their lives, and once they get out into life and the bombs and shells are falling, they have enough to move on. Some people, as we all know from our friends and others, *don't*.)

I feel that Bill got into the "Anglo" world—all those plays, big success and stuff—and when he began getting into trouble, factual troubles and *secret* troubles, his fallback position was 'way, 'way back in his fantasy Armenian childhood, Aram folktales.

When my father, 1946, '47, was close to fifty and was in Los Angeles playing at being a screenwriter, a fifteen-year-old girl from Missouri drove a car up on the sidewalk near the Beverly-Wilshire and knocked him down, and he had a bad leg thing, and he had a cane. His leg got better, *fine*, but he never gave up the cane, kept it for the rest of his life. He said, "I like it."

Bill—I don't know at what stage he got the mustache—but that was the same thing. As a kid, I remember a picture of Bill. He was really damned handsome, looked like Gershwin. You said, "That guy's a lot of trouble." And out of that comes this old folktale person. And what produced Akim Tamiroff out of that is the story of Bill's adult life.

Each of his several cities provided relief from any and all of the others, and in his two principal homes, Paris and Fresno, he saw to it that his stage was small and private.

IRWIN SHAW: When he lived in Paris, he'd never answer his phones, so you couldn't invite him. You just had to bump into him by accident. You bump into him by accident, he'd hang around with you all night. He was a lonely guy, wandering around Paris. I never saw him with a *woman* in Paris. I would see him, and I'd say, "Come on, we're going out to dinner with so-and-so. . . ." We had one marvelous meal out in the open in the Bois de Boulougne: Bill, Bill Styron?—I'm not sure—Gore Vidal . . . Blair Fuller, a writer for *The Paris Review*. Bill Saroyan did most of the talking, and enchanted everybody.

Herbert Gold, another of the surrogate sons (although only sixteen years Bill's junior), recalled a suspenseful occasion, a Paris dinner party designed to star Saroyan and to feature Mary McCarthy, an arrangement requiring her implicit consent, for Miss McCarthy's tongue can be as sharp as her pen point, and Saroyan, loud and dominating as usual in his increasingly rare social appearances, gave her ample opportunity to correct him on matters of fact and opinion. Without a hint of condescension, she was uncharacteristically silent, yielding to the old lion, who had obvious difficulty understanding what others said between his monologues.

The occasional visiting journalist would rediscover his presence in Paris and conduct an interview, and always would be told that Bill was writing. He wrote unceasingly. Robert Creamer, the editor who had arranged Saroyan's World Series assignment with *Sports Illustrated*, would open an envelope from Fresno or Paris to find a fragment of memoir, such as a recollection of driving a Model-T over Pacheco Pass, the difficult cut across the mountains separating San Francisco Bay from the Central Valley of Saroyan's youth. In its earliest years, Creamer's magazine had included art writing very nearly disconnected from sports altogether, but no longer. Saroyan was not the least bit senile, simply out of touch with the markets.

Reminiscence now was his stock-in-trade. A literary journalist who had once profiled him for the Manchester *Guardian* had become an editor for Praeger, and asked to see manuscripts. He received a curious batch of plays he considered unpublishable. The editor then asked if Saroyan could write, perhaps, more about himself? The result was *Places Where I've Done Time*, a memoir whose connecting thread is a chain of addresses and dates. *Places* would be followed by *Sons Come and Go, Mothers Hang in Forever*, as it had been preceded by *Not Dying*, books in which Saroyan ranged back and forth over his career, recapitulating the orphanage, confessing his displeasure with his children, occasionally attacking Carol directly. His son later would describe these books as "a multi-volumed literary libel against my mother." Whenever one of the publishers submitted material to Carol to discover whether she objected, she replied by letter, "Be my guest." But in most cases, the editors and lawyers would step in and delete the most defamatory material. W. J. Weatherby, the editor who commissioned *Places Where I've Done Time*, found Saroyan a reasonable author, who revised willingly and quickly, even when the demand was to cut away obviously heartfelt material about the marriages.

"I am an old man, sixty-seven years of age. I have failed. My children have grown up and gone away and don't love me. I have no wealth. I have no fame. I have no real reason to be glad." He was speaking to another of the surrogate sons, Garig Basmadjian, in Paris in 1975.

"And yet I go on. I've got a room and in the room there is a table, and in the room there is some paper and there is a pencil and I take the paper and I write down over here . . ." And now Saroyan took a pencil and wrote for Basmadjian: "*The world is a great big fat falsehood.*"

"Yeah, that's interesting. So I'm writing now. I got nothing. The room is cold. Now, how can I be miserable? I cross out *The world is a great big fat lie*, and I say it may hurt somebody's feelings, so I put over there *the world is really not real*, and then I look at that, and I am working.

"And I say the world is really not real. It is certainly not real the way Howard Hughes and Paul Getty and Calouste Gulbenkian thought it was real. They were wrong. And so I'm off to the races. There's something going on. That's the beginning of art. Or I take the pencil and make a drawing. I think about the drawing, or I start to write a poem. Now I do write poems and I keep them, and I almost never look at them again."

The Paris apartment filled up with Saroyan's drawings and manuscripts, the multitude of journals addressed to himself, the plays, which now were frankly documentary. These final dramatic efforts pose problems as works of living theatre, technical problems, because of their loose theatrical construction, and questions of taste, because of their scatological language. In *Haratch*, set in the offices of the Parisian journal of that name, every stock Armenian appears on stage, from the mild poet to the fiery-eyed terrorist sympathizer, a deft gallery of Saroyan's real-life acquaintances. In *Will There Be a Wedding?*, it is the Armenians of his Fresno childhood, of his own family, who live and speak, and in their own names and voices.

When he wrote back to America, to Arlen, for instance, he was at pains to emphasize how very much he was writing, and the writing itself had expanded by now to fill every square inch of his paper. He typed single-spaced from corner to corner, citing the savings, and he dated and noted his work as precisely as a telegraph message, "timing off," as the boys in the Postal Telegraph office had called it.

Much of his time at the typing table was spent in correspondence. A routine inquiry for anthology rights could result in a delightful stream-of-consciousness essay. A young editor who solicited an introduction from him found herself reading an informal book proposal, which was, in itself, a witty confession of his own peccadilloes as a gambler. And, as Kevorkian had realized, he remained a jealous caretaker of his own reputation. Basmadjian had asked Saroyan casually if he acknowledged the influence of Samuel Beckett on *The Cave Dwellers*, a connection several critics had suggested, and not in an unkind way. "Sometime when you have a taped interview with Mr. Samuel Beckett," Saroyan wrote to his young friend, "you might find it permissible to ask him if he was influenced in the writing of *Waiting for Godot* by the scene between Joe and Mary L. in *The Time of Your Life* in which the very essence of *Waiting for Godot* is presented in a profoundly simple way." Basmadjian did, in fact, get a chance to ask Beckett for his opinion of Saroyan, and Beckett replied, "He has made me smile on several occasions," closing the matter.

Garig Basmadjian had grown up from the boy whose poems had provided wrappers for Saroyan's wet rocks on the shore in Israel. Now, as a highly-acclaimed Armenian poet, he journeyed to Soviet Armenia to confer with the other young leaders of the national literature, and these trips gave him the opportunity to see his sometime mentor, Saroyan, in his incarnation as secular patriarch. Saroyan had journeyed to the new Armenia in 1935 and had found, in the analysis of certain Armenian-American writers, the impulse to return to his beginnings for the first time. (The *Aram* cycle resulted.) He had gone again in 1960, and had weathered pointed inquiries from the Passport Office of the State Department as to how he was quoted in the Soviet press. As usual, Saroyan's remarks had been strictly apolitical, but sufficiently broad to sustain a bit of propagandistic *braggadocio*, suggesting that his heart was in the highlands of (new) Armenia. Now, as the end of his life neared, he journeyed there again in 1976 and 1978.

GARIG BASMADJIAN: He really was a living legend for Armenia. No one—not one of the Armenian classics, dead or alive—had the impact that Saroyan had in Armenia. If you find an Armenian who doesn't revere Saroyan, tell me about him, and we can put him in a museum. They genuflected in Armenia. They love it. The man, they loved him more, because he is a different animal to them. To the Armenians who haven't been to the West, he was a completely different man, with his mustache, his allure, with his voice, with his clothes. Whatever he said was funny to them.

Just one word that he said echoed very far, and they tried to find philosophy in it. Anything he said was accepted as something extremely deep, and the word went downtown and more intelligent people made it better, and then the story went.

Basmadjian observed high Communist party officials and lowly cab drivers courting Saroyan's attention, hanging on his every word, and he also observed the older writer's crippling suspicion of almost everyone chosen to make his stays in Yerevan happy. "People who gave him their lives, their time, *everything* in Armenia, just to keep him happy, he comes to Paris and tells me, 'I'm sure that he is a worker of the KGB.'" In one case, a timid writer in the welcoming delegation was so tongue-tied in the presence of the great Saroyan that Saroyan concluded that the young man was the KGB agent: his silence was inauthentic for a real writer. He was ejected from the hotel suite at Saroyan's bellowed command, bewildered, humiliated.

As Basmadjian's poetic reputation in Armenia grew, so did his personal fortune in Paris, where he had established a successful art gallery. Now Saroyan's feelings toward the young man cooled. Basmadjian saw this as a replay of Saroyan's relationship with his real son. "It could be, from the inside, he loved me," Basmadjian recalls, "because, from too many people: 'He talked about you.' 'He sent you this. . . .' In Armenia he talked about me.

"But *with* me, he was a difficult man. We couldn't sit together and talk for five minutes. He would immediately make a fight with me. He always wanted to . . . *degrade* me or something. I don't believe that it was the competition that disturbed him. The creative force of anybody. It's not the Armenianism or the competition that he avoided. He didn't want the creative force around him. Why? I don't know. We have to think about it."

In the secret stream of Saroyan's writings, the journals that flowed into publishable memoirs and into plays intended for the stage of the imagination, the death theme now asserted itself, spilling over occasionally into his conversations with Basmadjian. In their talks, Saroyan could slip in and out of Armenian, speaking as frankly as he might have wished to do with his son, or to have done with his own father. He had confessed before to considering suicide in a reasoned way at the time of his second divorce from Carol, and he had written of having felt close to death one casino night when empty traveler's check folders littered the floor of his hotel room. He thought now of how others around him had died. . . .

WILLIAM SAROYAN: I have had some very good friends who have had heart attacks, and they know that they are not going to recuperate, and they cry like babies. Now I ask myself, if it happens to me, will I do it, too? It could be. We don't know. But it's such a humiliation to cry before death. You cry about other things. A man should cry. But because you are going to die, it's such a terrible thing.

I have noticed that dying people have an irritability which is rather large, and one can use that as a measure, a probable closeness to death. I'll give you an illustration: I had a Cadillac, I was taking my mother and my sister from Fresno to San Francisco, and I turned the Cadillac up to get to Skyline Boulevard. My mother said something when I turned. It was so irritable, unlike her, that I figured she had a slight stroke then, and this was retaliation to that stroke, and she died of a stroke. Apparently this was a hint, and I said, "That kind of unreasonable irritability isn't toward the event of turning, it's toward the event of death." And I've seen that happen to other people. And of course, to be perfectly honest, I've seen it happen to me, and it makes me realize, "Watch it!"

Somebody said, "We die when we want to. We don't die until we want to."

There was a girl in the Bagdasarian family, and Dikran was dispatched to help this little girl die of TB. She had been in the hospital and her family had become bankrupt, and he told me one of the saddest stories in the world. . . . Little Penny says, "Uncle Dikran, just don't ask me to die."

And I'll give you another little story: A friend of mine had many daughters and the daughter who was most like a butterfly was famous for playing a little piece called "The Butterfly." She got leukemia, and I visited her two days before she died. Her little brother and father visited her the day she died. Her eyes closed and this is what she said—her little brother's name was Vahan—"Vahan, I've got to go now, I've got to go," and she died.

Also, my Grandmother Lucy died at the age of eighty-eight, and this is what she said at the end: "*Ul chem grnar.*" Isn't that beautiful? "*Can't hang on.*"

He returned to Fresno each year at the time of the grape harvest, although the vineyard was gone now from across the street from his twin tract houses on West Griffith Way. To one of the surrogates, such as the novelist Herbert Gold, Saroyan would explain that he kept the extra house in case his son or daughter decided to visit him, the implication being that such a prospect was unthinkable on their part, not his. In fact, both houses were filled with the documentation of the life of Saroyan. His workplace was a simple white table in a big room with multiple towers of paper. He had begun to keep copies of his correspondence after a pleading letter from the Library of Congress and the affair of Aram's dealings with UCLA had established its value in his mind. The detailed evidence of his life was here, in these two private places where even Archie could be turned away at the door without a word. The cousin who had been as close as a brother learned to read Saroyan's answering face, to say quickly, "I'll see you later, Bill," and to hear Saroyan say, "Thanks, Arch," as Archie headed back for his car and the three-hour drive to Palo Alto. Only a few old friends would receive visits or have their invitations answered, and because his worsening hearing made the telephone something of an ordeal, Saroyan would bark even at a call from his brother, Henry. The phone number was unlisted, to the uninitiated, because he wished to avoid direct calls from agents or from students working on term papers. To the children of his neighborhood, to the denizens of the library and the regular customers of a nearby shopping mall that he favored, he was the old man with the white mustache who rode a bicycle. On page 88 of the Fresno telephone directory he was "Aram Garoghlanian, 2729 W. Griffith Wy..........227-4765."

He made friends with another young surrogate son, another Dickran Kouymjian, who had been born in Eastern Europe of Armenian-American parents from Chicago, and who now directed the Armenian Studies concentration at Fresno State University. Kouymjian is a scholar of wide-ranging skills whose particular specialty is iconography. Not only was he fluent in Armenian, capable of understanding clearly Saroyan's Bitlisi dialect, but, Saroyan was surprised to discover, Kouymjian also split his time between Fresno and Paris, where his wife kept their apartment. Kouymjian returned to California for the fall term at the university just as Saroyan was returning from his own Paris home. For the last dozen years of his life, Saroyan confided in Kouymjian and found the confidences kept. He discussed his unhappiness with his children, as he did with all the surrogate sons, and he spoke of what he considered to be Carol's betrayal, although journal entries Kouymjian was permitted to read described in unembarrassed detail the physical delight Bill had found in his lovemaking with her. Kouymjian and another young man, David Battan, a local scholar and collector of Saroyan's works, were his ideal readers. There was the young Armenian, Kouymjian, who acknowledged Saroyan's mastery of the broad sweep of matters Armenian, even if he could be faulted on the fine details, and who could laugh with delight at the mixture of satire and respect in the character sketches of the *Haratch* play. In the young non-Armenian, Battan, there was a sympathetic and eager expert on Saroyaniana who completely shared, in a more objective fashion, Saroyan's mystification over the eclipse of his reputation. Battan was permitted to read exactly what Saroyan wanted everyone else to be able to read, unpublished works in the old style, such as *Another Aram*, a volume that would complete and continue the sequence of stories only partially collected in *My Name Is Aram*, and which Saroyan intended to be illustrated by more of Don Freeman's wonderful drawings.

To any invitation to appear on a platform at a dinner or semipublic event, Saroyan's answer was an automatic no, although he found it necessary and appropriate to attend an appearance of a delegation of writers from Soviet Armenia at the Fresno Convention Center, insisting on sitting in the audience. If asked by old friends such as Aram and Alma Arax, Saroyan was willing to attend a dinner, but only after trimming the guest list to suit himself and making it plain that the floor was to remain his throughout the evening.

On a day that Professor Kouymjian was in the process of moving his office at the university, one of the five students he had recruited to assist him answered the office telephone. A moment later, obviously excited, he handed it to the teacher: "It's William Saroyan, Doc!" All five of the young men had grown up in Fresno's Armenian-American community and now had moved into formal study of their ancestry, and without even having glimpsed the archetypal Armenian, Saroyan. "Can I bring these five wild Armenian kids over?" Kouymjian asked.

"Bring 'em over!" Saroyan shouted into the phone, and the professor used the prospect of the meeting to make the work go quickly.

DICKRAN KOUYMJIAN: Five students, and he went around the table asking their names, spelling them. Went around the table trying to figure out their genealogy. "Aren't you such-and-such's nephew?" He was a walking encyclopedia on cousins, relationships, family ties, even though he didn't mix that much with the general public. He was asking questions to get that knowledge as quickly as possible, question after question.
What did he want to know?
Everything. Everything. He wanted to know about . . . everything. What do I mean by everything? What were these kids doing? Why did they want to do *that*? What did their parents think about what they were doing? How they felt about Armenian things . . .

Despite his complete grasp of spoken Armenian, Saroyan remained ignorant of the written language until the very end, and so it was Kouymjian who brought him the news written only in that language, pamphlets from the Beirut militants who believed in avenging the genocide. "Far from expressing any moral condemnation of it—I don't want to suggest that he was for it—he just wanted to know everything about it," says Kouymjian, "and he grew excited by the idea that there was a commitment on the part of these young people who should have been assimilated out by the third or fourth generation, all of a sudden feeling that they should be more aggressive in bringing up the old question that has never been resolved, the unpunished genocide and the loss of the land because of that genocide."

In 1977, perhaps becoming aware of the illness that would eventually claim him, but otherwise in sound health in the eyes of his few close acquaintances, Saroyan began a final thematic memoir. As a trivial interview and the summer visit of his children had provided framework for *Not Dying*, and as a list of all his addresses had given structure to *Places Where I've Done Time*, Saroyan now began to free-associate in writing as he pondered *Variety*'s necrology register for the year 1976, the show-business newspaper's listing of everyone who had died that year in the entertainment industry.

In 135 chapters, he writes about his personal experiences with a handful of the year's dead, speculates about the identity of others (*Variety* gave only the names, alphabetically, nothing more), and drifts on into reminiscence about people from his past whose names only *resemble* those in *Variety*'s final accounting. Old grudges surface. The death of one lawyer reminds him of the death of another—the one who had helped Carol in one of her legal battles against him—and he is delighted to gloat over his own personal survival in the face of the lawyer's passing.

Do we mock the dead by staying alive, by reading their names in lists, by remembering them in the world, by speculating about those we never knew? Do we perhaps take pleasure from our own survival and even from their sad or joyous failure to do so? Bet your life we do. And don't let us hang our silly living heads in shame, making our ugly faces even uglier by a sense of guilt. What is true of us may very well be helplessly true of us, and more connected with laws we do not know too well, and with natural conditions that at least slightly exempt us from any need to be ashamed or astonished.

The book, titled *Obituaries*, is a unique exercise in sustained internal monologue, published by Creative Arts in Berkeley, a small literary house that honored Saroyan's wish not to be corrected on his factual errors. What did it matter that Rod Serling appears as "Rod Sterling"? Everyone knows whom Saroyan meant, and the point of mentioning him at all was to speculate on his Armenian good looks, which in truth were not Armenian at all. Saroyan describes his day, comments on his life, ruminates over Ross Bagdasarian's entirely unexpected death from a heart attack, and relates his own snap-of-the-fingers decision to quit smoking in 1968. Bobbing along in the stream of consciousness were unbidden, unexplained, and completely isolated little passages such as, "Forget it, brother, that way madness lies, or childish absurdity, a child crying it out: 'Cut it out, Papa, you son of a bitch—stop choking Mama just because she is a liar.'"

Saroyan confessed, for the first time in print, that he had left Fresno High School after multiple expulsions, not simply to seek his fame and fortune. He wrote of the secret pleasure a son feels at the death of a father and of the trick to staying alive, the simple matter of managing to wake up another morning. Early in the fifties, when he was in his own forties, Saroyan had begun to explain his motive as a writer as a battle of life against death, the desire to make a mark, to leave behind his own equivalent of Armenak's homemade notebooks of poetry and aphorisms. Now, in his energetic meditation on the deaths of dozens of colleagues, many of them far younger than he, Saroyan spoke in a voice that even the critics were obliged to acknowledge. The reviews— including an inside-front-page feature in the *New York Times Book Review*—were more than respectful, and went beyond nostalgic reprises of his career. *Obituaries* was an important book, a judgment made plain by its nomination for an American Book Award in Autobiography. (Saroyan lost the prize to Lauren Bacall's more traditional effort.)

When the literary journalists asked him what was next, he replied that he was at work on a book called *Births*, the logical subject of a sequel, and that this book might be followed, in turn, by *Marriages*, *Divorces*, and then, finally, *Murders and Suicides*. How could he explain the journals and the plays, the correspondence and the housefuls of unpublished words? There was a book called *Births*, published only after his death, but its tone was querulous and unfocused because the implicit subject was now his own death.

After the publication of *Obituaries*, Saroyan received a request from *The Tonight Show* to make an appearance. "I'll do it," Bill told Shirley Wood, the program's producer, "only if Johnny's there." (Johnny Carson, the show's longtime host, was often on vacation.) Ms. Wood agreed to this demand. "And I want you to fly me down there"—to Los Angeles—"and make sure there's a limousine to pick me up." Ms. Wood, charmed by Saroyan's crustiness, said the limo would be there. Saroyan's appearance was advertised in *TV Guide* and other advance television listings, but at the last minute he reneged on his promise, giving no particular reason. *The Today Show*, too, wanted him as a guest, but Saroyan, after first agreeing to do it, made several extraordinary demands that forced them to abandon the idea. "It's too late," one could imagine him thinking, "both for them and for me."

Aram Arax and Cousin Archie both had admonished him to take better care of himself. The play royalties never had stopped, and despite the high cost of air travel between Paris and Fresno, Saroyan had income that was more than adequate for his needs. Archie, however, began to worry about what he saw on the occasions when he was admitted to the houses on West Griffith Way. The clutter was increasingly dense. On a visit to Paris, which Bill had insisted that Archie and his wife make, the Minasians spent their first days sorting out things, although Saroyan would insist that every receipt and old magazine had its meaning. Now, in Fresno, they would attack the disorder on a hit-and-run basis, begging Bill as they left to spend a bit of his money on a once-a-week cleaning woman. Even more worrisome to Archie was the matter of his cousin's diet. He ate from cans and prepared simple meals like the bulghur and onions of his boyhood; but all leftovers were kept until eaten, and sometimes Saroyan could not eat them before they had spoiled, and he would become sick.

ARAM ARAX: Saroyan never took care of himself. I hate his teapot, and I have a poem on that, "Killer Teapot." Every time that teapot was on, the whole day, he was drinking tea.

I said, "Saroyan, why don't you do it, why don't you go restaurant?" He said, "That costs too much money."

I said, "You are a rich man."

Maybe this is gossiping a little bit, but he killed himself by neglecting his diet or anything else.

When he came back from Armenia in 1978, the Writers Union gave him a beautiful Armenian rug, and he brought it to Los Angeles and the customs house says, "You can't take this home unless you pay fifteen hundred dollars." He says, "I have no money, I can't take it."

Imagine. A rug that is worth maybe fifteen, twenty thousand— maybe more. *Beautiful* rug. He didn't pay it.

A year later, I get a call from Los Angeles that friends are going to take the rug, they're going to pay whatever it is, and they're going to bring it to Fresno. "You had better contact Saroyan, if he's home." I call him up. I says, "William, they're going to bring you your rug."

He got very happy. He says, "Let them come. But what am I going to do with them?"

"Take them to restaurant."

He says, "No, *your* house. Alma cooks well. We're going to be guests in your house," and I said all right.

They brought the rug to his house, beautiful rug, and I said, "William, let's give them something to drink."

He says, "All right, I've got tea. I'll give *tea*."

"No, you've got cognac—you've got nine bottles of cognac there. Open one of them."

"No, they are *sacred*."

There was no time left for an occasion to drink the brandy. He had cancer of the prostate, a disease with a high cure rate, but instead of undergoing the simple operation his doctor recommended, he boarded the airplane for his last season in Paris. When he returned to California in the fall of 1980, he began to place his affairs in order, taking an advertisement in *Variety* to offer for sale the beach house at Malibu, now something of a wreck atop pilings. The rent, earmarked for Cosette's well-being, had long gone unpaid, and the house itself eventually would have to be demolished. But Saroyan was in a playful spirit, as he had been when forced to sell the worthless hilltop property near Fresno, which he had bought to stave off the first divorce. His nephew Henry told reporters who called, "I think it's his way of letting everybody know he's still alive. Everybody thinks, you know, that Faulkner, Steinbeck, and Saroyan all died in the same car crash." But the ad itself said plainly that the money was to go to the William Saroyan library and estate.

At Fresno State University he was shown a large, special room on the top floor of the new library, the place where the contents of the Paris apartment and the two Fresno houses were to be brought and sorted and handed to the scholars who would decipher their meaning, to the editors who would publish the rejected and never-seen plays and stories and novels, to the biographers Saroyan addressed and teased throughout his published lifetime. The royalties and the money from the sale of the Malibu property were intended to finance the study of Saroyan and his works. A will was written, signed, witnessed by a delegation from the university, but Saroyan evidently sensed a diffidence on the part of his local school, and by the time of his death it seemed preferable to his executors and trustees that the material be sheltered at the University of California's Bancroft Library in Berkeley, the leading facility of its kind in the West.

He had quarreled with Aram Kevorkian, as he had with all his other lawyers in the past, but the two men reunited now in Fresno on the nineteenth anniversary of their first meeting, in April of 1962, when they had found the apartment on rue Taitbout. Kevorkian hailed from Philadelphia's Armenian community, and his first view of Fresno and Saroyan's milieu startled him. "I realized that he was the only artist in the family, perhaps in the city, and you wonder how his talent flourished, nourished in such surroundings. I could well understand, when

I saw that context, why the family thought it was a joke that this guy wanted to be a writer. What impressed me in *Obituaries*, the significance to me was, he was saying, 'I've shown once more that I can do my thing, even if no one reads it,' and that was the Saroyan that I knew."

Kevorkian was shocked to learn that Saroyan was withholding news of his final illness from his family. Only the Fresno cousins who did the shopping and cared for the yard were permitted to see the emaciation and the feebleness. At the clinic where he was undergoing x-rays, Saroyan realized that the mustachioed young technician was a fellow Armenian, and he began the usual interrogation: "Where did your family come from? How do you spell your name?" The tests revealed that the cancer had become generalized, reaching the soft organs as well as the bones. There was no longer any chance of recovery.

Although it was strictly against Saroyan's wishes, Kevorkian telephoned Lucy in Beverly Hills to tell her that her father was dying. She spoke, in turn, with the Fresno doctor caring for Saroyan, who told her that the liver tumor left him very few weeks, and she telephoned Aram in Bolinas to tell him the news. Aram began the journal of his father's death that was published as *Last Rites*, and its earliest entries chronicle Lucy's attempt to visit her father and comfort him. The cousin working in the yard and the neighbors for many houses around could hear Saroyan shouting cruelly at his daughter, "You've come here to exploit my death." He rejected the food she had cooked, sent her away with this injunction for his son: "Tell Aram not to come, not to write, and not to phone. Tell him he'll kill me if he does."

"I like last sayings," he had written in *Obituaries*, "even though I must consider most of them spurious, inventions of the survivors, members of the family, exploiters of truth and falsity alike." In mid-April, 1981, he telephoned the San Francisco bureau of the Associated Press to dictate his own exit line. He had cancer, he had to explain to them, and he wanted his last words withheld until the obituary itself: "Everybody has got to die, but I have always believed an exception would be made in my case. Now what?"

When his cousin Ruben found him unconscious on the floor in one of the West Griffith Way houses, he was taken to the Veterans Administration hospital in Fresno, where the diagnosis given to the press was stroke, but this was soon corrected.

HENRY SAROYAN: I talked to him during the initial stages, but I did not know that he had cancer of the prostate. He went to the University of California, to a mutual friend of ours, and I was never told what the diagnosis was. But at that time it was possible for him to have that simple operation, but he would never submit to it.

And, naturally, it got worse and worse and he was—so I understand, I didn't see him—he got emaciated, something terrible. . . .

And I've never understood why he took that attitude, but it may have been his philosophy that "If this is my fate, this is my fate, and I'm not going to mess around with it." I don't know.

Bill's son, Aram, made a plan. He had to see his father and he would go to Fresno with someone Bill might not reject—Cream, the younger of the two daughters.

Saroyan's nurse announced, "This is your granddaughter, Cream." Saroyan was all eyes, huge eyes in a face wasted from the disease, and his eyes were locked on the delicate creature his son had brought to see him.

"And . . . you know your son," the nurse said, because after a few moments in the room Aram remained ignored.

"I'll never forget him," Saroyan told her, and turned his eyes toward his son in a look Aram read as both vulnerable and defiant.

Saroyan allowed his son to lift his glass of fruit juice to his lips, but he also used the child to taunt Aram. "What does *your* father do?" Saroyan asked her. "What?" "What does *your* father do?"

"He writes screenplays," she whispered.

"What?"

"She said, 'He writes screenplays.'"

"Ah."

Later in the visit, though, he told his doctor while Aram and Cream were in the room, "I'm . . . letting go," he told the doctor, in front of them. When it came time for them to leave, after an hour of sitting with him, he appeared to be asleep, but when Aram pointed for Cream to kiss him—there—she did and his eyes popped open.

Father and son regarded one another, and Aram moved forward and kissed him, too.

"Goodbye, Pop."

And Bill flung his arm over his son's shoulder, and the two men were in wholehearted embrace, Aram shocked by the softness of the neck muscle he remembered from childhood hugs as broad and hard, by the terrible lightness of what was left of the man.

"Thank you, Aram."

"Thank *you*, Pop."

"It's the most beautiful time of my life . . . and death."

There was another visit, for Bill to see Armenak, and Lucy saw her father, too, although no deathbed reconciliation could erase for her the horror of the day she had been turned away at the door in Fresno.

It was Saroyan's niece, Jackie Kazarian, Zabel's daughter, who was with him on Monday morning, May 18. She had spoken with the night nurse about him every evening since he went into the hospital, but on that particular Sunday night, she sensed it was important that she be at his side, since the children were back in their usual cities, getting daily reports by long distance from the doctors. Bill had indicated he wished to see no one, and at first Jackie was uncertain that he recognized who she was; he no longer could speak.

She slept in the chair by his bed, and he awoke soon after she did. She held his hand, told him she loved him, and opened a "bless you" cookie, whose message she read to him: "Bless you with health and happiness." Jackie left to tell the floor nurses that Saroyan was awake now, and when she and a nurse returned they found him dead.

"Now what?"

On the morning of May 20, 1981, Gerald Pollinger, Saroyan's literary representative in London, opened the letter addressed and mailed to him the week before. "Dear Gerald," he read, "By the time you read this, I will be dead." The communication that followed was brief, asking that Pollinger continue in his capacity as literary agent for the estate. It was signed, simply, "Bill."

The obituary began on the front page of the *New York Times* and filled another page inside.

Large tributes were organized in Fresno, San Francisco, and New York City, where even prominent Turks and utter strangers, such as Mayor Koch and Henry Kissinger, attended out of respect. Herbert Gold was asked to speak at the service in San Francisco, held under the doleful gaze of a giant portrait of Saroyan in his last years. Novelist Gold's invitation to speak had arrived in the name of humorist Harry

Golden, and he was taken aback at the request that he make his remarks in Armenian; he decided to say nothing at all. Archie followed the progress of one memorial service from a small church to a large public auditorium as ambitions for it grew. "What is it?" Archie asked. "Tribute, tribute, tribute. Lionize, lionize, lionize. It's all fake. What they're doing is lionizing themselves, for Christ's sake." Archie approached apoplexy when he viewed a formal exhibition of Bill's ink doodles mounted in a small gallery at the university in Fresno. The posthumous tributes increased in their absurdity. A year after his death, there was a ceremony in Yerevan to install the pewter urn containing Saroyan's ashes in a monument on a hill above the city. As he had feared in life, he was claimed in death as a champion of socialism, and the first secretary of the new Armenia's Communist party was among the urn bearers. (Nothing was made of the fact that the urn contained only half of Saroyan's ashes.)

The will was filed for probate and the Saroyan Foundation duly constituted, with a San Francisco businessman, Robert Setrakian, in charge. As expected, Saroyan had left everything to himself. The Fresno houses would shelter exchange students from Armenia; the house where Cosette still lived would become foundation headquarters. Nothing whatsoever was left to Lucy. The Bolinas house remained in Saroyan's name, now the property of the foundation, and for use by Aram and his family in a life estate. Of $150,000 in cash, payments were to be made at the discretion of the trustee in the event that one of the six beneficiaries (Cosette, Aram, Lucy, and Aram's three children) was in need of "support, care or maintenance." The inventory of the houses and the apartment was filed early in 1984 and ran to more than three hundred pages. Within its listings are millions of words of unpublished Saroyan. "I will be discovered again and again," he had written, and a rich trove awaits its certified examiners.

In 1982, Aram's journal of his father's death was published as *Last Rites*. In this book, and in a picture biography the following year, Aram propounded his theory that Saroyan's emotionality had been frozen by the orphanage years, that he was a man unable to feel. When *California* magazine printed an excerpt, it published it under what its editors referred to as the platonic, or ideal, title: "Daddy Dearest," emphasizing Aram's quarrels and discontent with his father. Michael J. Arlen had felt that, however correct Aram's facts were, anything but praise for his dead father would earn him enmity, and so it has been. Older members of the family—Bill's contemporaries—detest the book for its frankness.

Lucy wrote the foundation's lawyer with a simple request: would they send her the bathrobe he had worn when they last met? Months passed, but at last a box arrived with an apologetic letter, explaining that it first had been necessary to have everything catalogued and appraised. In the box was a child's bathrobe with a wornout seat. Her own? Aram's? It was an utter mystery, something from one of the garages on West Griffith Way, late and inadequate and not at all what she had asked for; as if what she needed could have been put in a box by a lawyer.

LUCY SAROYAN: It has nothing to do with Papa. I've never seen this bathrobe in my life. I don't know what this is or whose it is.

I haven't yet dealt with the levels that you're supposed to deal with. I haven't yet felt the anger and the rage and the rejection—I suppose the rejection, but I can't get mad at Pop about anything. I think it's going to be really healthy when I go, "That son-of-a-bitch really ditched me, completely *ditched* me." And he really did.

ARAM SAROYAN: All of this, this whole saga in a way, has to do with what I think of as a certain tendency among a lot of us who are Americans. We came over here, most of our families started out here, after some difficult reality somewhere else, and the whole idea was to look ahead and to make a life in the New World.

And, maybe as a result of that beginning, I think that many of us have an almost inborn tendency to shrink from any kind of reflective posture in relation to our own history. And I think Pop, as much as he became an official Armenian, really neglected to look at his own father's life, and, in looking at it, to come to terms with his own torment growing up the son of this man who was dead before my father was three years old.

The strange thing is that on a certain level, in his own family, he was condemned to perpetuate that deprivation. He could not be the father that he himself would have chosen to be in the best of all possible worlds.

And, look, I see my father in myself sometimes, in my relationships with my own children. But I think maybe the way through that is really to be able to look at one's history, one's individual past, and to be able to say, "Damn it, I got hurt there." That's a lot of what writing *Last Rites* was for me. Because until you acknowledge the pain in yourself, you can't acknowledge that you're perpetuating pain in other people's lives.

Until you can acknowledge that it hurt you, you don't know that it hurts anyone else when *you* do it. And that was Pop's problem, in a way. He just couldn't stop long enough to say, "Damn it, I'm *hurting*."

LUCY SAROYAN: I was always defending my father, I was always protecting my father, always taking his side, wanting to be with him. He was my hero. To a certain extent, he still is. I feel that I am able to, for some reason, able to forgive—able to forgive him . . . *anything*.

It wasn't Papa as a writer that was important to me at all. That was irrelevant to me. It was by the way he was that I knew he was a great man.

From the minute I can really remember his essence, I knew that he was larger life. He was better than Santa Claus. As good as God.

Lucy as actress. (She has been willing to dispense with glamour in character roles, such as the nagging wife in *Blue Collar*.) (Haya Harareet)

ACKNOWLEDGMENTS

First, our thanks must go to the members of William Saroyan's family who agreed to speak with us for this book, especially his former wife, Carol Matthau, his son, Aram Saroyan, and his daughter, Lucy Saroyan. While engaged in completing his own study, *William Saroyan*, Aram Saroyan generously acted as ambassador and explainer to his family on our behalf and also was kind enough to share the family's photograph collection, which helps to enrich this volume. Going over the ground covered in our questions cannot have been a pleasant task for these most important of our witnesses, and our obligation to them is enormous.

It should be emphasized that no one, including the close family members, was granted the right to delete material from our manuscript, except in the case of their own directly quoted remarks. We appreciate this ratification of our journalistic and literary independence.

Next, our thanks to those for whom the study of William Saroyan has been a task of many years, persons to whom we must certainly have appeared to be ill-informed newcomers. Dickran Kouymjian of California State University, Fresno, offered a unique perspective to us, not only as a scholar of Armenian art, history, and current affairs, but as Saroyan's friend and colleague in Paris as well as America. His insights and advice at the very beginning of our journey were especially helpful, as were those of his fellow Fresno scholar David Battan, who generously shared information and materials gathered for his own forthcoming work on the same subject. In Fresno, Aram and Alma

Arax offered both hospitality and perspective, and from Boston, James H. Tashjian's valuable interviews and his assembly and annotation of Saroyan letters and materials in the special issue of *The Armenian Review* and the collection *My Name Is Saroyan* were a rich source of chronology and fine data. We also are grateful to David Calonne for sharing with us at an early stage his study *William Saroyan: My Real Work Is Being*.

In Paris, Hagop Papagian and Michelle Lapautre were generous with their time and memories. Our very deep thanks are due to Garig Basmadjian, both for his personal interpretation of Saroyan and of his own difficult friendship with him and for the text of, and permission to quote from, his 1975 interview with Saroyan, an incredibly rich encounter, whose depth can only be hinted at in the chronicle at hand.

Patricia Angelin kindly arranged, and then conducted, the interview that brings Julie Haydon Nathan center stage. And Sam Hudson kindly steered us toward Lillian Gish.

We thank James Hart, director of the Bancroft Library at the University of California at Berkeley, for the courtly and almost painless way he denied requests for material from the Saroyan archives, as cataloguing circumstances and the terms of Saroyan's will decreed that he must, and for his kind offer of his library's available resources. The basic reference library for the book was that of California State University, San Francisco. Chronology and fine detail on Saroyan's show-business career were developed at the Billy Rose Collection of the New York Public Library's Performing Arts Branch, Lincoln Center, whose staff were tremendously helpful, especially in our picture searching. (The jacket photo is a special treasure, which turned up in an unexpected corner of their collection.) And Gladys Hansen and her staff in the History Room of the San Francisco Public Library made California picture searching a pleasure. Thanks as well to Ron Mahoney and his colleagues at the library at California State University at Fresno, whose collection roots the Saroyan story in his Armenian past.

Our thanks also are due to the friends and colleagues who eased and assisted in our travels (and absences): to Duane Big Eagle, Frank Lowe, Marshall Clements, Steve Friedman, Donald S. Ellis, Pennfield Jensen; and to Mike Ferring, Carl Twentier, Darryl Compton, Mimi Beck, Bob Hodierne, and (especially) Tom DeVries, all of whom made possible Larry Lee's long and repeated leaves from KRON-TV. In Boston, Bill and Carol Henderson were kind hosts and White Mountain guides, and in New York, Bill Whitehead was a generous host and a shrewd and deeply appreciated literary counselor.

Not all of our sources speak directly in these pages, but to Raymond Healy, Armina Marshall, W. J. Weatherby, Lydia Freeman, Don Gold, Karen Moline George Mardikian, and many others, who might not care to be credited by name, our thanks as well, and to their spouses and companions who added special insights of their own as we hurried through their venues with our recorders.

Our agent, Peter L. Ginsberg, is due all credit for the original spark for this book, and for his skill in steering it toward its ideal editor, Larry Ashmead. Our thanks as well to others at Harper & Row: our old friend, Ani Chamichian, and our new ones, Margaret Wimberger and Craig D. Nelson. Finally, on the home fronts, our love and gratitude for forbearance in the face of long absences, closed doors, and blank stares to Mary Lou Gifford and to Michael Sugihara.

CHRONOLOGY

1908 August 31: William Saroyan born in Fresno, California, to Armenak and Takoohi Saroyan.

1911 Armenak dies in Campbell, California. WS; his brother, Henry; and his sisters, Zabel and Cosette, are placed in a Methodist orphanage in Oakland. Takoohi goes to work as a domestic servant.

1916 Takoohi and her children are reunited in Fresno, living in the heart of that city's Armenian community. She works in packing houses, her sons as newspaper boys and, later, telegraph messengers.

1925 After repeated disciplinary expulsions, WS leaves Fresno high school without a diploma, and works in the vineyards and offices of his uncles.

1926 WS leaves Fresno for Los Angeles, a brief stint in the California National Guard, and, after a short reconciliation with his family, goes to San Francisco, where he works as a clerk-typist with the Southern Pacific. Finally, he works as a messenger, then manager, for Postal Telegraph, the company he had worked for in Fresno with his brother.

1927 Henry brings Takoohi, Zabel, and Cosette to live in San Francisco.

1928 *Overland Monthly* buys WS's first published sketch. In August, with money borrowed from an uncle, he leaves at age 19 to seek his fortune in New York.

1929 Disheartened and homesick, WS returns to San Francisco and his family. Begins a series of low-paying, short-lived jobs while haunting the public library and putting in long hours at his typewriter.

1932 The Armenian journal *Hairenik* ("Fatherland") in Boston accepts poems from WS.

1933 *Hairenik* publishes his poetry, his first stories ("A Fist Fight for Armenia," "The Broken Wheel"), and a sketch of Grandmother Lucy, *Noneh*. In October, WS translates his sketch for a novel, *Trapeze Over the Universe*, into the short-story masterpiece "The Daring Young Man on the Flying Trapeze." First ventures into Los Angeles and San Francisco literary society.

1934 *Story* publishes "The Daring Young Man . . ." and "70,000 Assyrians," and other magazines quickly begin to buy his backlog and fresh output. "The Broken Wheel" is collected in O'Brien's short-story annual. WS's triumphant debut collection, *The Daring Young Man on the Flying Trapeze*, appears in October, published by Random House, and is an immediate critical and commercial success.

1935 WS journeys to New York and on to London, Paris, Scandinavia, Moscow, Yerevan. Back home, he visits Mexico City by train. Emergency appendectomy.

1936 WS's second collection, *Inhale and Exhale*, appears from Random House, but not in the form he wished, and he breaks with his editor and publisher. His next collection, *Three Times Three*, appears that year from the Conference Press, the brainchild of three Los Angeles college students. WS works as a salaried Hollywood writer, first for B. P. Schulberg and then at Columbia Pictures.

1937 *Little Children*, his next story collection, appears from Harcourt, Brace.

1938 *Love, Here Is My Hat* appears as an experimental quality paperback, price 25 cents, from Modern Age Books and, in the fall, *The Trouble with Tigers*, a hardbound collection from Harcourt, Brace.

1939 April: *My Heart's in the Highlands* opens as a Group Theatre workshop production and receives enthusiastic reviews and an extended run. WS writes *The Time of Your Life* in a six-day stint, joins its rescue in Boston from a disastrous New Haven tryout, and sees it open to triumphant notices in October. A summer trip takes him to Europe, including Ireland. Aborted musical revue collaboration with Vincente Minnelli.

1940 *Love's Old Sweet Song* opens on Broadway in April to mixed notices, but in the same week Saroyan receives both the Critics Circle Award and the Pulitzer Prize for *The Time of Your Life*. But three new plays, *Sweeney in the Trees*, *Something About a Soldier*, and *The Hero of the World*, all fare poorly in summer tryouts. *My Name Is Aram*, a suite of short stories lightly fictionalizing his boyhood, is published in December to enthusiastic reviews.

1941 A new play, *Across the Board on Tomorrow Morning*, fails in tryout at the Pasadena Playhouse. In April, WS produces and directs *The Beautiful People* to generally warm reviews. That fall, after severe gambling losses, he agrees to prepare a screenplay for M-G-M.

1942 February, meets Carol Marcus. March, shoots his short subject, *The Good Job*. April, *Razzle-Dazzle* (collected short plays and sketches) published by Harcourt, Brace. May, public split with M-G-M. August, *Across the Board on Tomorrow Morning* and *Talking to You* open the Saroyan Theatre to immediate disaster. *Hello, Out There* staged in September. October, sworn into United States Army as drafted buck private.

1943 February, marries Carol Marcus; novelization of *The Human Comedy*, his M-G-M screenplay, is published to rave reviews. Army duty in New York, psychiatric observation. Birth of son, Aram, September 25. November: *Get Away, Old Man*, play satirizing Hollywood, fails on Broadway.

1944 February, ships for Army duty in Europe. In London, circulates in literary society, simultaneously writes propaganda novel, *The Adventures of Wesley Jackson*, and journal of its composition, *The Adventures of William Saroyan. Dear Baby*, stories, published by Harcourt, Brace.

1945 Hospitalized in Luxembourg, returned to United States, released from Army in September.

1946 Daughter, Lucy, born January 17 in San Francisco. *Adventures of Wesley Jackson* published to reviews challenging his patriotism.

1947 In residence at Millneck, Long Island, for the first half of the year, writing with great difficulty. Allegorical play *Sam Ego's House* receives Los Angeles showcase production.

1948 *The Time of Your Life* film opens, a financial failure. *The Saroyan Special*, an anthology with no new work, is published by Harcourt, Brace. Heavy gambling losses and Carol's attempt to divorce him after his impulsive decision, soon abandoned, to move to a farm near Fresno. September: moves with his family to New York City.

1949 April: breaks with Carol and goes to Europe, returning in September and spending six weeks in Nevada to secure a divorce, suffering $50,000 in gambling losses.

1950 *The Assyrian and Other Stories* is published by Harcourt, Brace and hailed by critics as a return to form. Begins writing on assignment for slick magazines, negotiating with Hollywood. Writes *Tracy's Tiger* and *Rock Wagram* in a month-long burst of work at midsummer.

1951 Campaigns for Carol to remarry him, which she does on April 2. Saroyan and family return to Los Angeles. *Tracy's Tiger* and *Rock Wagram* published. "Come On-a My House," song whose lyrics he co-authored with his cousin, tops Hit Parade. In October, Carol brings divorce proceedings against him.

1952 Divorce granted. Carol and the children are installed in a house in Pacific Palisades and Saroyan buys himself a house on pilings at Malibu. *The Bicycle Rider in Beverly Hills*, in which he first reveals his orphanage years, is published by Scribner's.

1953 *The Laughing Matter*, a bitter melodramatization of his marriage, is published by Doubleday.

1954 *A Lost Child's Fireflies*, a play written in 1950, is given a summer production in Dallas with an all-black cast.

1955 "A Few Adventures in the California Boyhood of William Saroyan" is broadcast on the *Omnibus* series with child actor Sal Mineo as Saroyan.

1956 *Mama, I Love You* is published by Little, Brown.

1957 *Papa, You're Crazy* published by Little, Brown. *The Cave Dwellers*, his first New York production since 1943, opens.

1958 Leaves his Malibu home for a trip around the world, working on the memoir, unpublished in its original form, entitled *Fifty-Fifty*.

1959 Leaves America for Europe, styling himself a tax exile. An abortive movie project in Yugoslavia is followed by a script for Darryl Zanuck that becomes a successful stage play in Vienna. *The London Comedy* is produced in London, and he collaborates with Henry Cecil on a second stage comedy, *Settled Out of Court*, also produced in London.

1961 Teaches at Purdue University in Indiana, where students produce his didactic comedy, set there, *High Time Along the Wabash*. Buys Paris apartment.

1962 Autobiography, *Here Comes There Goes You Know Who*, published by Simon & Schuster. Half-hour teleplay, "The Unstoppable Gray Fox," is broadcast on *The General Electric Theater*.

1963 Publishes *Boys and Girls Together* (Harcourt, Brace & World), and lives, briefly, in Third Avenue penthouse.

1964 *One Day in the Afternoon of the World* published by Harcourt, Brace & World.

1966 Publishes the memoir *Short Drive, Sweet Chariot* (Phaedra) and forms the William Saroyan Foundation.

1968 Publishes a collection of occasional pieces, *I Used to Believe I Had Forever, Now I'm Not So Sure* (Cowles).

1971 Publishes *Don't Go, But if You Must, Say Hello to Everybody* (*Letters from 74 rue Taitbout* in U.S.), Cassell, London, and New American Library, New York.

1972 Publishes *Places Where I've Done Time*, Praeger.

1973 Publishes *Days of Life and Death and Escape to the Moon*, Dial.

1976 Publishes *Sons Come and Go, Mothers Hang in Forever*, McGraw-Hill.

1978 Publishes *Chance Meetings*, Norton.

1979 Publishes *Obituaries*, Creative Arts.

1980 Nominated for American Book Award for *Obituaries*.

1981 Dies of cancer in Fresno, May 18.

1983 Posthumous publication of *Births*, Creative Arts; and *My Name Is Saroyan*, Coward-McCann.

1984 Posthumous publication of *The New Saroyan Reader*, Donald S. Ellis/Creative Arts.

NOTES

Works of William Saroyan Frequently Cited in the Text

Boys & Girls   *Boys and Girls Together* (novelized memoir), Harcourt,
                  Brace & World, 1963.

Don't Go   *Don't Go, But if You Must, Say Hello to Everybody* (mem-
                  oir), Cassell, London, 1969. (Published in U.S. as
                  Letters from 74 rue Taitbout, New American Library,
                  1971).

Here Comes   *Here Comes There Goes You Know Who* (autobiography),
                  Simon & Schuster, 1962; Pocket Books, 1963. (Paper-
                  back pagination cited.)

I Used to Believe *I Used to Believe I Had Forever, Now I'm Not So Sure* (oc-
                  casional pieces), Cowles, 1968.

My Name   *My Name Is Saroyan*, Coward-McCann, 1983.

Places   *Places Where I've Done Time*, Praeger, 1972.

Sons Come   *Sons Come and Go, Mothers Hang in Forever* (memoir),
                  McGraw-Hill, 1976.

CHAPTER ONE: SAROYAN

4 "Tree," etc. *The Beautiful People*, p. 30.

9 "Bill came to believe," Bennett Cerf, *At Random* (Random House, 1977), p. 117.

9 *The White-Haired Boy*. Malcolm Goldstein, *George S. Kaufman, His Life His Theater* (Oxford, 1979), pp. 333, 339–40.

10 "The Blaring Young Man." E. Y. Harburg in Sidney Skolsky's syndicated column of May 11, 1942, as quoted in full in *Variety*, May 13, 1942.

11 "After the first act," 2. 1940 Cerf, *op. cit.*, p. 116.

17 "I was speechless," Robert Giroux in *Publishers Weekly*, January 8, 1982, p. 65.

17 "Art must be democratic," WS in New York *Herald Tribune*, May 7, 1940.

18 "[T]he most charming and original evader," Nathaniel Buchwald in the *Daily Worker*, May 7, 1940.

19 "The present state of the world," *My Name*, p. 275.

20 "Are they in that box, Miss Hepburn . . .?" *Sons Come*, pp. 142–44.

20 "If you and others," San Francisco *Chronicle*, August 11, 1940.

21 ". . . Holder of the First Prize," from "The Saroyan Prizes," originally published in *The New Yorker*, August 31, 1940, and subsequently in *I Used to Believe*, pp. 1–3.

26 "Act I. By God," WS in "A Slightly Saroyanish Look at a Budding Drama Season," New York *World-Telegram*, September 7, 1940.

27 "[N]o instance of a love," Brooks Atkinson in the *New York Times*, September 1, 1940. "It so happens," WS in the *New York Times*, September 8, 1940.

29 "Last night, Clifford Odets came up to me," *Sons Come*, pp. 179–80.

29 "I'll have him in my next play," WS in "His Unwritten Play Pursues Saroyan Through the Town," New York *World-Telegram*, October 19, 1940.

30 "Look, I need the publicity," *Sons Come*, p. 180.

34 "If I can't borrow $15,000," WS in *Variety*, October 30, 1940.

CHAPTER TWO: IMPRESARIO

37 "I soon discovered," Herb Caen in the San Francisco *Chronicle*, May 19, 1981. "[E]ven if he had, I wouldn't let him," Duggan quoted by Lawrence Langner in *The Magic Curtain* (Dutton, 1951), p. 326.

41 "He certainly can't be picking grapes," in "Saroyan, Generally Adequate, Mute at His Biggest Build-Up" by S. M. Weller, New York *Herald Tribune*, April 25, 1941.

45 "George Jean Nathan saw it," *Razzle-Dazzle* (Harcourt, Brace, 1942), p. 61.

48 "I hadn't played more than half a minute," and Slemons, Loring, and Blair anecdotes following, from "That Man Saroyan," New York *Post*, July 10, 1941.

54 "I am a truck driver," quoted in "The Man Who Wasn't There: Pass Seeker with Double Talk," New York *Herald Tribune*, May 4, 1941.

56 "I am going to begin writing," WS in New York *Herald Tribune*, April 27, 1941.

57 "My husband liked the show," quoted in "9 Take Up Saroyan on Refund Offer," *New York Times*, July 3, 1941.

58 "The sun is very close to the earth," WS from the preface to *Hello, Out There*, as reprinted in *The Time of Your Life and Other Plays*, pp. 276–81.

CHAPTER THREE: MOVIEMAKER

60 "I think I would be wasted in the Army," WS to the Associated Press (as published in the Baltimore *Evening Sun*, May 10, 1941).

60 "We'll see whether Saroyan meant what he said," quoted in the New York *Telegraph*, August 15, 1941.

61 "The amusing thing about moving pictures," WS: "Of Personality," the *New York Times*, July 6, 1941.

62 Freed's sponsorship of WS at M-G-M in *The World of Entertainment, Hollywood's Greatest Musicals*, by Hugh Fordin (Doubleday, 1975), pp. 58–60.

63 "I wasn't spending anywhere near enough," *Sons Come*, pp. 145–46.

63 "Very often, more often than not," *I Used to Believe*, pp. 203–204.

65 "Mayer likes a good cry," WS quoted in "Mr. Saroyan's Thoroughly American Movie" by Patrick McGilligan in *The Modern American Novel and the Movies*, pp. 156–67.

67 "They gave me a crib of a room," WS in conversation with James H. Tashjian, quoted in *My Name Is Saroyan*, pp. 382–84.

67 "What is this man saying?" quoted in "My Grandmother Lucy Tells a Story Without a Beginning, a Middle or an End," in *My Name Is Saroyan*, pp. 296–99.

75 "A gay, sophisticated and cosmopolitan world ," Maury Paul quoted in *Little Gloria, Happy at Last*, by Barbara Goldsmith (Knopf, 1980), p. 575.

85 "[V]ery pretty, but not commercial," WS quoted in Associated Press dispatch, May 5, 1942.

86 "I sincerely recommend immediate purchase," WS in *Variety*, May 13, 1942.

87 "It was a movie scenario Saroyan had written for M-G-M," Giroux in *Publishers Weekly*, January 8, 1982, pp. 55–56.

89 "The factual story by itself is so eloquent," WS quoted in "Saroyan Silenced for Once," New York *World-Telegram*, June 30, 1942.

89 "If such plays don't come out," WS quoted in "Saroyan in 1-A," New York *Herald Tribune*, July 22, 1942.

92 "[I]nept people," WS in "Mr. Saroyan Says Au Revoir to Stage," *New York Times*, August 24, 1942.

93 "I don't want to go home," etc., *Boys & Girls* (Harcourt, Brace 1963), p. 34.

CHAPTER FOUR: SOLDIER

97 "They're all scared," WS quoted in "William Saroyan Is Off to the Army," by Carolyn Anspacher, the San Francisco *Chronicle*, October 30, 1942.

99 "All I know of what you have become," Eugene O'Neill quoted in *O'Neill, Son and Artist*, by Louis Sheaffer (Little, Brown, 1973), p. 537.

99 "They got me up at 5:30," WS quoted in "Pvt. Saroyan Can Write a Book on Bed Making," the San Francisco *Examiner*, November 11, 1942.

99 "I've just sent my typewriter to the laundry," J. D. Salinger quoted in *William Saroyan* by Aram Saroyan (Harcourt Brace Jovanovich, 1983), p. 77.

108 "One morning at five I couldn't get out of bed," WS in *Places*, pp. 83–84.

112 "The family line 2." *Places*, p. 202.

113 "How come you don't salute them all?" Mary Welsh Hemingway, *How It Was* (Knopf, 1976), p. 91.

115 "Colonel Stevens, permission to talk," *Sons Come*, p. 183.

116 "Armenian? But didn't the Turks. . .," *Sons Come*, p. 158.

120 "Here's Bill Saroyan," Carlos Baker, *Ernest Hemingway: A Life Story* (Scribner, 1969; Avon, 1980), p. 561 (Avon ed.).

CHAPTER FIVE: MARRIED MAN

130 "From the beginning they scare you to death," WS quoted by Paul L. Speegle in the San Francisco *Chronicle*, June 2, 1946.

130 "Right now, there's no healthy protest," WS quoted by Earl Wilson in his syndicated column of July 11, 1946.

131 "[T]he most preposterously phoney damned job," *Obituaries*, p. 351.

135 "Everybody knew that after three years in the Army," *Places*, pp. 45–47.

136 "It's kind of a symphony, isn't it?" quoted in James Cagney, *Cagney by Cagney* (Doubleday, 1976), p. 122.

143 "He had no heart for the work," *Boys & Girls*, p. 52.

145 "The studio thought Cagney had to use his fists," interview with Luther Nichols in the San Francisco *Chronicle*, June 13, 1948.

150 "But Molnár's dead," "Sons and Fathers" in *I Used to Believe*, pp. 206–209.

152 "She just happened to be who she was," *Places*, p. 46.

155 "Look at you, all white and pink and perfect," *William Saroyan* by Aram Saroyan, p. 97.

155 "The little bride had confessed it," *Places*, p. 150.

CHAPTER SIX: *TSOOR* WILLIE

For much of the fine detail in this chapter on the Armenian community of Fresno in its homeland and its new country we are indebted to Richard Tracy LaPiere's *The Armenian Colony in Fresno County, California: A Study in Social Psychology*, an unpublished doctoral dissertation submitted to Stanford University in 1930.

180 "Pinhead, Pinhead!" *Don't Go*, p. 60 ff.

182 ". . .my cheek felt the impact of his rough hand," *Here Comes*, p. 144.

184 "He is Mad Baro all over again," *Here Comes*, p. 85.

186 ". . . [t]his is all that remains," *Here Comes*, p. 34.

188 "In Fresno the financial power of the community is found in the hands of Jews," Aram Saroyan in *Asbarez*, February 24, 1923, quoted in LaPiere, *op. cit.*, p. 408.

189 "inaccessible to all races of Asiatic origin," quoted in *Asbarez*, March 24, 1911, as quoted by LaPiere, *op. cit.*, p. 393.

190 "A badge that cost a dollar?" *Don't Go*, p. 100.

195 "So you're William Saroyan?" *Here Comes*, p. 67.

196 "Miss Clifford, whoever you are these days," *Don't Go*, p. 85.

196 "This is not punishment," *Here Comes*, p. 70.

197 "The woman in charge of transfers was required to ask," *Places*, p. 49.

201 "Get out and stay out. When are you leaving?" *Here Comes*, pp. 48–51.

CHAPTER SEVEN: WRITER

202 "What are you crying for? He's not here," *Don't Go*, p. 5.

203 "Hang your cap up," *Places*, p. 37.
205 "I wrote working-class Armenian writing in English," *Here Comes*, p. 21.
205 "The revelation was blinding," *Places*, p. 42.
206 "Pete, there's style for you," *Here Comes*, p. 18.
207 "You are Armenak Saroyan's son," *Here Comes*, p. 91.
207 "Why aren't you writing?" *Places*, p. 20.
219 "So you're Walter Winchell?" *Sons Come*, p. 88.
219 "They like me, it must be that I am really a good writer," *Don't Go*, p. 105.
219 "We hear 'Valse Triste' a lot on the radio in America," *Sons Come*, p. 99.
222 "Get in there and knock the critics for a loop," Hemingway quoted in Baker, *op. cit.*, p. 816.
223 "No, I'd rather not read Veblen," WS quoted by Budd Schulberg in *Writers in America: The Four Seasons of Success* (Stein & Day, 1983), p. 79.
225 "I'll never see you again," *Sons Come*, p. 106.
225 "There's this Boston man, Nat Hawthorne," *Sons Come*, p. 108.
234 "Be a poet," WS quoted in R. Lewis, *Slings and Arrows*, p. 116.
234 "What the hell is the matter with the actors?" WS quoted in Langner, *op. cit.*, p. 323.
237 "I understand him easy. . . .I hate women who try to think," WS quoted by Walter Holbrook in the New York *Herald Tribune*, October 22, 1939.

CHAPTER EIGHT: EXILE

252 "Ross and I have made about fifteen thousand dollars apiece out of the song so far," WS quoted in "Everything a Song," *The New Yorker* ("The Talk of the Town"), September 8, 1951, p. 31.
254 "Suicide was suicide, divorce was divorce," *Places*, p. 135 ff.
256 "Morning is best when it begins with the last hours of night," *The Bicycle Rider in Beverly Hills* (Scribner, 1952).
257 "I was forty-three years old," *Places*, p. 137 ff.
266 "I haven't been a playboy," WS quoted in the *New York Times*, February 19, 1959.
270 "I buy trash books, I make a drawing," WS in unpublished 1975 interview with Garig Basmadjian.
270 ". . .a city of enlightenment," *Don't Go*, p. 91.

CHAPTER NINE: FATHER

279 "My past was kicking me around," *Here Comes*, p. 199.
289 "What happens to kids?" *Chance Meetings* (Norton, 1978), p. 31.

CHAPTER TEN: SAROYAN

303 "Cut it out, Papa, you son of a bitch," *Obituaries*, p. 210.
307 "You've come here to exploit my death," Aram Saroyan, *Last Rites* (Morrow, 1982), p. 22.
308 "This is your granddaughter, Cream," Aram Saroyan, *op. cit.*, p. 136 ff.

BIBLIOGRAPHY

Arlen, Michael. *Passage to Ararat* and *Exiles*, Penguin Books, New York, 1982.

Bode, Carl (ed.). *The New Mencken Letters*, Dial Press, New York, 1977.

Cagney, James. *Cagney by Cagney*, Doubleday, New York, 1976.

Carey, Gary. *All the Stars in Heaven: Louis B. Mayer's M-G-M*, Dutton, New York, 1981.

Clurman, Harold. *The Fervent Years: The Group Theatre and the 30's*, Harcourt Brace Jovanovich, New York, 1975.

Edmiston, Susan, and Cirino, Linda D. *Literary New York: A History and Guide*, Houghton Mifflin, Boston, 1976.

Flamm, Jerry. *Good Life in Hard Times: San Francisco's 20's and 30's*, Chronicle Books, San Francisco, 1975.

Freeman, Don. *Come One, Come All!*, Rinehart & Company, New York, 1949.

Garfield, David. *A Player's Place: The Story of the Actors Studio*, Macmillan, New York, 1980.

Gibson, Margaret Brenman. *Clifford Odets, American Playwright*, Atheneum, New York, 1982.

Gish, Lillian (with Ann Pinchot). *The Movies, Mr. Griffith and Me*, Prentice-Hall, Englewood Cliffs, N.J., 1969.

Goldberger, Paul. *The City Observed*, Vintage, New York, 1979.

Goldsmith, Barbara. *Little Gloria . . . Happy at Last*, Knopf, New York, 1980.

Goldstein, Malcolm. *George S. Kaufman, His Life, His Theater*, Oxford, New York, 1979.

Grace, Carol (Carol Marcus Saroyan Matthau). *The Secret in the Daisy*, Random House, New York, 1955.

Hewison, Robert. *Under Siege: Literary Life in London 1939–45*, Weidenfeld & Nicolson, London, 1977.

Kazin, Alfred. *Starting Out in the Thirties*, Atlantic Monthly Press, Boston, 1965.

Lewis, Robert. *Slings and Arrows: Theatre in My Life*, Stein and Day, New York, 1984

Mantle, Burns. *The Best Plays of 1939–1940, The Best Plays of 1940–1941, The Best Plays of 1941–1942*; Dodd, Mead, New York.

Meredith, Scott. *George S. Kaufman and His Friends,* Doubleday, New York, 1974.

Nathan, George Jean. *Encyclopedia of the Theatre,* Knopf, New York, 1940. *The Theatre Book of the Year, 1943–1944,* Knopf, New York, 1944.

Saroyan, Aram, *The Street: An Autobiographical Novel,* The Bookstore Press, Lenox, Mass., 1974. *Last Rites: The Death of William Saroyan,* Morrow, New York, 1982. *William Saroyan,* Harcourt Brace Jovanovich, San Diego, 1983.

Schulberg, Budd. *Writers in America: The Four Seasons of Success,* Stein & Day, New York, 1983.

Shaw, Artie. *I Love You, I Hate You, Drop Dead!,* Fleet, New York, 1965.

Sheaffer, Louis. *O'Neill, Son and Artist,* Little, Brown, Boston, 1973.

Tashjian, James H., (compiler). *William Saroyan: My Name Is Saroyan,* Coward-McCann, New York, 1983. Editor. *The Armenian Review,* Saroyan Memorial Issue, Volume xxxiv, No. 3, p. 135, September, 1981.

Trilling, Diana. *Reviewing the Forties,* Harcourt Brace Jovanovich, New York, 1978.

Wilson, Edmund. *The Thirties,* Farrar, Straus and Giroux, New York, 1980.

INDEX